TEACHING ABROAD

Hong Kong University Press thanks Xu Bing for writing the Press's name in his Square Word Calligraphy for the covers of its books. For further information, see p. iv.

I wish to dedicate this book to those partners with whom I have shared team teaching, interdisciplinary approaches, and videoconferencing:

Dr. Iska Alter, Dr. Geeta Chanda, Dr. King Kok Cheung, Dr. Staci Ford, Dr. Gina Marchetti, Dr. Caroline Muir, Dr. Priscilla Roberts, Dr. Tom Stanley, and Dr. Wendy Zierler — American Studies, The University of Hong Kong

Dr. Henrik Lassen, Dr. Roy Sellars, and Dr. Jane Winther — English Studies, The University of Southern Denmark in Kolding

Dr. Li Ai-Li, Dr. Pan Yining, Dr. Wen Qiang, and Dr. Zhu Weibin — The Lingnan Foundation "Transnationalism and America" Project, Sun Yat-sen University in Guangzhou.

TEACHING ABROAD
International Education and the Cross-Cultural Classroom

Gordon E. Slethaug

香港大學出版社
HONG KONG UNIVERSITY PRESS

Hong Kong University Press
14/F Hing Wai Centre
7 Tin Wan Praya Road
Aberdeen
Hong Kong

© Hong Kong University Press 2007

Hardback ISBN 978-962-209-854-1
Paperback ISBN 978-962-209-855-8

British Library Cataloguing-in-Publication Data
A catalogue record for this book is available from the British Library.

Secure On-line Ordering
http://www.hkupress.org

Printed and bound by Lammar Offset Printing Ltd., Hong Kong, China.

Hong Kong University Press is honoured that Xu Bing, whose art explores the complex themes of language across cultures, has written the Press's name in his Square Word Calligraphy. This signals our commitment to cross-cultural thinking and the distinctive nature of our English-language books published in China.

"At first glance, Square Word Calligraphy appears to be nothing more unusual than Chinese characters, but in fact it is a new way of rendering English words in the format of a square so they resemble Chinese characters. Chinese viewers expect to be able to read Square Word Calligraphy but cannot. Western viewers, however are surprised to find they can read it. Delight erupts when meaning is unexpectedly revealed."

— Britta Erickson, *The Art of Xu Bing*

Contents

Acknowledgements

I would like to acknowledge the funding of two important foundations that have supported my work and are critical for global cross-cultural relations and international understanding. These are the Fulbright Commission that supported my research in Denmark from September 2003 until December 2004, and the Lingnan Foundation that supported my work in Hong Kong and mainland China from December 2004 until July 2007. I would like to thank especially Marie Mønsted and Barbara Lehman of the Fulbright Commission and Danish American Foundation in Copenhagen and Dr. Leslie Stone of the Lingnan Foundation at Yale University whose support has made a profound difference in my life and those of other scholars.

I would also like to thank Clara Ho of Hong Kong University Press for overseeing this work through the production process.

Introduction

We travel together, passengers on a little spaceship, dependent upon its
vulnerable resources of air and soil; all committed for our safety to its
security and peace; preserved from annihilation only by the care, the
work, and I will say the love we give our fragile craft.

— Adlai Stevenson

About a decade ago the language historian Bill Bryson noted that, "the third
edition of the *American Heritage Dictionary*, published in 1992, contained
10,000 words, about 5 per cent of the total, that had not existed twenty
years before" (1998, 417), and he estimated that, as a result of technology
and science since that time, the English language has grown "by up to
20,000 words a year" (1998, 417), far more than suggested by the 1992
dictionary.

Besides technology and science, the expanding English language has
added words related to international developments in business, politics,
and education. Words such as "globalization," "internationalization,"
"intercultural," "multicultural," "cross-cultural," "transcultural", and
"transnational" have either come into existence recently, gained new
currency, or acquired new meanings. The meanings of these words are in
flux and sometimes hotly contested because the cultural milieu and
international changes they represent are not coded in agreed-upon ways
or distanced by time.

As part of this new international scene, multinational corporations,
computer and telecommunication companies, and investment banks
increasingly cover the globe even as hundreds of thousands of university
academics, schoolteachers, and students go abroad. These international

workers, academics and teachers, and students are themselves intercultural and think in international and transnational rather than national terms and make a big difference socially and politically.

Robert Satloff has argued that, since September 11 "experts have debated how to win the battle for hearts and minds among the world's 300 million Arabs and 1.2 billion Muslims. Everyone seems to have the magic bullet" — but American education abroad, he thinks, is far better and less expensive than high profile and costly political alternatives:

> What makes American schools a strategic asset is the fact that non-Americans flock to them. Of the nearly 100,000 students enrolled in such schools around the world, more than 70% are not American, fairly evenly divided between local and third-country students. . . .
>
> Students at these schools learn how to ask questions, be curious, solve problems and accept differences. They study Thanksgiving, George Washington and Martin Luther King while finding a way to celebrate the various nationalities each brings to the classroom. Every student leaves with a facility in English and an appreciation for critical thinking and cultural diversity that represent American education at its best. (Satloff 2003, 9)

Satloff's depiction of students in international schools is one that most transnational educators would understand — they are sophisticated, mainly urban learners whose parents readily see the value of international education, want their children to be well versed in the subjects, and are fully engaged in educational processes. These children are already globalized, so that international schools are able to accomplish diplomatic goals effectively.

Although Satloff cannot give statistics about the total number of international schools because "no single organization keeps track of all international schools around the world" (Greenlees 2006), they grew from about 50 in 1964 to some 1,000 in 1995, with "50,000 teachers and half a million students distributed around the world, being 'equivalent in size to that of a nation with a population of 34 million, but with the significant difference that 90% of the students passing through the system go on to higher education'" (Hayden and Thompson 1995, 333).[1] This three-decade

---

1   Hayden and Thompson are here quoting M. Matthews' 1988 University of Oxford MSc Thesis, *The Ethos of International Schools*, and using those 1988 statistics, but they also use the same figure of 1,000 international schools for 1995.

period of growth to 1995 is a mere shadow of what has taken place at the primary and secondary level from that time because, according to estimates, there are currently about 3,000 schools globally, with at least 100 new international schools opening world-wide between 2005 and 2006 and enrollment in Asian international schools alone jumping 14% in the same year (Greenlees 2006). During these past two decades, the enrollment in all of these schools has increased exponentially, so that the total enrollment might well be two million.

There has been equally significant expansion at the university level as well. In 1995 Pamela George predicted that approximately 50,000 American academics would "participate in more than two hundred programs facilitating international exchanges" (1995, 1), and in 1998, William Gabrenya argued that "the movement of students across national boundaries for educational purposes has increased steadily since World War II, reaching well over 1 million persons per year by the 1990s" (1998, 57). The actual number during the rapidly globalizing '90s exceeded these predictions, and international student enrollment in higher education in the USA alone went from 34,232 in 1955 to 481,280 in 1998 (Spaulding et al. 2001, 195). Recently, the *New York Times* noted that 565,000 students from foreign countries were currently studying in American universities and 191,000 Americans were studying at international universities (Finder 2005). Add to these numbers the immigrant flow into the USA each year, and the number of foreign and naturalized-American students mingling with native-born students in American classrooms is staggering, not only in large urban areas like New York City, Chicago, Los Angeles, or San Francisco, where substantial immigration has always been a fact of life, but in small towns and villages across North America. Added to this are those students who go to other countries such as the United Kingdom and Australia, with the UK receiving 195,000 non-EU students in 2004 and Australia receiving 303,324. Australia alone predicts that this international student body will rise to 810,000 by 2018, and the UK predicts 677,000 by 2015 (Ryan and Carroll 2005, 4).

In a related vein, in an article called "Let the Chinese Students Come," written in 2003, Yale University President Richard C. Levin celebrates the 25th anniversary of Deng Xiaoping's Open Door Policy that "permitted not only the inflow of capital, but also, for the first time since 1949, the flow of students and scholars in both directions." He notes that, "since 1978, tens of thousands of Americans have enrolled in educational institutions in China, and more than 580,000 Chinese have studied in U.S. colleges and universities" (*International Herald Tribune* 2003, 8). Indeed, China's

Ministry of Education statistics show that, in 2001, 61,869 undergraduate and graduate students from 169 countries studied in 363 Chinese universities (China Service Centre for Scholarly Exchange 2001) and, by 2004, that had grown to "110,844 overseas students" from 178 countries studying in mainland China, an increase of "42.63% over the previous year." The figures for 2005 are even more impressive with "more than 140,000 overseas students [studying] in China," and "119,000 Chinese [going] abroad for study" (*South China Morning Post* 2006). These assertions, reinforced by a host of studies about the impact of a growing and developing educational system in China, remind readers not only of the increasing movement of students between the USA and China, but hundreds of other countries as well.

This flow of educators and students across national borders has its rewards, but is not without problems and risks. To go outside one's own country is to discover a wealth of different cultural expressions, but it also means leaving certainties and securities behind — those physical and emotional comforts taken for granted within our home culture. To cross a national boundary and live in another country, quite possibly on a different continent, is to create a gap between new and old experiences and perceptions. This gap may shrink or expand in time, but it can never be eliminated, and those who set out to experience a new culture are forever likely to feel that they are simultaneously part of more than one culture but are never entirely at one with their culture of origin. In other words, educators who go abroad will live on the margins and inhabit the gap, even while experiencing the benefits of transnationalism.

Part of "inhabiting the gap" is giving up comforting cultural perceptions and understandings. For instance, although "America" in this book specifically refers to the USA and "North America" to Canada, Mexico, and the USA together, I have become uneasy with these definitions. Most Americans take the term "American" for granted as referring to inhabitants of the USA, but some from the USA and other countries think the term should not be used in that sense. Still, rhetorically it works better than always referring to "citizens of the United States." Similarly, there are times when I use "Asian" and feel discomfort about the cultural complexity and diversity subsumed under that term. In general, I will use that term only to refer to an area and not to something like a so-called Asian value system, which would be impossible to define or defend. For the purposes of this book, then, America is a country and Americans the inhabitants of that country, Asia is a continent, and East Asia a part of that continent — but I am always on the alert about the shifting sands of meaning and attitude regarding these usages.

Those who inhabit international spaces learn how to question local assumptions and issues and ways of expressing them, but it is important to feel part of those neighborhood relations, educational processes, and everyday work in the operation of society. Those going abroad will experience on a personal level the distinctions inherent in the terms "globalization," "internationalization," and "transnationalism." Globalization is the most rhetorically loaded of the three terms and usually refers to the rapid international transfer of goods, commodities, culture, and political ideologies. Those who celebrate globalization see multilateral trade leading to growing economic and political equality across the planet. Those who reject it believe that the benefits of globalization accrue mainly to the United States and other developed and developing countries and that underdeveloped countries suffer as a result (Alexander 2004, 1). Those who disapprove of globalization find it a form of exploitation, extreme capitalism, and economic colonization and therefore dislike the term applied to non-economic and non-governmental sectors.

Because "internationalization" suggests reciprocity rather than cultural and economic hegemony, it is a relatively neutral term and well adapted to broad cultural and educational issues. Educators increasingly use this term but also like "transnationalism," suggesting a reciprocal, almost arbitrary and unintentional (as opposed to schematically controlled) flow of knowledge and cultures across national boundaries. Terms closely related to transnationalism are "transculturalism" and "transculturation." Francoise Lionnet says that transculturation means "constant interaction, transmutation between two or more cultural components with the unconscious goal of creating a third cultural identity" (15–16). Although these terms mute the mediation of nationalist discourses that transnationalism suggests, they suggest a cross-national discourse, which, as with "internationalization," lacks many of the negative indicators that "globalization" bears.

When educators describe internationalization in education, they often do so in terms of the need for equality of race, ethnicity, and gender, and for the separation of church and state in the classroom, but without significant consideration of the more comprehensive educational challenges of an intercultural classroom. For example, France's struggle to integrate its Muslim population into classrooms, while protecting secular values, provides a rough sort of lesson. The issue occupying the French and German press in 2003–04 was the Muslim wearing of headscarves in their countries, and the consequent French government report recommending a ban on headscarves worn by Muslim girls, yarmulkes by Jewish boys, and large crosses by Christians, as a means of protecting secularism in the classroom and workplace. The press was occupied with the issue of headscarves, but said little else about implications for the education system, except that there could be a threat of more private religious schools in the wake of this ban in the public schools (Sciolino 2003, 1).

Surely in these international contexts, there should be greater concern about teaching style, student responses, and classroom relations, which are even more important for education than religious symbols, and this is the area that has been least recognized and researched. Of all the areas of globalization and internationalization, the classroom may well be the least discussed. Everyone knows, and has an opinion about, the interface of politics and business as reflected in national trade policies and the World Trade Organization (WTO); and most also understand the migration of students from all parts of the world as they pursue their academic interests. However, surprisingly little has been said about the international classroom — whether that classroom is in Morocco, China, Bolivia, South Africa, Denmark, Canada, or the USA. It is this paucity of discussion about the intercultural classroom that provides the impetus for this study, and I hope that my observations can be thought-provoking to all teachers and incorporated into conversations about classrooms at every academic level, although my own experience on three continents is with the university classroom. I have taught American studies — culture, literature, and history — at universities in the USA, Canada, China (both Hong Kong and mainland), and Denmark; have given papers, lectured, and discussed educational perspectives in a dozen different countries (including several places in China, Poland, South Korea, and Vietnam); and have grounded my observations in what students in other countries often call the "American style" that favors student participation over teacher control. Along with others in various international settings, I have increasingly crossed national and cultural boundaries — a phenomenon for teachers and students alike.

In their book about international education, Janette Ryan and Jude Carroll define international students as those "who have chosen to travel to another country for tertiary study" (2005, 3), and, in her book about Fulbright professors going abroad to teach, Pamela George defines cross-cultural contexts as "those in which academics from the United States teach in countries, cultures or in languages which are not their native ones" (1995, 3). These excellent sources focus on students and contexts, but I am interested in the teachers or pedagogues who go abroad to teach because they engage cross-cultural dynamics in ways that those who stay at home do not, even if they teach culturally diverse and international students.

Those cross-cultural educators who go abroad must adjust to new cultures while trying to preserve and promote some of their own, and do so in a way that is not "culturally imperialistic" (McLean and Ransom 2005, 45), but those remaining at home can expect students (in whatever mix of international and local/home students) to adjust to their own country's beat. Teachers who stay at home and deal with international students can assume the so-called "deficit approach," that "implies that any 'problem' is the student's, that it is the role of academics and language support staff to 'correct' the problem and that it is the student's responsibility to 'adjust'" (McLean and Ransom 2005, 45). Those who remain at home may not have to interrogate familiar pedagogical formulations: "the academic culture inherent in their discipline seems obvious and expectations are rarely made explicit . . . [for] we have learned how to behave in tutorials and lectures, expectations of the postgraduate-supervisor relationships, out-of-class etiquette, and attitudes to cheating and intellectual property" (McLean and Ransom 2005, 47).

As outsiders to a culture and in teaching ethnically and nationally diverse groups of students, cross-cultural teachers have to rethink culture, pedagogy, and identity, and reconsider their social and pedagogical assumptions in critical ways or risk failure. It is quite typical that teachers' evaluations plummet when they first go abroad because they have not thought sufficiently about the new classroom and adjusted their habits and standards. My assertion in this book that "cross-cultural" refers to teachers who go abroad is not meant to suggest a preference for the foreign over the domestic, or even to assume that it is not possible to have a cross-cultural experience at home, but only that in teaching abroad to students of other nationalities — whether monocultural or multicultural — teachers must self-consciously engage their pedagogical assumptions and strategies and develop new ones to cope with the particular new international context. According to Kam Louie, this can give them a deep understanding of the learning process: "teachers who gather cultural knowledge at the same time as they are imparting it are aware of the processes of learning about another culture, and that awareness deepens their rapport with the students" (2005, 17). However rewarding, this encounter with the cross-cultural classroom is often difficult; as one teacher noted in designing courses, "my major difficulty has been in designing a unit for our overseas programme. The students in that specific locality have had very different preparation from our local students but the unit must fit within the standard degree framework" (Toohey 1999, 4). As educators and students move around the world, they constantly must be aware of the fit of the local and the international and invent ways to deal with that.

The understanding of "cross-cultural" — and even transcultural — is different from "multicultural," which can be restricted to intercultural and often ethno-racial mingling within a particular country like the USA (Hollinger 1995, 13). Students in an American school may be African American, Asian American, European American, Hispanic, and Native American, representing different cultures and racial groups within the USA, without any of them, including the teachers, being international. This multicultural group probably shares and takes for granted characteristics of the national and local culture, which an international cross-cultural situation would not. "Transcultural" suggests the exchange of cultural components within or outside the boundaries of a single country, but "cross-cultural" implicitly has an international dimension (Charles Wei-hsun Fu 1990, 135; Ryan and Carroll 2005, 6) even when used with reference to seminars involving foreign professionals wanting to "assimilate as quickly as possible by enrolling in cultural training courses to learn the attitudes, accents, and auras of Americans" (Zia 2000, 210). Because of privately run, cross-cultural training seminars that prepare Americans for life abroad or for foreigners wanting to assimilate quickly into the USA, people fear that "cross-cultural" has come to refer only to American experiences and argue that the term and situations it governs should include the experiences of any expatriate encountering other national cultures. According to Gretchen Lang, one of the complaints of business cross-cultural training seminars is that the organizers forget about the perceptions and problems of nationalities other than Americans, even though they invite them to attend: "Martina Nelson, a German national whose family moved from Spain to the Philippines in 2000, said her one-day training seminar in Manila failed because the trainer geared her talk exclusively toward Americans. 'It was all oriented toward what an American expat would want to know,' she recalled. 'There was no one there who could understand what a European would want'" (2004, 13). In short, many want cross-cultural education to be universalist, incorporating the experiences of anyone who needs to understand how best to relate to other nationals, whatever the setting.

Pamela George uses the term "cross-cultural" to talk about teachers or pedagogues who are outside their native countries, are teaching students of a different nationality, and, therefore, are put in the position of rethinking their cultural imperatives and of negotiating core principles of education.

It is this understanding that I will follow in this book, and my comments are directed at those who intend to go abroad to teach. These foreign-bound teachers are my target audience, and it is my assumption and experience that they are interested in the historical and cultural conditions of a country and in need of practical advice about teaching abroad.

Teaching abroad offers rich opportunities for cultural understanding and communication for teachers and students alike because those who leave their home country and enter another need to be especially careful that they are not exploitative and arrogant toward those cultures, or guilty of thoughtlessly imposing their own home culture on others. Each culture has its own ideology, advantages, and limitations, and those who enter a new culture need to be aware of and sensitive to it, and able to critique it and their own culture as well, and to negotiate with it. Although social analysts often criticize cultural imperialism in politics and business, it can be equally present within the educational context. The first lesson to be learned by those who choose to leave their home country and live abroad is that they are outsiders and guests of their new domicile. Putting themselves outside their home country also places them on the cusp of their home value systems and the ones they enter, so that internationalization is at once a form of cultural engagement, both enlargement and marginalization. Those who work internationally are simultaneously insiders and outsiders in their home and guest countries.

Although a cross-cultural perspective can be applied to business, government, and non-government organizations, as well as school systems, I would like to focus my comments on the interdisciplinary classroom that lends itself to area studies (such as American studies, Canadian studies, Chinese studies, Scandinavian studies, etc.). Such academic domains as Media Studies and Communications can easily benefit from the same interdisciplinary perspectives, but for the sake of consistency, I will focus on area studies. As Heinz Ickstadt notes, international American studies was among the first to emphasize interdisciplinary teaching at the university level: "the founding of American studies institutes in Germany (Berlin, Frankfurt, Munich), Great Britain (Nottingham, Keele), Poland (Warsaw) and, most recently, Denmark (Odense) resulted from the wish to bring different disciplines (in most cases literature and history) together under one roof" (1996, 11).

In the process of discussing the cross-cultural classroom, I want readers to consider the role of the teacher, the relationship between the teacher and students, and the value of the local culture in relation to the international environment. By doing so, I hope to meet a critical need for pedagogical perspectives that involve not just the intercultural and multi-national classroom, consisting of students from many countries, but the increasingly complex international cross-cultural classroom that thinks about and promotes everyone's involvement in a way that draws out their best qualities, consciously incorporates and respects their cultures, and looks carefully at classroom practices that might be perceived to advance or undermine those values. In this regard, it is important to remember that, in the cross-cultural classroom, everyone is an outsider because when teachers and students are from various countries, there is no inside space that can be taken for granted. As such, teachers and students alike need to be educated into a self-conscious awareness of local conditions and be reminded of particular cultural dispositions and pedagogical preferences. It is also critical to remember that the cross-cultural classroom is about respect for each culture and a willingness to learn at every step. These, I think, must be the most important values for education in the twenty-first century.

A first step in thinking about the cross-cultural classroom is to reflect on familiar assumptions about education. As Philip Jackson (1990, 8–9) has remarked, it is easy to take the activities of classrooms for granted because they are generally consistent spaces across any given nation:

> The labels: "seatwork," "group discussion," "teacher demonstration," and "question-and-answer period" (which would include work "at the board"), are sufficient to categorize most of the things that happen when class is in session. . . . [These] major activities are performed according to rather well-defined [national] rules which the students are expected to understand and obey — for example, no loud talking during seatwork, do not interrupt someone else during discussion, keep your eyes on your own paper during tests, raise your hand if you have a question. Even in the early grades these rules are so well understood by the students (if not completely internalized) that the teacher has only to give very abbreviated signals ("Voices, class." "Hands, please.") when violations are perceived.

Such conventions are understood as second nature by the public in a given country, but need to be rethought in crossing different cultures.

National culture, then, looms large as a consideration, and I will be referring to that often, but local conditions also play a large part. For example, as a professor, I taught at the University of Waterloo, one of the most highly respected educational institutions in Canada, especially well known for its computer, engineering, and mathematics programs and its cooperative education, work-study features. Students there are smart, hardworking, practical, and able to engage in effective classroom discussions, but some colleagues argued that the institutional emphasis on technology resulted in a greater pressure for lecturing than characterized other institutions dominated by the arts. This was not my experience, but it serves as a reminder that all learning is contextually embedded, and local conditions affect pedagogy and the style of education, even when national curricula and pedagogical considerations appear to dominate.

First of all, then, this book intends to think out cross-cultural issues and problems to help educators teaching abroad avoid pitfalls and make the right decisions for a creative learning environment. To go away from one's own local environment and study or teach in a different culture is to experience a new way of apprehending life or undergo a paradigm shift, as Thomas Kuhn (1996) would call it. I wish to make the reader aware that one of the most important paradigm shifts is the internationalizing of education and the considerable degree to which we live in a global economy with teachers and students moving around the world all the time and experiencing these paradigmatic changes.

Second, I want to help the reader consider cultural identity or what Hollinger calls chosen "affiliations" (1995, 7) at personal, social, and national levels in order to create the most stimulating and effective classroom experiences for teachers and students alike. Because teachers and students can be exhilarated by mixing cultures or frustrated because that international classroom is resistant to the tried-and-true ideas and techniques that worked so well at home, self-assessment can help create better pedagogical goals and directions. In this book, I do not intend to address the subject matter of a classroom, though many of my comments are oriented towards humanities, area studies, and interdisciplinary work.

Finally, I propose to blur customary writing genres as a way to rethink intercultural communication and bridge writing cultures and classrooms. I will begin this study with the history and culture of the Chinese higher education system, and common assumptions about classrooms in the East and West. The final chapter is grounded in postethnicity theories of identity. Between these scholarly chapters, I will personalize the study, presenting my own experiences as well as scholarly comments by others who write about international education to raise issues, provide insights, and offer practical advice about effective tools and techniques for teaching in the cross-cultural classroom. Teaching at any level is deeply personal as well as scholarly, and it is my intention to combine the two — to cross writing and cultural boundaries in discussing the international cross-cultural classroom.

Chapter 1, "Internationalizing Education: The Example of China," reflects upon the recent intensification of global educational initiatives. University education has become a huge enterprise in the West during the twentieth century, and many countries in the world, including China, owe at least some of their university system to its influence. As the example of China indicates, the development of universities has not always been easy and has been linked to political winds. Recently, however, this country and others like it have been working hard to ensure that they keep pace with the rapidly changing world of science, technology, communications, and economics, both in sending their youth and professors abroad, as well as bringing experts to China for short or long terms. This receptivity to global changes has also affected certain other areas such as law and American studies, and has made English language study one of the most important subjects in the contemporary curriculum.

This goal of internationalization has extended to the creation of new programs and the restructuring of courses of study, faculties and colleges, and entire universities. The national government of China has also indicated that it wants to incorporate certain aspects of Western pedagogy and has backed that up with additional resources to its top universities, making many of its classrooms more interactive and giving individual students a greater opportunity to participate. Still, not all universities have benefited and, even in those that have, such traditional areas as literature and history have not shared equally in this development of programs, addition of human capital, economic support, or shifts in pedagogy — which suggests that such change and growth may be more heavily weighted toward the research universities and toward technology and economics rather than arts and social studies. The emphasis on change in education and the dialogue with Western forms of pedagogy may not extend equally, then, to all sectors of the university or to the country as a whole.

In Chapter 2, "The Individual, the Group, and Pedagogy," I look at the differences that an awareness of individuals and groups can make in the classroom. Many accept Geert Hofstede's dichotomy between collectivism and individualism, suggesting that, if North Americans go to Thailand to teach, for example, they must take into account the values associated with this collectivist social structure which is so radically different from the North American individualist structure. As I will note, I have difficulties with this bifurcation and prefer to think of a loose distinction between *communitarian* and *individualist* values. Nevertheless, the perceived difference between the individual in the USA and the group in China does account for certain strengths and weaknesses in each system.

Chapter 3 examines "The Classroom Environment: Physical, Emotional, and Intellectual Spaces," which builds on group and individualist perspectives. The space where learning takes place is important because inadequate and poorly planned space clearly hampers the educational process, but more important for the cross-cultural classroom is the need to think of students' cultural dispositions in relation to the space. The use of space is never completely neutral because of local and national cultural expectations and constraints, and teachers need to locate preferences and become sensitive to resistances in order to create an effective classroom. If the cross-cultural classroom only involves going between Germany and Denmark, for instance, or between South Korea and Japan, then taking into account similar preferences may be good enough. However, if a teacher goes from the West to the East, the USA to China, or an individualist to communitarian society, very different cultural expectations can come into play, perhaps necessitating different uses of physical space. How best to organize the activities of the cross-cultural classroom within a given space is thus a particularly important issue, for some cultures give priority to lectures while others prefer unstructured, student-oriented spaces.

Space, however, is not only physical and cultural; there is also a mental dimension, and students clearly need to feel that their learning does not suffer from inadequate teaching, a poor learning environment, and oppressive attitudes. They need to be assured that theirs is a level playing field, where they can learn about themselves and their cultural heritage and where they can be assured of equal treatment, regardless of race, class, gender, religion, or age.

In Chapter 4, I delve into "The Teacher-Oriented Classroom," the dominant pedagogical strategy of most cultures. Some teachers and students like to emphasize the give and take of lively student exchange, but, in most places in the world, teachers ground education with lectures as the best way to transmit information, create knowledge, and establish a basis for discussion. It is important in the cross-cultural classroom to understand this reality and see how creative lecturing can foster a positive learning environment. A single teacher in the classroom may seem the easiest and most efficient way of educating students, but team teaching can provide dynamic education, and this is especially the case where various disciplines are incorporated in a course of study — in short, where interdisciplinary learning takes place. Team teaching may not be applicable to all classroom environments, but it is especially appropriate for various kinds of area studies — American studies, Canadian studies, Chinese studies, etc. —

14   *Teaching Abroad*

provided that the teachers really do work together as a team rather than give quick walk-through presentations without collegial interaction.

Team teaching, as such, may play an important part in "The Student-Oriented Classroom," discussed in Chapter 5, helping students to discover how to relate respectfully and enthusiastically with a variety of students and faculty in an interactive environment. Most North American educators take it for granted that a discussion-oriented classroom is an excellent mode of learning, but that is not a universal assumption. Students in Asian countries and Scandinavia, for example, are taught to work as groups, but often do not like to "stand forward" individually in the classroom, whereas American students may tend to jump into a discussion and dominate it. Even in the USA, however, such student-oriented discussion can have problems. In a recent account of the wireless keypad in the American classroom, Katie Hafner (2004) argues that "although some sceptics dismiss the [wireless keypads] as novelties more suited to a TV game show than a lecture hall, educators who use them say their classrooms come alive as never before. Shy students have no choice but to participate, the instructors say, and the know-it-alls lose their monopoly on the classroom dialogue." Implied in Hafner's comment is a view that a student-oriented classroom can lack balance because quiet students do not talk and loquacious students talk all the time. In a cross-cultural classroom, this tendency can be amplified, and as many non-Americans think that the classroom is stacked against them, teachers must be particularly sensitive to the class dynamics and create strategies to include everyone. The strategies include exercises in problem solving, group work, and presentations (both group and individual) and might also involve student responsibility for classroom activities and assessments. By incorporating team-building techniques into the classroom, with teachers and students alike responsible for creating, participating, and assessing their effectiveness, students may feel part of the classroom environment in ways they never have before. Recognizing, however, that learning extends well beyond the classroom space is extremely important, and electronic technology (e-mails, blackboards, and teleconferencing) can supplement the traditional space in amazing ways. So, too, can field trips to other countries.

Whether in a teacher- or student-oriented classroom, cross-cultural education can benefit from film, the subject of Chapter 6, "Film in the Cross-Cultural Classroom." Although "reading and 'riting and 'rithmatic" have traditionally been seen as the basis of knowledge, these are never completely transparent subjects, so media aids make language, numbers, and science available to the imagination and understanding in particular ways. All forms of media — music, documentaries, films, and computer applications — can enhance learning in the cross-cultural classroom, but teachers also have to be cautious about cultural predispositions and sensitivities. Students in countries without a history of film criticism often think that films exist only for entertainment and not for social critique and, consequently, may not take film viewing as serious study. Also, certain films cannot be shown in particular countries without offending local tastes or may be barred by national censors. Thus, while the cross-cultural classroom provides an excellent opportunity to enhance learning, the teacher needs to be cautious in ascertaining the appropriateness of all the materials. I am a particular fan of film adaptations as a special kind of cross-cultural tool to raise issues about gender, ethnicity, regions, and identity, but even here the teacher must think carefully and consult widely about appropriate forms.

The cross-cultural classroom is never complete without "Assignments and Assessments," the subject of Chapter 7. Everyone assumes that students require assignments and assessments, but these are subject to cultural expectations and preferences. Some cultures are strongly oriented to large reading assignments and some to small ones; and some like final examinations, whereas others prefer ongoing or continuous assessment over the duration of the course. Teachers must work hard to understand and evaluate particular cultural demands, so that students never have the feeling that the expectations of their culture are being ignored even while they become receptive to new methods, matter, and ideology. For that reason, teachers may have to use a variety of methods of assessment. They also have to be aware of attitudes to cheating and plagiarism as well as official school policies — and lack of them — and penalties for committing them, whether the guilty parties are teachers or students. Plagiarism can be one of the most difficult and disconcerting assessment problems that teachers abroad may have to face. Another aspect of assessment is that of the classroom itself, and teachers and students alike should be involved. This is not as common internationally as Americans, for example, may assume. As it is important to everyone that learning be a positive experience, part of the closing activities of the year might include an assessment of the goals, accomplishments, and attitudes in the classroom.

The possibilities and demands of the cross-cultural international classroom impact upon personal, social, and national identities, so in the concluding chapter, "Descent, Consent, and Cross-Cultural Affiliations," I will discuss the unique and rewarding aspects of affiliated identities, those which, as David Hollinger stresses, are capable of change and multiplicity.

Students and teachers alike in international classrooms must be aware of the values inherent in cross-cultural education and the positive changes to individual identities, but they must also be aware of personal and professional risks.

In short, teachers abroad need to consider the program in total — the cross-cultural classroom environment, the students, the kinds of learning that take place, an annual review of the entire process, and resultant issues of identity. The cross-cultural classroom is one of the most interesting developments of globalization and internationalization, but it is also one that requires awareness and sensitivity. By thinking about these aspects all the time, teachers and students alike can benefit more fully from the educational process.

1

Internationalizing Education: The Example of China

For the past decade, scholars have been writing about the impact of globalization and the changing face of business and international relations. Before 9/11, much of that research painted a positive picture of globalization, but some analysts were critical of nationalist agendas, muddled strategies, and disappointing long-term effects — as they should be in undertakings of this magnitude. In the past few years, assessment has been more balanced, but most commentators still subscribe to a positive view of the economic and political effects of globalization, even if there is a long way to go.

Less has been said about the changing face of international education, but those who do write about it often focus on technology, business and commerce, and politics that feed directly into economic, political, and legal spheres. In these areas, there is a great deal that education owes to globalization, both concerning American influences on educational systems abroad and those students who come from abroad into American classrooms. In this chapter, I look at the impact of the American education system on recent developments in education abroad, especially concerning the incorporation of American educational priorities, university structures, and academic cultures as seen in the example of American studies in China.

Because, as mentioned in the "Introduction," globalization is often configured in images of technology, global capitalism, and cultural dominance, "internationalization" is increasingly the preferred term for talking about the field of education because it suggests cross-fertilization rather than cultural dominance (Welch 2002, xiii). It is with this understanding that I would like to position my comments about the interface between university systems and their goals at home and abroad.

I am interested in ways that North American educators or those from anywhere in the world can be seen to influence — but not attempt to dominate or overpower — and take on board the various cultural practices of other countries in their own classrooms. I am interested in the problems of learning situations and the transferability of knowledge when teachers and students are from different cultures and nations because "both the general culture in which a student grew up and the specific cultural setting of his or her learning environment . . . have a significant impact on learning, retention, and the transfer of information," as do social interaction skills and application of knowledge (Casmir 1998, 10). This aspect of intercultural communication, especially when the teacher is the foreigner, is what I find most valuable about the international cross-cultural classroom.

There are many ways of measuring internationalization, but, in this chapter, after giving a brief history of the modern Chinese university, I will focus on curriculum development and international exchange, and stress American studies and interdisciplinary inquiry within the humanities and social sciences. I will first look at the late nineteenth and early twentieth-century development of the Chinese university and include recent attempts to redesign, rename, and amalgamate programs and universities. I will then concentrate on curriculum design, the development of American studies and interdisciplinary inquiry, the flight from traditional humanities and social science subjects, international collaboration and student exchange, and the promise of the Internet amidst the paucity of library resources. I will elaborate also on the urgent desire of the Chinese to improve their educational system and will focus on many of these issues affecting universities in later chapters, with the understanding that tertiary changes have a strong relationship and bearing upon those in the primary and secondary levels as well.

In making these comments, I will draw on recently published research, the official reports of and e-mail exchanges with Fulbright Fellows in China and Europe from 2000–06, and my own experience of teaching at universities in mainland China and Hong Kong from 1995 to 2007. Finally, I will make some specific recommendations for developing relationships between international programs, such as those in the USA and China.

The Development of Chinese Universities in the Late Nineteenth and Twentieth Centuries

Although for many centuries China had a highly developed education system to prepare the elite for work in the civil service, mass education was not introduced until the Manchu Dynasty and the Westernization Movement (1860s to 1908). After the Nanking Treaty of 1842, ceding Hong Kong to Great Britain, and the Beijing Treaty of 1850, Western missionaries and educators promoted the education of wealthy Chinese sons in the USA and England, the development of foreign-language colleges in China, and the introduction of science in the curriculum. It was in this early period that the first student from China came to study in the USA. On January 4, 1847, the 18-year-old Yung Wing boarded a ship to study at Yale University, where he stayed for seven years, receiving his degree in 1854. Through the Early-teen Youth Studying in America Project and subsequent endeavors, Yung Wing and others were responsible for sending many more young men to the USA, beginning with a group of thirty in 1872 (Qian 2002, 11–14).

Although the origin of internationalization in Chinese universities clearly lies in the nineteenth century — whether in Hong Kong, mainland China, or Taiwan — the real impact of international education came with the abolition of the Chinese civil service examination system in 1905 and the subsequent introduction of Western educational influences. The emphasis upon science and technology in the development of universities in the 1930s and the addition of law, business, communication, and journalism accelerated the internationalization of the twentieth and twenty-first centuries. This development follows a similar, though not identical, pattern in other Asian countries such as India, Japan, South Korea, and Thailand that introduced Western characteristics in education with the expansion of American business interests and occupation of the Philippines and English, French, German, and Dutch colonization in Asia.

As a case in point, the British founded the University of Hong Kong (HKU) in 1911 as the first university on the island, and the Americans, French and Germans started universities in Chinese coastal and/or urban centers such as Tianjin, Shanghai, Beijing, Tsingtao, and Guangzhou as early as 1895 (Lin 2002, 1; Hayhoe 1999, 266; Becker 2002, 29–33). Although HKU was established as a secular university, foreign missionaries working in China throughout the nineteenth century founded numerous Christian primary and secondary schools and universities, and many of those maintained links with their international denominational sponsors until the Communists assumed power in 1949, when China nationalized all schools and its universities were forced to abandon links to religious groups and foreign powers.

As with most Asian countries, Chinese university education begins largely as a modern enterprise with a considerable debt to the educational systems of the West for structure and curriculum (Yang 2002, 136–37). The flowering of Chinese universities, however, was interrupted by the Japanese invasion (1937–45), the Chinese Civil War (1945–49), and the post-1949 reorganization of national higher education along the lines of the Soviet model. These were times of great upheaval and stress, followed almost immediately by the Cultural Revolution (1966–76), when Western influences were not only discouraged but harshly punished. The ministries of the government and provincial authorities controlled the structure and content of universities, and, in most places, it was against the rules to read books written in the West, play Western music, or listen to foreign radio broadcasts. Western-oriented curricular reform, international research, and faculty exchanges were out of the question. In general, those restrictions started to ease with the resumption of US-China relations in the early 1970s and were lifted completely after Deng Xiaoping adopted the Open Door policy in December 1978, but the Tiananmen Square incident (June 4, 1989) temporarily turned back the clock when it was felt that Western culture bore a considerable measure of responsibility for student activism and the tragic results. As one form of protest, the Chinese government (PRC) in 1989–90 cancelled the well-known American Fulbright Program, but renewed it again the following year, and internationalization continued.

Regarding the period from 1937 to 1980, Hong Kong differed significantly from the Mainland: Hong Kong education, the product of British curriculum and structure, did not renounce its colonial origins and, indeed, continues to bear that imprint in its three-year undergraduate curriculum and cultural practices, though it is moving to a four-year system in 2012. Moreover, although this colonial imprint is pronounced, Hong Kong retained it by choice and was never subjected to the constraints of the Mainland's Cultural Revolution.

With the death of Mao Tse-tung and the accession of Deng Xiaoping to leadership, mainland universities began a process of reform influenced by the transnational economy and "globalization of social life and institutions" (Postiglione 2001, 23). Although some Chinese universities were not ready for internationalization, most welcomed outside contacts, influences, and financial assistance, "developed an intellectual elite" who kept track of academic and political developments in the USA (Roberts 2004, 423), and began to develop links with foreign universities. Since the

1980s, China has encouraged internationalization and sent many Chinese abroad to study. Recently, these overseas-educated Chinese have returned home in great numbers. According to *USA Today,* in 2002 "more than 18,000 of China's best and brightest returned home, 47% more than in 2001, double the figure for 2000, and more than triple the 1995 mark." *USA Today* celebrated this return of the Chinese by announcing, "China's brain drain days are over" (Lynch 2003, 6A). By 2005, Jun Wang reported in Hong Kong's *South China Morning Post* that, "lured by zero-interest business loans and tax cuts in China, more than 190,000" of the Chinese who studied abroad "had returned by the end of last year, according to the Ministry of Education" (2005). These "sea turtles," as they are called, bring back ideas and attitudes about education that can help transform the system, but this phenomenon is not without some problems. One rising young star with a PhD from the University of Texas came back to lead a research facility at Jiao Tong University, only to resort to reproducing research and a microchip from an American corporation while claiming to have invented his own. If Chinese returning with PhDs earned elsewhere are often publicly feted and given preferential treatment and high salaries at universities, at least some have not profited ethically from their study and experience elsewhere.

Returning scholars mean increased opportunity for reform at the rapidly growing universities. In a 2003 article defending a liberal federal policy on student visas against those who wanted to restrict it after 9/11, Yale President Richard C. Levin asserted that the USA should welcome students from abroad because scholars returning to China can contribute greatly to education reform: "Although we have no hard evidence to prove the point, those of us who work in universities have learned from experience that the Chinese who study here are likely to return home favoring greater openness, freer exchange of ideas, and good relations between China and the West" (2003, 8). Although Levin does not define "greater openness" or "freer exchange of ideas," these general goals are important to the refashioning of an educational and political system at many different levels.

Returnees to China, however, have worried about access to a truly international education at the most basic elementary and secondary levels, to say nothing of university education: "Now, the biggest hurdle often is the difficulty of finding an affordable quality education for returnees' children. China's poor schools are the reason many of the country's future elite go abroad in the first place. Many schools employ a rigid system of rote memorization, ill suited to a modern economy . . . As a result, many people leave their children and spouses abroad, especially at first" (Lynch 7A).

Increasingly, the PRC has argued for educational reform at every level, with the Ministry of Education itself seeking to reform the university system, including that of humanities and social sciences (Hayhoe 1999, 258). According to reports of the Communist Party, "China's membership in the World Trade Organization (WTO) makes improving higher education a top priority and will probably lead to more cooperation with foreign universities, including increased trade of educational and training services, potentially resulting in further improvement of teaching and scholarship" (Postiglione 2002, 149). China has recently made great strides in the manufacturing of high technology equipment for export and domestic markets but knows that, to make a significant leap into invention and product design, it will have to foster creativity in its education system. As Xu Kuangdi, President of the Chinese Academy of Engineering, told the political journalist Thomas L. Friedman "we have to build more products from our own intellectual property" by "improving the innovative capability of the younger generation," and Friedman himself adds, "which will require some big changes in China's rigid, rote education system. Chinese officials, [Xu] said, are thinking about such changes right now" (2004). As Paul Mooney reports in "The Long Road Ahead for China's Universities" (2006, A42), they certainly are doing so, but some self-defeating notions of rote memorization carry on.

In implementing reform, the Ministry set out in 1998 to identify 10 key universities and 100 leading research centers important for economic and social development and top-quality higher education, to reform the administrative system, and to improve research capacity and international reputation (Yang and Yeung 2002). One of the most important areas of reform has been curriculum design, which is now being left to the individual institutions, thereby increasing autonomy and academic expression (Hayhoe 1999, 258–59). Accordingly, Sun Yat-sen University in Guangzhou, one of China's top 10 research universities, has been given a special mandate to transform educational methodology.

This reform is especially timely as the entire university system rapidly expands. China has taken on board the West's recommendation that it adapt populism and educate more of its students at the highest levels. This is a brave and challenging move for, with a population of some 1.3 billion people, China in 2002 already educated more than one quarter of the world's university students (Postiglione 2002, 151). According to Min Weifang, Vice President of Peking University, in 1994 there were 1,080 regular higher learning institutions in China, and one year later there were 1,156, an increase of 76 institutions in one year (1997). Since then, the central government has raised the total number of colleges and universities to 2000, increased student numbers to 16 million, and poured "an estimated $11.6-billion [into universities] during the five-year period ending in 2004," tripling their acreage. They hope to "double the percentage of young adults enrolled in college, to 40 percent, by 2020" (Mooney 2006, A42), creating one of the largest higher education systems in the world" (Min 2001) and educating up to one-half of all university students in the world.

Internationalization in education in China is timely and generally positive, although not everyone there agrees with all of the reforms in management and administration, financing of higher education, internal resource distribution, or curriculum development. There are some China watchers, too, who worry about a stratification of higher education structures and a marketization of the higher curriculum as municipalities race to specialize in popular academic areas. Although schools of medicine, education ("normal schools"), engineering, agriculture, military strategy, and foreign languages still exist, most specialized colleges and universities do not limit themselves to these traditional areas. The central government has given responsibility to local institutions to choose their specialties, decide enrollment, and appoint staff. The names "University of International Business and Economics" (Beijing), "Shanghai Jiao Tong University Law School," the "Nanjing-Johns Hopkins Center of Chinese and American Studies," the "Tsinghua School of Journalism and Communication" of Tsinghua University, the "Center for American History and Culture" of Nankai University, and the "Xi'an University of International Studies" suggest many new directions within old universities (Shanghai Jiao Tong, Tsinghua, and Nankai universities), institutional renaming to define and market university identity (Xi'an), or new universities needed to keep pace with the changing times and market trends. Renaming is, of course, also designed to attract attention from foreign universities, international donors, and foundations offering financial and human resources.

Because some 2,000 diverse colleges and universities exist in China, regional governments have attempted to bring together several under one roof, creating large flagship universities that are common in North American education. A few years ago the comprehensive Sichuan University combined with Chengdu University of Science and Technology, creating a university of 22,000 students, the largest in China at the time (Hayhoe 1999, 259–60). Recently, in Guangdong province, several colleges and universities have been brought together as the new Sun Yat-sen University, resulting in an even larger student body of some 34,000 students, almost half of them in the graduate and professional schools. Plans are afoot, too, to raise the enrollment to 60,000 students with the completion of an additional campus at Pan Yu, an island in the middle of the Pearl River, together with other universities from Guangzhou. Even in Hong Kong with its nine universities, the government has proposed amalgamating three of them — the Chinese University of Hong Kong, the Hong Kong University of Science and Technology, and the Hong Kong Institute of Education — to form a multiversity of 25,000 students. This latter merger will probably never happen, but the point is that such mergers create a new type of comprehensive Chinese university with a potentially more varied curriculum.

This tendency to redesign universities by adding new colleges or to create large comprehensive universities out of small ones is similar to strategies of American education. Indeed, one Fulbright Fellow located at the University of International Business and Finance in Beijing noted that "these schools are trying to create a template consistent with US schools."

Lingering Structural Constraints: Financial, Ideological, and Linguistic

Building new campuses and creating ever-larger universities, however, has not put to rest some of the major concerns about international education in China because many systemic problems linger concerning funding, the impact of political ideology on the classroom, and the relative lack of English speakers within the universities.

The first constraint on the improvement of the university system is funding. Although at the turn of this century the government has invested remarkable amounts of money on education, distribution is uneven across the country, and the central, regional, and local governments together do not spend as much on education as is necessary to be competitive with other developing countries in the same region. In 2006, for instance, the central government of China spent 4% of its national budget on education, but in 1998 Vietnam was already spending 12% of its national budget and has since increased that amount. It is true that the cities in China, rather than the central government, are expected to bear the main financial burden for education, and Beijing and its surrounding cities, as well as Shanghai and Guangzhou on the industrialized eastern seaboard, do fund excellent educational systems from primary through to university. However, education in the center and west of the country, as well as in towns and villages of the east (as opposed to the principal cities), is often under-funded, and students are not given adequate opportunities to excel in learning. Although the central government's so-called 985 and 211 Projects give liberal support to some 100 top-level universities, those listed below them cannot afford first-rate education.

Even top research universities suffer from internal differential funding. The well-known Nanjing-Johns Hopkins Center of Chinese and American Studies, established in 1986, has its own building and Master's program, and hires visiting American professors, ensuring a highly qualified, high-profile American presence, but the School of Foreign Studies at the same university employs native speakers or "foreign experts" with minimal qualifications and pays them an extremely small amount. Few of these universities hire foreign academics as permanent staff, whereas universities in Hong Kong, Japan, and Thailand hire qualified foreign academics to teach in major programs on a regular basis because parents demand foreign expertise to ensure quality education.

A second constraint is the imposition of ideology on the classroom. Many governments in Asia have centralized bureaucratic systems, and China is no exception, leading to direct intervention in university affairs to promote state ideology and national unity (Morris and Marsh 1991, 261–63). Chinese universities often have dual administrative structures in their faculties headed by Deans and Communist Party Secretaries. Though interference with academic freedom varies from university to university and province to province, political oversight and censorship are thus built into the academic structure. For instance, some universities actively discourage students from using the Information Resource Center at US embassies and consulates, while others do not. Similarly, one Fulbright Professor in Shanghai was advised by his Dean not to distribute to his students certain Western newspaper articles downloaded from the Internet, but, during three years in Guangzhou, I was never given any such instructions, and the courses I taught and the content were not censored.

In many places, political ideology bears considerably upon curriculum, and, in this respect, it has important implications for pedagogy. Although China has a great desire to achieve international standards and join the global academic community, the Communist Party apparatus wants to control what students learn and what professors say. A recent *New York Times* article illustrated this dilemma: although major Chinese universities were trying to attract senior academic talent from abroad (primarily of Chinese descent), qualified candidates and established professors in China complained of a lack of academic freedom. According to Howard French in "China Luring Scholars to Make Universities Great" (2005), "China is focusing on science and technology, areas that reflect the country's development needs but also reflect the preferences of an authoritarian system that restricts speech. The liberal arts often involve critical thinking about politics, economics and history, and China's government, which strictly limits public debate, has placed relatively little emphasis on achieving international status in those subjects." He concluded, "Chinese say — most often euphemistically and indirectly — that those very restrictions on academic debate could hamper efforts to create world-class universities" and, in support, he cited Lin Jianhua, Peking University's Executive Vice President, who commented, "right now, I don't think any university in China has an atmosphere comparable to the older Western universities — Harvard or Oxford — in terms of freedom of expression" (ibid.). He added, "We are trying to give the students a better environment, but in order to do these things we need time. Not 10 years, but maybe one or two generations" (ibid.).

Even when Chinese students do not suffer from overt imposition of ideology on their curriculum, they lack public spaces where they can openly discuss and debate public issues, restricting their ability to enter local, national, and international debates. According to Howard French (2006), all "politics, even school politics, is banned on [electronic] university bulletin boards," and China has "as many as 50,000 state agents who troll online, blocking Web sites, erasing commentary and arresting people for what is deemed anti-Communist Party or antisocial speech." Some universities also have sizeable corps of volunteer students who provide similar assistance in monitoring websites in the name of "socialist morality" (ibid.).

A third constraint on the development of international universities is linguistic. Apart from foreign language departments and business schools, there are too few Chinese professors and students who can speak fluent English. Thus, teaching across disciplinary lines can be difficult. A Fulbright Professor who taught political science in a major Beijing university said he had no Chinese colleagues who spoke English, and other Fulbright Professors in the fields of law and history complained that they did not know if their students understood half of what they said in class. Nonetheless, my teaching experience at Sun Yat-sen University has been different: I lecture in English to American studies/History open courses of between 60 and 130 students, each drawn from across the university (especially in business, the sciences, and medicine) who are articulate and engaged, and I team-teach these courses with two European and Australian colleagues from the Department of Communications and Design and four Chinese colleagues from the Department of History. This exception, however, does nothing to mitigate the magnitude of this problem in other places, but with the central government's decision to begin English training at age six in the major eastern cities, this situation will undoubtedly change in a generation.

Curriculum Reform

Despite these real weaknesses, China is changing rapidly, almost daily, and wants to develop a template consistent with American education in structural and administrative models and in curriculum design. Accordingly, richly developed curricula are being established all over China in response to both internal development and international forces. The University of International Business and Economics in Beijing tries to standardize its MBA programs with those in the USA and has a joint-EMBA program with the University of Maryland. Also, the Tsinghua School of Journalism and Communication has set up institutes to deal with international issues, placing a heavy emphasis on the international dynamics of media communication in research and course work. Although the Tsinghua School was only established in 2002, there are already 20 full-time faculty members for 200 students, a faculty/student ratio that universities in North America and Europe would envy. Considerable money has been spent to establish this School of Journalism, and the facilities are state-of-the-art. Also, law schools across the country have been attracting professors from abroad to help transform international law in China.

A further feature of curriculum reform, one that serves people across the vast distances of China, is distance education, and Chinese universities are linking up with American institutions to start projects and create common courses. Fudan University, in Shanghai, has become part of the intercollegiate classroom system of the Global Knowledge Network, based in Australia; Shanghai Jiao Tong University and the People's University of China have linked up with Cornell University's Human Resources Center to deliver courses using teleconferencing technology; students of history at the University of Hong Kong and anthropology at the College of William and Mary meet weekly through videoconferencing technology; and students of American studies at the University of Hong Kong meet weekly with students at the University of Southern Denmark-Kolding for courses on Asian American culture and Globalization. These are very specific cases in which curriculum reform is enhanced electronically by professors and students, and in which international and Chinese professors share the same goals and learn from each other's pedagogical practices. In addition, there are projects in China that involve many different international relationships; for example, Sun Yat-sen University, the University of Southern Denmark, the University of Waterloo, and the College of William and Mary are exploring a four-university MA that involves a mandatory student exchange in the second year.

However, the constraints noted in the subsection on "Lingering Structural Constraints: Financial, Ideological, and Linguistic" (see pp. 24–27) continue to operate here. It is mainly the universities in Beijing, Guangzhou, and Shanghai that attract visiting professors, including the Fulbright (in the fall of 2005, 80% of the Fulbright Professors went to these three cities), that enter into agreements with international universities, and that provide an impressive menu of curricular choices. What students can do varies widely in China's education field and is subject to funding and political pressure.

An area of curriculum reform that would not be difficult to finance is the reduction in the number of courses that Chinese university students are required to take. There is a long-standing pattern in Chinese education that students should take up to eight courses a semester, "giving them little opportunity to focus deeply on any one of them" (Mooney 2006, A42). Because many faculty members do not require students to read particular essays or books in conjunction with a course and because they do not include readings for examinations, they assume eight courses to be a reasonable load. Students, however, commonly indicate that it is unmanageable, and, as a result, concentrate only on those courses required in their major area and pay little attention to university electives or "open courses." In keeping with that perspective, administrators do not penalize students for open courses that they have failed, and department committees overlook them when students apply for graduate programs — the net effect being that only the five or six courses in the major each term really count.

Some universities have begun to address this issue of requirements. The Arts Faculty of the University of Hong Kong has lowered the number of courses a student must take each semester from eight to six, allowing instructors to include more reading material in the syllabus. Similarly, the University of International Business and Economics in Beijing "has slashed the number of required courses from 160 to as few as 120," and "Master's-degree programs, with the exception of law, have been cut from three years to two" (Mooney 2006, A42). As universities cut the number of required courses, all courses begin to count more equally, encouraging students to be more responsible in seeking a well-balanced package of electives and required disciplinary courses.

American Studies

Increasingly, a marker of internationalization in curriculum throughout China and all of Asia is the cultivation of international studies, global studies, American studies, Asian studies, European studies, and many others. Upon resuming study of the West in the 1980s, Chinese universities began to focus on international issues and, especially, to form American studies programs, departments, and centers, so that by 1990 at least 15 existed in China, although these were initially limited to economics, politics, and international affairs and sometimes restricted to earlier periods of US development. As evidenced by the American Studies Network in China sponsored by Julia Chang Bloch's US-China Education Trust, that number has risen to at least 28 universities (including Hong Kong). These include:

- Beijing Foreign Studies University
- Chongqing Technology and Business University
- China Foreign Affairs University
- East China Normal University
- Fudan University
- Guangdong University of Foreign Studies
- Guizhou University
- Jinan University
- Luoyang Foreign Languages University
- Maoming College
- Nanjing University
- Nankai University
- Northeastern University
- Peking University
- People's University
- Shanghai Institute for American Studies
- Shanghai International Studies University
- Shanghai Jiaotong University
- Sichuan International Studies University
- Sichuan Normal University
- Sichuan University
- Southern Yangtze University

- Sun Yat-sen University
- Tongji University
- The University of Hong Kong
- Xi'an International Studies University
- Xiamen University
- Yunnan University

This Network is attempting to coordinate research activities and program alternatives among the various member universities and strive for common goals, countering John Deeney's observation on behalf of the Hong Kong American studies delegation to China in 1996 (consisting of J. Deeney, R. Horwitz, G. Mills, P. Roberts, and G. Slethaug) that American studies in China was weak, fragmented, and restricted to broader USA-China relations, economics, and political science. Even now, most universities concentrate on those "traditional" areas: for example, Beijing Foreign Studies University specializes in Sino-American relations, and the Institute of American Studies at the Chinese Academy of Social Sciences and Fudan University focus on international relations. In the late 1990s, however, American studies developed and diversified. East China Normal University, Shanghai International Studies University, Xi'an University of International Studies (formerly Xi'an Foreign Studies University), Northeastern University, Nankai University, Nanjing University, Sun Yat-sen University, Sichuan Union University, and Xiamin University now include American literature, film, and culture, although popular culture is still underrepresented. In addition, Shantou, a recently established small university in Guangdong with considerable private support, is a pioneer in creating an American-style liberal arts curriculum and credit system.

American popular culture and contemporary society are still underrepresented in part because of a lack of interdisciplinary initiatives — as is the case in most universities internationally — and in part because of inadequate resource materials such as documentaries and videos. Another reason for the dearth of teaching on popular culture depends on the vision of university education in China. Education in China has been seen as a way to raise the culture economically, philosophically, and spiritually, and American popular culture is not perceived as assisting in that quest. While China wants to take its rightful position on the international stage and is trying to build a strong, internationally recognized university system to help with that, embracing Western — specifically American as opposed to North American and European — cultural and educational imperatives is sometimes met with resistance. Occasionally, these are rejected outright because not everything from the American educational system can readily fit, because the expertise and experience are not available, or perhaps just because they come from the USA. In short, there can be many reservations about Western culture and things American in a China that wants its own identity in education as well as the broader culture.

Although largely free of the early political challenges of mainland China, Hong Kong did not begin to develop American studies until a decade ago and, even then, in only one of the universities. The University of Hong Kong (HKU) initiated American studies in 1992, and the program began to flourish in 1995. Initially, this program, located within the Faculty of Arts, restricted itself to literature and history, but then expanded into other areas. Those teaching there in 1995 realized that students were unfamiliar with US culture apart from television and films, and, following an American studies tour of programs in China in the spring of 1996, thought that the University of Hong Kong would be unique among Chinese universities if it stressed American cultural issues.

HKU initiated a program that would consider history, literature, popular culture, gender and class, multiculturalism (especially Asian American culture), business, and globalization. This became a popular program, and the total enrollment in courses climbed from 10 students in 1995 to as high as 1,000 in 2002–03. The program developed links with mainland Chinese universities (Xi'an, Northeastern, Nanjing, and Sun Yat-sen) and with American universities (the College of William and Mary, UCLA, and Yale) through visits, e-mail student exchanges, Fulbright Professors, symposia, and regular academic exchanges involving students and staff.

This program also became well known for its experiments in team teaching. In many courses, two or three faculty members from various disciplines share in the delivery of materials and sit in on others' presentations, so that students learn the value of many voices and shared knowledge. Students also learn to feel comfortable with the discussion of ideas among faculty members and develop confidence in their own abilities to participate.

Interdisciplinary Inquiry and "American-Style" Teaching

Although interdisciplinary teaching is increasingly spoken of as a preferred pedagogy in the USA — though by no means a fact in the classroom —

Hong Kong and mainland China universities have been slow to adopt that method, are largely ignorant of the effort and techniques required, and have shown great reluctance to fund it adequately. According to Min Weifang of Peking University, "because of the heavy influence of the former Soviet Union, the narrowly defined fields of study have produced short-sighted students both in knowledge and skills, and the curriculum still does not allow much room for individual differences and interdisciplinary learning" (1997). Min adds, however, that, recently, some "Chinese institutions have been cutting obsolete and redundant specialties, merging related ones, expanding applied programs, and creating interdisciplinary fields of study" (ibid.).

Hong Kong does not have the same grounding as mainland Chinese education, but in practice "the problem oriented, imagination driven, interdisciplinary approaches favored by American studies academics in the United States are, if not largely unknown, certainly not readily accepted or used" (Ford and Haulman 1996, 52). This has begun to change at the University of Hong Kong, to some degree as a result of the success of interdisciplinary work and team teaching in American studies. It has also begun to change at the City University of Hong Kong, where those in psychology, social work, East Asian studies, political science and sociology all work together. Both of these universities have increasingly made interdisciplinary study part of their priorities. However, adequate funding for interdisciplinary programs continues to be a struggle, and individual disciplines are unwilling to give up their traditional methods, status, and funding to make way for these new endeavors. Sadly, many universities include token interdisciplinary efforts but restrict their enrollment by reserving funding for traditional disciplines.

Interdisciplinary inquiry is also moving forward in mainland China, but at a slow pace. Students from cognate departments (history and politics, for example) sometimes co-mingle for particular purposes and events; some departments arrange for guest lectures from outside their areas; and symposia and lecture series are established to highlight the relationship between theory and practice in related disciplines. To its credit, the central government in Beijing is aware of the value of different kinds of pedagogy and has urged universities to begin adapting new ideas and techniques.

Team teaching and self-conscious exploration of ways to break out of the traditional classroom format and conventional lecture style can be important parts of interdisciplinary study in the cross-cultural classroom. Some call this "American-style teaching" and contrast it with "Confucian teaching" in which students are addressed as a group, hold their teachers who give formal lectures in high respect, and are mainly receivers of information. The rule of departments is strongly entrenched within universities across the globe, and this is also the case in China, which means that cross-discipline consciousness and interdisciplinary inquiry exist only in a limited sense. However, "there is a recognition that problems exist in university teaching. Scholarly papers, government reports, and popular newspapers make note of the fact that teaching methods are still traditional and content/examination-oriented and that modern society needs innovative thinkers" (Postiglione 2002, 157). At very official levels, then, "learning as a social activity" is increasingly challenging "knowledge-based teaching," but this may not be true in the average classroom. Michael Pettis, a professor of business at Peking University, says, "it will be a long time before China is spending as much as the United States on education, but even then it won't help China much if the system continues to penalize intellectual discovery in favor of rote learning" (Mooney 2006, A42).

One Chinese university that has taken up this particular challenge is Sun Yat-sen University in Guangzhou. Located in the middle of a special economic zone, this university has begun to take important steps in liberalizing its educational system. An amalgamation of several universities, it is streamlining its operation to avoid the usual redundancies of multiple institutions. More importantly, it has accepted a national mandate to liberalize the classroom and has shown special interest in interdisciplinary study and team teaching, and has worked with the Lingnan Foundation of New Haven, Connecticut, to initiate new teaching areas and styles. Two humanities and social science departments — History and Anthropology (including Communications and Design) — stand out in their wish to take steps to link American and local academics in their classrooms, creating real cross-cultural opportunities. In this regard, the goal of "American-style teaching" is to create what might be called an international learning environment and interactive space for learning — reconfiguring seating in the classroom space (sitting in a circle or breaking into small discussion groups); involving students pedagogically through questions and answers, individual and group presentations, and self-conscious reflection on the teaching process; and implementing problem-based inquiry. Undergraduates often value student-centered learning as long as it does not threaten them or destroy their sense of group solidarity (Slethaug 2001). Different cultures may also have a different sense of goals: in my experience, Americans tend to prefer open-ended topics, with students choosing their own focus, Danes want more certainty in establishing parameters and goals, and Chinese want still more explicit directions. This may not be everyone's experience, but at least one Fulbright Professor remarked that her students in China were very willing to participate in classroom discussions as long as they were provided with specific directions about focus and expectations.

Internationalization of the classroom must therefore consider the cultural context of the students, their expectations, and course requirements in the same way.

The Market Economy and the Flight from Arts and Social Sciences

Despite numerous possibilities in curriculum design, interdisciplinarity, and new pedagogical methods, internationalization in education has often focused more or less exclusively on curriculum development rather than "old-fashioned teaching," so that "the quality of teaching remains a problem" (Mooney 2006, A42). Various reasons exist for this emphasis, not least the government's wish to use universities to develop a strong economic base, but uppermost is student interest: in the booming days of globalization and the dot-coms, university students gravitated to business, computing, and other technical areas in order to position themselves for attractive job offers in the private business sector. In a tight job market, students will do the same thing in order to be marketable at all.

This interest in things practical means that business and finance departments have flourished in recent years, both in the USA and abroad, and, although much of this emphasis may relate to regional and national standards and rules, increasing attention is paid to international trade, finance, and business law. With numbers of Western companies seeking to take advantage of the international market, students want to stay abreast of important international theories and practices as well as new developments. Many universities are, however, realizing that the cultural and social dimensions are especially important and are taking steps to internationalize them. This is also a place for programs to play a part in teaching students about social issues and culture — including business culture — because international companies often wish their employees to understand their corporate culture and business practices. Chinese universities with these programs often want Fulbright Professors and fellows and other foreign scholars with this kind of background and frequently invite them back for a second time. It is equally true that universities in North America and Europe are requiring students who want an international focus in their education to take language and culture courses in countries where they hope to work.

Perhaps this new realization about the need to investigate culture and society will stem student flight from the humanities and social sciences at home and abroad. In 1996 Staci Ford and Clyde Haulman remarked that at the University of Hong Kong, American studies, in certain respects a representative Arts program, was not seen as "a very practical course of study, particularly in the energized market economy of Hong Kong" (1996, 51). Despite students' concern that American studies was not as strategically placed in the market as business, its enrollment rose because of its innovative curriculum and interdisciplinary teaching, while in many traditional humanities disciplines, enrollments declined. Literature programs declined, for example, and, though linguistic study remains strong in certain places abroad, it has declined within the USA and countries like Denmark as well. This is especially the case in mainland China where concentrating on literature is sometimes considered impractical and a waste of time, except as an aid to learning the English language.

As a result of the student movement to practical areas, institutes of foreign languages and traditional humanities and social science departments often find themselves without adequate libraries, funding, and other kinds of resources, while practical programs thrive. An article in Hong Kong's *South China Morning Post* quotes Peking University President Xu Shihong as "blasting the unfair treatment arts faculties received in China's education system." The article reports, "the resources available to arts faculties [have] been squeezed because science faculties [have] been awarded most of the funding and grants . . ." (Staff Reporter 2003, A5). In most cases, however, it is not the science faculties, but professional faculties or colleges in business, law, engineering, and medicine that receive a disproportionately large share of resources.

Taken together, student flight and reduced funding "combine to reveal a dispirited picture of internationalization among arts, humanities and social sciences" at certain universities (Yang 2002, 147). This is not a positive observation, and it may not be universally true, but it has a ring of truth for many universities in China specifically and Asia as a whole. Indeed, colleagues in Denmark and Germany complained bitterly about the diminishing resources for humanities and the expansion of IT and business departments.

International Collaboration and Faculty Exchange

On a brighter note, in order to ensure cross-fertilization of curricula between universities at home and abroad, many faculty members have studied or taken sabbaticals abroad and carried out international research under American university or foundation grants in order to import the latest methodologies into their classrooms. The Ford Foundation, the Fulbright Program, the Lingnan Foundation, the Luce Foundation, and the United Board for Christian Higher Education in Asia all support these scholars, as do national organizations such as the Danish American Foundation that send students and faculty abroad for extended periods. In the 1980s, of some 80,000 Chinese students and scholars who visited the USA, almost 55,000 stayed, but the volume of those going abroad and returning home has accelerated, so that, as mentioned earlier, 190,000 Chinese had returned by 2005 (Wang 2005). As China has become more prosperous, the universities receive better funding, and external controls on teaching and research diminish, well-educated scholars have returned with their masters and doctorate degrees. These scholars usually maintain relationships with universities where they studied — in the USA, for example — and continue to collaborate with faculty members there and contribute to conferences and symposia. Such on-going study and research in the West is considered a perk for high-achieving Chinese.

Increasingly, however, faculty members and students are not wholly reliant on going abroad to gain access to new ideas and research. In the latter half of the twentieth century and the beginning of the twenty-first, research facilities have improved in many Asian and European countries, including China, to the point that some in finance, communications, law, and technology-driven subjects are better than in the USA.

Other countries also hope that foreign scholars and students will come there as well, and this is increasingly the case. Although many universities abroad do not have the budget to cover the airfare of visiting scholars, they pay generously for accommodation and meals for short visits. These sometimes involve a conference, a few days of lecture presentations, or scholarly exchange. For example, over 200 dignitaries, professors, and lecturers visit the East China University of Politics and Law each year, allowing ample opportunity for consultation on curriculum and on-going collaboration on research. This does not seem an exceptional instance.

As previously noted, the number of students coming to China has also increased dramatically, and, for the most part, they have not been part of official exchange programs. Many of the highly regarded Chinese universities that lie within the key metropolitan areas of Shanghai, Beijing, Guangzhou, and Nanjing attract students from the USA wanting to study Chinese language and culture and have established language programs with American universities. These have been expanding in recent years, though some have a fixed enrollment. For example, the Johns Hopkins American Studies Master's program at Nanjing admits 50 Western students (mostly American) and 50 Chinese, offering an excellent opportunity for international cross-fertilization. Other departments within the same universities may not be so fortunate. At Nanjing, almost no international students enroll in the English Department, despite their offering American — and even Asian-American — subject matter.

Hong Kong has for many years been a transit point for scholars going to the Mainland or to other points in Asia. As such, visiting scholars are a regular feature of all Hong Kong universities and come for a single lecture, a week, or several months. Hong Kong faculty members collaborate with those in the USA on any number of projects. Here, too, a growing number of Americans study Chinese language and culture, but, because the lingua franca in Hong Kong is Cantonese, not Putonghua, and because in the past the universities made little effort to attract or accommodate foreign students, most go to mainland universities instead. Few undergraduates from China go to the USA as part of their programs, although many hope to broaden their international exposure after undergraduate training. For example, although the Chinese legal system is not based upon British/American common law, students at Shanghai Jiao Tong University Law School know that to understand international law in relation to their own system, they need to study further in the States or the UK, so they try to work in an overseas educational experience after their legal training in China.

Contrary to experience on the Mainland, undergraduate student exchanges are a growing feature of Hong Kong education. All universities in Hong Kong actively encourage student exchanges, and the government has started a program to help students to go abroad for a term or a year. The University of Hong Kong has more than 1,000 international students in a student body of some 15,000. The discrepancy in student exchanges to the USA between Hong Kong and the Mainland is almost solely based on income because, even with tuition rebates, most Chinese undergraduates still cannot afford to study for a year at an American university. This problem of financing study abroad at the undergraduate level is true for most students, including those in North America and Europe. At the graduate level, more scholarships and fellowships are available to assist those who wish to pursue their studies in a foreign country.

Library and Internet Resources

A significant challenge for the cross-cultural classroom and the internationalization of humanities and social sciences in developing countries is the paucity of library resources about American culture and society or almost any other society, even at well-known Chinese universities, although Sun Yat-sen University has recently become the beneficiary of some 500,000 books culled from the library collection at Harvard. Because a "growing proportion of the budget goes to salary payments, there is a serious shortage of funds for both non-salary instructional expenditures and necessary facilities, library books, and equipment. This situation has resulted in underequipped laboratories and libraries" (Min 2001). With few exceptions, national and provincial governments have not been able to provide sufficient money for books, journals, microfilms, and microfiche. As a result, universities depend upon donated books for collections that are dated, haphazard, and scant with no field systematically represented. If there are resources, these are often — and understandably — put toward the acquisition of texts in the local language rather than English. This means that teachers and scholars who go abroad for extended stays must bring their own lecture handouts, articles, and books — and even plan to provide them for their students.

In any event, undergraduate students often have little access to their university library collections, although graduate students can often access whatever is available. Tier one universities (e.g. Beijing, Fudan, Nanjing, and Sun Yat-sen in China) do have more resources than universities lower in the hierarchy, but frequently few or none have outstanding — or often even adequate — collections of materials in English. Individual departments usually try to build up small collections of value to the faculty and graduate students, but they are very limited. This fact alone dissuades many Westerners from studying anything other than the particular language and culture of their host country, but it also means that foreign teachers do not have easy access to the basic materials to talk about their own culture, society, and social problems. Without basic documentaries, cultural commentaries, and films, foreign students cannot gain an adequate sense of another culture, and that is equally true in the USA. Without access to materials about foreign countries, students at home may well have inappropriate notions and, if foreign students are in the classrooms, their cultures and habits are misapprehended.

Developed countries may not have the same problems with access to library materials as those in developing countries, but they also may have collections that are spotty and lacking in instant access. Libraries in large university centers routinely acquire books and journals and build substantial collections, although relatively few around the world are comprehensive. Even in Europe, universities sometimes have inadequate libraries for international research — this can be true of colleges in the USA and Canada as well — although, by contrast, the JFK Institute in Berlin has two million documents pertaining to the study of Kennedy and the USA, making it one of the top European libraries for the study of American culture.

Despite the bad news about libraries in some countries, there is a silver lining. If an interlibrary-loan system exists, some of the difficulties in acquiring books can be allayed, but these loans can sometimes take months to arrive. For those who have access to computers, the Internet and World Wide Web have opened an amazing window of opportunity. By accessing URLs (uniform resource locators) — Netscape, MacWeb or Internet Explorer, for example — to reach websites, students at home and abroad have access to an untold wealth of documents, allowing them to roam at virtual ease in documents of the USA and other countries. The portal Google alone can help students find billions of documents and is in the process of electronically copying millions of books for public dissemination. Although electricity and computer connections are unpredictable in some places, although Iran, Saudi Arabia, and Yemen use filtering technology to block politically and culturally sensitive sites, and although China has worked with Microsoft, Google and Yahoo to limit access to politically sensitive information, most Internet documents are available throughout the world. There is, of course, no quality assurance on these sites, and students may not have a skilled eye in looking for authoritative material and cannot easily distinguish uninformed from informed responses, but no one can question that, for undergraduate and graduate students as well as faculty members, the Internet has proven enormously useful in providing information and facilitating internationalization. The following are a few sites that, in addition to a portal like Google and Google Scholar, might prove helpful:

- The American Studies Association website
  http://crossroads.georgetown.edu/
- Lists of intercultural e-mail connections among students for personal exchange, projects, and classes:
  http://www.stolaf.edu/network/iecc/
- Resources on ethnic and cultural studies:
  http://www.educationindex.com

Internationalization in education, then, is an increasing reality, and many foreign countries, including China, continue to create educational opportunities for its young people and to welcome students from abroad into its programs. Although many growing programs are market-oriented or geared to professional development, China has been developing new alternatives and diversifying its offerings at an enormous rate, looking particularly to faculty members and institutional models from the West to assist in this monumental undertaking. Although many from various cultures may disagree with the greed and nationalism of globalization, they will likely look on internationalization in education with favor. Education is clearly an area for positive cooperation between China and the USA and can lay the foundation for international relations.

2

The Individual, the Group, and Pedagogy

The rapid pace of change in globalization has entailed shifts in education as well as economics and politics, and many countries, including China, are seeking new structures, areas of study, and modes of pedagogy to enhance existing systems. All educational systems have useful aspects, and the challenge is what, how, and when to introduce new elements so as to preserve the valuable features of the existing system. That China is working to integrate Western educational values into its traditional structures — from the top level of the national government to the most local of districts and from senior university institutions to basic primary schools — suggests something important about this transforming moment of its culture and global culture in general. As usual, however, China wants to ensure that the best of traditional education is not compromised.

China's desire to be careful about the process of integrating international education makes sense, not only to protect the best in its current educational system, but also to defend its own ways of thinking deeply imbedded within the individual and cultural unconscious. Richard E. Nisbett's provocative book *The Geography of Thought: How Asians and Westerners Think Differently — and Why* (2003) raises profound questions about these patterns. On the basis of his psychological studies at the University of Michigan, Peking University, Kyoto University, Seoul National University, and the Chinese Institute of Psychology, Nisbett argues that, while societies may not be hard-wired for thinking in particular patterns, the East Asian regard for group interdependency, collective agency, social harmony, and holistic complexity — as opposed to Western individualism, social agency, and focus on isolated specifics and details — each goes deeply into culture, is physically and psychologically observable, and functions as a "self-reinforcing, homeostatic system" (2003, xx). Nisbett's research team compared the perceptions of Chinese and American students as they studied pictures of fish underwater and found that American students focused on the fish while the Chinese observed the field-dependence, that is, the relationship of the field to "the behavior of the object" (2003, 24). As Robert Matthews notes, this difference revealed "fundamental differences in perception, logic and even models of reality between eastern and western cultures, with implications for business people trying to bridge the divide" (2006). To that should be added the implications for intercultural communication and basic educational philosophy, because putting these differences together in the classroom might create productive new education models and results.

In deciding to teach in China, Western educators need to be aware of these ways of thinking, social patterns, traditional precepts in culture, and related forms of pedagogy that influence the classroom at every level, as well as what local administrators, teachers, and the public might hope to gain from other countries. These "cultural values and situational factors" (Salili 1996, 86) — the field dependencies — are decidedly important for instruction, and, if some anthropologists and psychologists are correct, the most important of these considerations is the relationship of the individual to the social group in various nation states. It is critical to come to grips with this notion in the classroom for it entails ways that students relate to each other, their sense of authority and hierarchy, the power distance between students, and other aspects of the way they learn.

Many anthropologists believe that Western societies characteristically elevate the role and function of the individual, while other societies place more emphasis on the primacy of group. This view has support within the research community as evidenced by Nisbett and is also quite prevalent in the popular imagination; for instance, Tommy Koh, Executive Director of the Asia-Europe Foundation, cites the 1995 study of Asian and Western values by David Hitchcock, the Centre for Strategic and International Studies in Washington, DC. Of personal values, Koh summarizes, "Asians emphasized the importance of respect for learning, honesty and self-discipline, whereas Americans emphasized achieving success in life, personal achievement and helping others," and he notices that, "on societal values, there were three differences. First, 71% of the Asians compared to 11% of the Americans emphasized the importance of an orderly society. Second, 82% of the Americans compared to 32% of the Asians emphasized the importance of personal freedom. Third, 78% of the Americans compared to 29% of the Asians emphasized the importance of individual rights"

(1999). The importance of an orderly society for Asians and the lack of importance of personal freedom and individual rights suggest that independence and individualism are of less concern than that the entire social unit functions well.

Some anthropologists have given labels to the particular differences. As Theodore Singelis and Richard Brislin remark, "individualism and collectivism are the most widely called on constructs in explaining cultural differences," and they see them as closely conjoined to primary values and cultural ideology (1998, 67). These, in turn, are deeply tied to the goals and dynamics of society and indicative of, and responsible for, the way people relate to each other and learn.

First articulated in Geert Hofstede's *Culture's Consequences* (1980), the comparison between collectivism and individualism has been used in various contexts and refined by different writers, and the concepts have entered academic culture strongly, although not without controversy, especially because they have become almost irretrievably linked to national identities. According to those who favor the neatness and breadth of this construct, collectivists see themselves as part of, and answerable to, a group and make their decisions on that basis, whereas individualists see themselves as responsible for their own consciences, goals, and achievements (Hofstede 1997, 50). Thus, collectivists perceive themselves as interdependent, placing individual wishes in a secondary position to those of the group, while individualists see themselves as independent, put their own goals ahead of the group, are often competitive, and strive for their own success. The collectivist wants to move forward with the group, and the individualist chooses to succeed on her/his own merits. This attitude plays itself out in many different ways.

Although I recognize the value of generalizing about social tendencies and of categorizing societies as promoting individualism or collective behavior, I am uneasy with the sweep of this construct and many of its implications and prefer the thinking of Stella Ting-Toomey in *Communicating Across Cultures* (1999) who continues to use the terms, but nuances them by focusing on social relationships. My own concern with the terms "individualism" and "collectivism" is based on several reservations. First, individualism and collectivism form a binary pair, suggesting an either/or character to society, as if only one of these alternatives exists in any given place, though Hofstede for one is careful to point out a range of perspectives in particular cultures. Second, as with most binary splits, this one tends to give higher value to one term of the pair: for Western educators, this is normally individualism, and the binary split ascribes more importance to places where it is practiced (especially North America and Europe) and their institutions than to where its opposite flourishes — especially the East (East and Southeast Asia and the Middle East) or the South (Africa and South America). As Koh remarks, "the West has not yet come to accept Asia as an equal. The West has dominated Asia for the major part of the past two hundred years. Most people in the West, including its intellectuals, still regard Asia and Asians as inferior" (1999). These binary terms simply perpetuate that mindset. Third, collectivism resonates of a Marxist social model or Cold War attribution implying that this behavior is, at worst, socially programmed or, at best, lacking in independent thought. David Chidester (2005, 133) sees an American cultural bias in Hofstede's paradigm:

> Unavoidably, these oppositions, designed to be useful when doing business in a foreign culture, reflect the cultural interests of American business. It is easy to suspect that all of these oppositions can be distilled into a fundamental distinction between us and them, especially if *we* can appear as individualists in an egalitarian business environment that is nevertheless masculine in its strength and willing to take risks, while *they* register as collectivist, traditionally hierarchical, essentially feminine, and fearful of taking the kind of risks necessary for gaining profits quickly in the short term.

Despite such sweeping generalizations and related associations in this construct, the foundational idea demonstrates that the social system itself where the teaching is located, including group dynamics and context, is a useful platform for thinking about education and must be a primary consideration in the international classroom.

Perhaps, instead of thinking globally about individualism and collectivism, educators should think of dominant patterns of relationships that inform the classroom space. In every society, relationships are important, and most people do not want to violate them. Independence itself is an implicitly agreed-upon social relationship, even as is so-called collectivism. In some societies, in which independence and individualistic action are highly prized, people are often said to want to excel and further their own interests and careers, though they may wish to help others in the process, whereas in other societies, the rights of the group predominate. "Collectivist" and "individualist" social constructions, then, are focused on social attitudes, personal and social identities, human relationships, educational expectations, and classroom behavior.

In thinking about this issue in the cross-cultural classroom, I want to alter the terms and thereby reconfigure the thinking. First of all, I want to substitute "community" and "communitarian" for "collective" in order to rid the concept of links to social determinism and/or Marxist ideology. I want to think of groups as valuing independence or communitarian relationships to greater or lesser degrees, and I also want to make sure that these terms are not attached to hemispheric and national predispositions or particular ethnic groups in negative ways. Within any given society there will be a variety of reactions and a range of responses that may be generalized to present an overall, globalized and geographic picture, as does Nisbett. Second, I want to think of independence and individualism and communitarian relationships as existing on a value-free spectrum. To avoid simplistic binary oppositions, configuring social and classroom relationships in a circle rather than a linear spectrum gets rid of the idea of right and left, positive and negative, or right and wrong — all polarizing, binary pairs.

It is important to be wary of stereotypes about traditional social relationships concerning Western and Eastern culture. The culture of the USA is said to emphasize the individual, whereas Chinese, Japanese, Filipino, and Thai students are said to give high value to kinship, friendship, group relationships over personal power, "inter-relatedness" in a "dependence-emphasizing society" (Tang 1996, 183), and "cooperative learning contexts" (Salili 1996, 88), but neither construction is wholly accurate. Similarly, in areas of Europe usually thought of as orientated toward individual achievement — in Denmark and Sweden, for example — that stereotype breaks down because decisions are often taken by consensus, and individuals are often reluctant to put themselves forward over other members of the group. According to Aksel Sandemose, a Dane writing partly humorously and partly seriously in 1933, Danes have a deep desire to conform and observe the 10 commandments of the "Law of Jante" that drive them toward the group. These have recently been reconfigured to read:

1. You must believe everybody is somebody.
2. You must believe everyone is as important as everyone else.
3. You may be cleverer, but that does not make you a better person.
4. You must believe everyone is as good as you.
5. You must believe everyone knows something worth knowing.
6. You must think of everyone as your equal.
7. You must believe everyone can be good at something.
8. You must not laugh at others.
9. You must think everyone is equally worth caring about.
10. You can learn something from everyone.

(Dyrbye et al. 1997, 12–13)

This list of 10 commandments is tongue-in-cheek, but it does suggest that Danes, who think of themselves as independent, also value modesty, self-effacement, and respect for — and even deference to — others. This Law of Jante also suggests that, in finding their place within the group and acting as a group, Danes value one person's opinion as much as any other's and, as a result, believe that society should be tolerant. It also implies that one individual should be careful of stepping out in front of another, whether in the classroom or the social arena.

Perhaps this view has practical implications, too, for Danes do try to reach consensus on issues, focusing more on the importance of community and social responsibility and less on independent action than might be said of other Western cultures. High taxes (up to 60% income tax), redistribution of wealth, and the social welfare state are manifestations of their regard for the primacy of human relationships and social responsibility. So, while researchers generalize to study culture, this description of the Law of Jante in the center of a liberal western European culture that values independence shows how treacherous it is to talk about "Western" versus "Eastern" social attitudes toward individualism or communitarian relationships.

Although China tends to be more hierarchical than Denmark, students in both countries share a reluctance to assert themselves too forcefully, show off in front of others, or put others down in public. As Hofstede (1997, 61–62) remarks, "a typical complaint from . . . teachers [who move from individualist to collectivist cultures] is that students do not speak up in class, not even when the teacher puts a question to the class. For the student who conceives of him/herself as part of a group, it is illogical to speak up without being sanctioned by the group to do so. If the teacher wants students to speak up, she or he should address a particular student personally." Hofstede is quite right about how to ask questions, for both Danes and Chinese willingly participate when asked questions individually or as part of small groups, unless they really do not know the answer. The issue is not so much about individualist or collectivist societies but about the degree to which students will actively jump into a classroom conversation and the ways in which standards of politeness and social cohesion govern behavior.

The fact that various cultures defer to the group in the classroom does not mean that their attitudes toward education are congruent. Although they might not want to seem assertive in putting themselves forward in the classroom, Chinese students will work very hard and are quite competitive in their homework and examinations, whereas Danes do not necessarily celebrate competition. Danes will work hard and do not want to be seen as slackers, but they do not want to stress personal competition in the classroom. One Chinese graduate student in Denmark expressed surprise that Danes seemed so much less competitive than she was used to in her Chinese classroom. To a Westerner, this might seem paradoxical — that an Eastern society putting great value on the group also values competition highly, and that a Western society that equally values the group and the individual does not emphasize competition. Educators need to be aware of these larger patterns of individualism and community relations, but they also have to be aware of particular preferences, precautions, and cultural resistances in the local culture and on an individual basis. In addition, they need to realize that social patterns do change, especially in modern-day China.

It is important to note, in this respect, that caution must be observed not only with respect to societies at large but also subcultures. This caution may be required less in thinking about Denmark, a small country with considerable homogeneity despite recent arrivals from the Middle East, but it is required with reference to large countries like China and the USA that, despite their superficial coherence, consist of disparate groups. Although the West often thinks of China as a large, homogeneous society, in addition to the Han majority, it comprises 55 different minority ethnic groups, each of them quite different. Similarly, the USA is not simply a country that uniformly promotes individualism in business, culture, and society, but one that differs from place to place and group to group. The 2004 presidential election illustrates some of the complications and implications. The so-called blue states of the northeast and west coast voted solidly for John Kerry, but George W. Bush carried the so-called red states of the south and middle America. Political analysts have spent considerable time reviewing this voting pattern, ascribing it to the liberalism and relativism of the multicultural urban centers as opposed to the conservative values of smaller, less ethnically diverse areas; however, in many cases, the election was won by slim majorities, suggesting that, whatever the predominant view that emerges over time, the USA is culturally diverse and not as cohesive as people might want to believe.

Within those regional voting blocks — whether urban or rural, multicultural or relatively homogeneous — are the interests of people from different classes, races, and ethnicities who have varying consciousnesses and dispositions — certainly not all of them giving high recognition to the independence and individualism said to characterize the USA. For example, Kenneth Lincoln notes that in Native American enclaves "personal concerns are native matters" (1983, 4), a view seconded by Arnold Krupat who finds that individual autonomy is subordinated to communal and collective requirements (1983, 261). Lincoln and Krupat believe that, unlike Euro-Americans, Native American communities share human and material resources and find their kinship in tribal councils rather than the interiors of private homes. Still, not all Native Americans can be said to share in tribal circles or participate in this kind of kinship relations. Many have moved away from their reservations to urban areas and are indistinguishable from the American majority and their ways of negotiating in society.

In a similar way, the nomenclature of "North American" does not account for the cultural differences of Canada and the USA, which are similar, but by no means identical, societies. Institutional practices within the larger society suggest Canada's communitarian tendencies: taxes are higher, more pervasive, and used for a greater number of social benefits than in the USA; the pan-Canadian education systems at all levels are mainly public and relatively inexpensive compared to the USA, and consist of few private grade schools, high schools, or universities; the publicly funded health care system benefits everyone, and individuals pay only modest amounts for basic medicine and care; and the cities are noted for careful planning, with individuals much less likely than in the USA to buy random acreages outside the city limits to put up structures. Canadians self-consciously think of themselves as more community-oriented and less individually assertive than Americans, but even that assertion is heard more frequently in Toronto than Calgary. Consequently, although national identities and patterns of relationships clearly do exist, exceptions occur throughout society — and must be taken into account in the cross-cultural classroom.

Such exceptions aside, in places that do emphasize the primacy of the group, social cohesion is important at every level, and adults as a whole, for instance, often take responsibility for the wellbeing, discipline, and education of the young — at home and in public. In Hong Kong and mainland China, grandparents, aunts, and uncles often live in the same household as the parents and children and will help with household tasks and family care and maintenance. If grandparents and other family members do not live in the same apartment, they may still live in the same building. Although the raising of children may be primarily a family concern, society as a whole may also accept responsibility. Accordingly, it is common to see adults on the streets of China publicly admonish children who are not their own, but are boisterous and thoughtless of others. On the contrary, in the USA, with its tendency to privilege individualism, the parents usually live separately from grandparents, aunts, and uncles and generally take care of their own children, and the public seldom takes upon itself to discipline a child.

In communitarian societies in general, and in particular that of China, elders are accorded great respect, and a hierarchy of age and gender traditionally exists from the oldest male to the youngest female. That hierarchy includes the right to speak, and it is common — although not always the case — that the oldest and/or males will have speaking rights while the youngest and/or females may not. Such hierarchies of respect or patriarchies may well influence whether individuals feel comfortable trying to raise their own status individually or work through their group.

Michele Gelfand and Karen Holcombe find that these predominant relationships and aspirations play out in different ways across cultures, creating various forms of "horizontal" and "vertical" individualism and collectivism — "horizontal" referring to the tendency for individuals to remain at certain social and economic levels, and "vertical" for aspirations of upward mobility. Within this profile, those who are vertical and individualist want to excel, become distinguished and acquire status — the classical definition of self-reliant American business executives; those who are horizontal and individualist are self-reliant and want to be on their own, but are not interested in acquiring status and are happy when others excel as well — a characteristic sometimes attributed to Scandinavians; those who are vertical and collectivist support the group, try to further their goals, and help everyone to progress — a characteristic of many East Asian cultures; and those who are horizontal and collectivist support the goals of the group, want to share their achievements, and subdue personal preferences for the sake of the group — a characteristic of many within an Israeli kibbutz (Gelfand and Holcombe 1998, 122). (Gelfand and Holcombe also argue that horizontal collectivists do not submit to authority and that vertical collectivists do, but it seems to me that such a division along these lines of authority does not work well in practice.) These cultural dispositions can continue into the classroom with consequences for teacher-student relationships, preferences for assignments, and speaking rights within the group.

There are many clues about the part that social relationships and group dynamics play within the classroom, but a basic indicator of cultural preferences and tendencies is how students relate to authority figures. Societies that value communitarianism pay particular respect to those who have special functions, responsibilities, and qualities, especially those who are older, well educated, professionally trained, politically influential, and economically well situated. Students in these societies often think of their teachers as akin to the head of the family or state, give respect to them, and keep a polite distance — sometimes a spatial distance as well as an intellectual and emotional one. In countries such as China and South Korea, students often expect teachers to dress and act formally, in keeping with their highly regarded social positions. The Western habit of dressing down, sitting on top of a desk, or putting feet on a chair to relax is considered disrespectful in these circumstances. By contrast, in a classroom where individualism is fostered, students often strive for equality with fellow students, may consider the teacher as a guide and friend, and value a relaxed style of dress and personal demeanor.

This perception of the teacher can even be observed in the students' form of address to the teacher. Few of my students in Hong Kong feel comfortable calling me by my first name, preferring honorific titles like Dr. or Professor. Even when I took some of those students on month-long field trips to the USA, almost everyone would continue to address me formally, although some would ask permission to be informal but fall back into formal patterns once back in Hong Kong. To break down any absolutes that may surround this observation about group dynamics, I should note that in China, once I had indicated that my first name was easier to pronounce than my last and that I was quite happy for them to call me Gordon or Mr. Gordon or Dr. Gordon — whatever they wished, students were delighted to do so. In more individualist societies, there may be great variations, depending on whether they are, in Gelfand and Holcombe's terms, more vertical or horizontal in nature. At the undergraduate level, my students in the USA and Canada — so-called vertical individualist societies — would usually begin by addressing me by my last name and honorific title, but, when they got to know me better, would call me by my first name, as would graduate students on a regular basis — without asking my permission. Most Europeans tend to be more formal in address, indicating respect and deference to authority and the diminished importance of individualism, but, in Denmark, arguably more horizontally individualist, all students call their teachers by their first names from grade school through university, indicating a deeply egalitarian social structure at every level of society. This indicator of horizontal tendencies carries over into all levels of society and represents a radical shift in patterns of decorum over the past 40 years. This use of formality or informality in address becomes a linguistic marker of other preferences in the classroom environment, and Danish students, for example, feel quite comfortable with casual relationships and classroom conversations with fellow students and teachers alike. According to Jude Carroll, teachers should do what seems comfortable, and students should "use the name suggested. Many teachers expect first names except in formal or public situations. Calling by first names does not signify friendship or imply an equal status between student and teacher" (2005a, 30), but students will not necessarily feel comfortable with informal naming, if they have been used to a certain level of formality.

Some Danish adults lament this first-name informality and think it has been carried too far, creating a society where children do not show enough respect to their elders. The Danes say this familiarity has grown from a more formal, hierarchical society in a matter of a mere two generations, so that older members of society remember what it was like to be part of a more rigidly defined social hierarchy characterized by formal address and clothing.

This change in Denmark is, if anything, less radical than that of China where, in the past century, political control and resultant economic changes have gone from rule by the Ching imperial dynasty, to the War of Liberation and civil conflict between the Koumintang and Communist parties, to the dominance of a Maoist Communist state and the ensuing, short-lived Cultural Revolution (1966–76) to the most recent stage, capitalism with socialist characteristics. These massive political and economic changes have been matched by changes in social patterns and individual behavior. For instance, during the Cultural Revolution, many people (mainly men) were sent from the cities to the countryside for re-education into fundamental Maoist peasant ideology, putting pressure on the traditional family. This pressure increased with the movement of farmers and laborers to the cities and migrant workers to the special economic zones to find work in the new manufacturing plants authorized by the central government. This massive movement of men, and sometimes women, put stress on family units, and family separation and divorce have skyrocketed in the wake of this sea-tide of change. Whereas grandparents traditionally have taken an active role in raising the grandchildren in Chinese families, now, with the movement of families around the country, perhaps only 50% of them have grandparents to help. This alteration of family patterns and responsibility has gone hand-in-hand with changes brought about by the one-child policy, in which urban families only rarely have more than one child and, consequently, lavish their time, money, and full attention on their increasingly individualistic children, the so-called "little emperors" and "little empresses."

All of these changes, plus the remarkable growth in personal income derived from globalization — expanding manufacturing, exports, and local consumption — mean that China and other South East Asian countries (including Japan, South Korea, Singapore, and Taiwan as well as Malaysia and Thailand) are subject to considerable flux; the old conceptions of a collectivist society that values stability, hierarchy, and respect for elders and other authority figures no longer have the same currency as they did half a century ago, or even five years ago. The impact of modernization, urbanization, mobility, and globalization has created a new social reality in which individualism is on the rise across the country and increasingly taken for granted.

The Pedagogy of the East

Although making generalities about regional and hemispheric preferences or about collectivism and individualism has always been risky, Asians are said to be famous for their "positive attitude towards education, their achievement motivations, and their willingness to spend most of their free time in the pursuit of study" (Lee 1996, 25). It is believed as well that East Asian cultures emphasize the need for students to work hard to achieve wisdom and success and place high value on the leadership role and responsibilities of the teacher in helping to accomplish that. An equally prevalent, and often contradictory, negative stereotype of Asian students is that they are "respectful of the lecturer's authority; diligent note-takers; preoccupied with fulfilling the expectations of the lecturers; uncritical of information presented in the textbook and by the lecturers; seldom asking questions or volunteering to contribute to tutorial discussions; and unaware of the conventions regarding acknowledging quotes and referencing sources" (Volet and Renshaw 1996, 205–6). Another negative stereotype is unconditional respect for examinations, which pervade the education system at every level, but it is respect for authority and unwillingness to challenge it that are often cited as special characteristics that hold Asian students back (Mooney 2006, A42).

These positive and negative stereotypes find their focus in Asian preferences for a teacher-centered classroom. According to Paul Morris and Colin Marsh:

> The prevalent teaching method remains highly expository with pupils' 'activities' confined primarily to listening, recording and answering narrowly focused, factual questions. This experience confirms the universal nature of the problem, namely that the most difficult part of the curriculum to initiate change is the styles of teaching and learning used.

In the PRC teaching methods are very teacher-centred — 'a dogmatic
Confucian pedagogical tradition which has fused effectively with the
Soviet mode of instruction . . .' (1991, 259)

In mainland China, Hong Kong, Taiwan, Korea, Vietnam, Singapore,
and Japan, this reference to the importance of the teacher and other so-
called unequal social relations — ruler-subject, father-son, older-younger,
husband-wife, senior-junior, leader-led — is called Confucian because of
the great emphasis that Chinese society has put on educating the young
and maintaining civility, public safety, and social stability since the
principles were first articulated by Confucius in 500 BC. Apart from these
"Confucian-heritage learning cultures" (Biggs 1996, 46) are other Asian
countries that share values: Thailand, which has never been subject to
Chinese rule (although in Bangkok about half of the population has some
Chinese ancestry), values these characteristics as part of the Buddhist
monastic tradition (Bhikkhu 2005), and this same tendency takes place
throughout much of Asia.

Lee Wing On remarks that another primary characteristic of Confucian
thinking is the notion of the "self" as "a significant reference point in a person's
value system" (1996, 33) and network of relationships. The cultivation of
the self and personal authenticity is key to the development of moral values,
personal responsibility, and commitment to the larger society.

Although Lee Wing On and T. R. Reid, among others, accept the view
that these personal, social, and educational values are Confucian, I will call
the educational paradigm that traditionally arises in these cultures "the
pedagogy of the East." I prefer to use this phrase rather than "Confucian"
so that it does not become confused with any particular system of ethics
or religious preference. Part of the reason for not wishing to call it
"Confucian" is that these values characterize non-Confucian cultures in
Asia and because Confucianism as a philosophical system is increasingly
remote from what actually goes on in Asian countries or what students see
as reality. Kam Louie says, "Confucianism has undergone some of the most
drastic transformations in recent decades, so that while many people
continue to eulogise its virtues, these virtues are often no more than values
and beliefs that have lost all currency in their host countries" (2005, 18).
To decide whether Confucian values were considered valid among young
people, I asked two classes of my third- and fourth-year university students
in Guangzhou (over 120 students) whether

- they viewed their social preferences and beliefs in society and education
  as a conscious or unconscious product of Confucian society;

- families or schools talked directly or indirectly about a Confucian heritage; or
- Confucianism had no bearing on their social and educational attitudes.

Only four students chose the first two alternatives, while the rest chose the third. They felt that their beliefs were part of a general social value system privileging hierarchy, stability, positive social relationships, and community morality. They did not want to call it anything other than Chinese — and felt that even the Chinese label might be increasingly inaccurate.

Traditionally, respect for the teacher has been one of the main values of the pedagogy of the East along with a corresponding acceptance of power distance between students and teachers, meaning that students feel more comfortable in a lecture-oriented classroom than a discussion-oriented classroom. In contrast, students in Canada, the USA, Australia, and New Zealand, for instance — who share in the pedagogy of the West — are said to have a more egalitarian cast, less sense of hierarchy, and a minimum power distance from the teachers so that teachers and students often share an informal relationship that can de-emphasize lecturing. Despite my having used this term "West" inclusively, it must be said that European schools and universities vary widely, though there is a common perception that Italy, Germany, and France tend toward a hierarchical ordering of the classroom that centers on the teacher, while Scandinavian schools and universities are informal and egalitarian.

Because education is such an important basis for personal achievement and contribution to society, parents in the East and West want classrooms that match their cultural values — or sometimes classrooms that overcome the limitations of their cultural value system. North American parents value individual academic achievement for their children and also appreciate the socialization of sports and recreation. Chinese want their children to develop personally in the classroom and are sensitive to the responses of the entire group, so that society as a whole will move forward in a harmonious way. Hong Kong Chinese parents often say that children do not have time for sports and recreation because learning must be their personal focus and family responsibility. It is their work. Education, then, in East Asia is often a personal and family responsibility and social duty, and students who do well academically enjoy a sense of personal pride, honor their families, and meet the expectations of the community. It is still true, however, that these children enjoy individual achievement.

Parents who value these Eastern ideals may want their children to commit material to memory at very early ages and assume that self-discipline and the teacher's discipline are required to ensure this kind of learning. As authority figures, teachers should be strict, and they should give students plenty of homework.[2] As John Biggs (1995, 6) remarks of the traditional Asian school:

> The structure of secondary school teaching, in particular, reflects a cold, non-personal mode of learning: organisation is by subject, not by age or even friendship groups. Because classes are taught by different teachers, no one teacher stays with a class long enough for warm relationships to develop between teacher and student; a 'good' teacher is traditionally seen as strict and distant. Do you think schools were designed to *prevent* teachers and students from seeing each other as human beings?

Even in the early grades, teachers still lecture to the students, and students may absorb the knowledge without high levels of individual classroom participation. As many studies have shown, there is nothing wrong with a strong emphasis on memorization because it trains the mind in important ways and, when a strong power of analysis is added, students can be well grounded and creative at the same time. A concern, however, is that too frequently memorization is required without analysis, and creativity is promoted without a foundation of memory training.

Western educators often assume that rote memorization is inherently limiting and call students educated this way "stuffed ducks" because they are force-fed information (Mooney 2006, A42), but many who study education in Asia, as well as the success rate of Asians studying in the USA and Australia (Volet and Renshaw 1996, 207–15), find that the best kind of memorization has many other components, including "understanding, reflecting and questioning . . . Memorization precedes understanding, and is for deeper understanding" (Lee 1996, 36). John Biggs himself, who sometimes is decidedly critical of the Hong Kong tendency to require rote memorization, argues in favor of "repetitive learning" that leads to recall used for creative and constructive understanding and "deep learning"(1996, 54, 63). Studies have shown that the best Asian students do memorize "deeply" rather than "shallowly" or on the "surface" (Kember 2004, 42; Marton, Dall'Alba and Kun 1996, 69; Toohey 1999, 9), thus achieving that much-desired combination of knowledge and

---

2 An interesting fictional treatment of these expectations is provided in M. Elaine Ma's *Paper Daughter: A Memoir,* for example on pages 70 and 117.

understanding. Many students are "cue seekers" who will memorize if they need to for an examination but are equally adept at spontaneous interaction and discussion if that is the required outcome (Tang and Biggs 1996, 160).

As a consequence of the emphasis on memory work, teachers who use the traditional pedagogy of the East arrange the classroom so that the students learn their responses from the teacher. Although it is becoming more customary in Hong Kong to have students sitting around tables as part of early education, it is still common for them to sit individually at carefully arranged desks, so that they can see and hear the teacher without causing a disturbance. A group of 20-year-old Chinese students told me that as young school children, they had to sit in the classroom silently with their hands folded, memorizing details of the teacher's presentation. Certain testing mechanisms ensured that students gave back to the teacher what they heard. All of these classroom techniques and spatial arrangements assist in transmitting the cultural authority of the teacher and the group. In this hierarchical model, the teacher is an expert and authority, and, Pamela George argues, the information is kept unambiguous, resulting in clear, direct, and, to some extent, predictable results (1995, 8).

The students' primary and secondary education typically involves the teacher talking to a group of students lined up in desks side by side in even rows, and this setting is comfortable for university students as well. In the most extreme form of this "performance for an audience," as in large classrooms and lecture halls, there may be little interaction between instructor and student beyond eye contact, body language, and some kind of verbal affirmation that the message is getting through, and that style may not alter significantly even in smaller classrooms. Teachers in elementary and secondary schools using this pedagogy are to maintain discipline in the classroom and not form close attachments with the students. This principle is made possible by a layout of the classroom that does not lend itself to informal chatter among students or casual relationships between teacher and students.

My students in Hong Kong referred to this lecture situation as the traditional "Asian model of teaching" because of its traditional position within Chinese education and its emphasis on the hierarchical prominence of the instructor and the respectful receptivity of the students. Because students from societies in East Asia tend to think of this model as Asian, I will refer to it that way, but without forgetting that it is a familiar classroom model for societies elsewhere that do not have this tradition, even for large classes in American schools and universities. In general, however, North

Americans at home and abroad prefer small, informal classes and try to break larger lectures into smaller units.

Before ending on this note and proceeding to the pedagogy of the West, however, I want to interrogate and, as Jacques Derrida would have it, put "under erasure" characteristics of Asian students, who, according to Kember (2004, 39):

rely on rote-learning
are passive
resist teaching innovations
are largely extrinsically motivated, which is usually regarded negatively
have high levels of achievement motivation
are high achievers
are good at project work
are willing to invest in education.

David Kember finds that, if the actual study patterns of Asian students all conformed to these stereotypes, they should not have such high levels of achievement locally and internationally. As noted above, his studies have shown that: their memorization is often accompanied by deep understanding; resistance to teaching innovation occurred mainly because they were not given opportunity and time to adjust; study and preparation for a career were seen to be harmoniously aligned; and achievement was desirable but not as a fulfillment of ego that typifies Western societies. In short, making distinctions between the pedagogy of East and West must not lead to stereotyping.

The Pedagogy of the West

When I asked Hong Kong, mainland Chinese, and Korean students what they considered a typical Western educational style, most thought it American-derived, interactive, lively, and ideologically linked to free expression. They also thought it to be characterized by strong interpersonal relationships, self-motivation, an informal atmosphere, a lack of hierarchy, and centered on the student. I will take up those issues in a moment, but first I want to stress one thing that they did not mention — the primacy of reading in the classroom.

American courses, like those throughout the Western hemisphere, usually require large amounts of reading for each class. Classroom lectures and discussion are frequently based upon reading assignments, and students are expected to read the material in advance of the class in order to respond critically to it. Teachers often state that students should have their own opinions. This tendency differs considerably from many places in Asia where the lecturer is expected to have read the required information, distilled it for the students, and put it in the context of appropriate theory, in which case the students absorb it second-hand. Because textbooks are relatively expensive in China and because libraries have few texts that Westerners might consider essential for their courses — especially those in English — lecturers need to bring articles and books with them and to give reading assignments that students can realistically undertake given cultural expectations and available time. As Chinese students have usually not been taught to skim material, they should be given "short texts in the beginning, with guided questions that elicit the level of analysis desired" (McLean and Ransom 2005, 56). From the lecturer's point of view, required reading for a course is perhaps the biggest difference between many Asian classrooms and those of the Western world. That, in turn, means more responsibility for lecturers in Asia. If they are the sole sources of the material and the interpretation of it, their function is unparalleled by anything in the West. This in itself accounts for one of the big differences between the current pedagogies of East and West.

There are other significant differences, however. As some Hong Kong students noted, American-style teaching (as opposed to Asian or British, both of which have formed the culture there) is more student-centered:

- "Quite interactive. Students can freely express their opinions. Very open discussion and active."
- "Lots of discussion in class. Teachers and students are just like friends."
- "It should be interactive, involving student participation instead of merely lecturing by professors. Also, teaching materials can include some videos . . . not only reading."
- "A lively atmosphere. Not too pushy, relatively freer, students are self-motivated rather than pushed to work on their studies."
- "More informal."
- "Lecturers know all the students' names. Students voluntarily raise questions and voice their opinions. Everyone . . . in the classroom is enjoying it. It's not an intense atmosphere."
- " 'Open' — one that encourages student participation and allows their voices to be heard."
- "American-style teaching tends to draw more on its immediate surroundings and less upon the textbook. . . . I associate freedom,

flexibility, multi-faceted aspects with the so-called American-style teaching . . . Teachers are teaching from the mind rather than off a textbook . . . [and] lecture material is not based so much on facts as it is upon reasons behind the facts."

- "Allows more space for students to think/Encourages students to think."
- "Students challenging lecturers is welcome."

From these responses in classes ranging from 25 to 150 students in Hong Kong and mainland China, it is clear that students do not automatically associate so-called American-style teaching with small classes, but rather a more informal, student-centered, individual-focused atmosphere, regardless of class size. In practice, in university classes of 30 to 50 students, North American instructors at home or abroad often combine lecturing and class discussion — although, of course, this practice is also based on the teacher's personality — and classes of 20 or fewer are less formally structured, both in presentation style and seating arrangement. Seats for classes smaller than 30 in flexible classrooms are sometimes arranged in a circle with the students taking an active role in questioning and responding. Many American instructors will say that they prefer the seminar approach or "circling the wagons," a visually descriptive term that goes back to frontier times in the USA when the settlers would put their covered wagons in a circle to provide a line of defense to keep out Indians, strangers, and wild animals. The circle thus becomes a metaphor for community, communication, equality, and participation. Seminars and circles are not yet common features in Chinese education, and, because the circle tends to be favored by some Americans, many students think of it as part of American-style teaching.

Whether in Asia, Europe, the Americas, or Africa, issues of space and seating arrangements may be mainly practical, based upon certain spatial arrangements, but they are ideological as well and speak volumes about the kind of social relationships that are valued and instructor/authority-centered and student/individual-centered learning. This is something that needs to be fully understood for an effective international cross-cultural classroom, and the teacher needs to be aware of the implications in developing classroom pedagogical models because students may have strong emotional attitudes about them. The teacher also needs to be conscious of the value attributed to these cultural and pedagogical practices in establishing space and using and assessing modes of learning for teaching is, to whatever extent, cultural and contextual. I will discuss this issue more fully in the next chapter.

There are probably many reasons for these preferences in style from country to country, but there are two major factors: (1) individuals (for example, from North America and certain European countries) are taught at an early age to engage in conversation in the classroom and talk with each other as a means of procuring information and thinking about knowledge; and (2) certain groups (again, for example, from North America and some European countries) have been taught to have faith in the collective knowledge and power of the group, while others may look more toward authorities as the source of information and advice. Sometimes students who come from hierarchical societies with a great sense of power distance between teacher and students do not understand class discussion as a means of discovering information and formulating individual opinions and, therefore, think that American students, for example, just like to talk, whether or not they know the subject matter. Students from societies that look for strong leadership from the teacher in the classroom as a means of moderating or curtailing what they think is useless conversation might not find conversation rewarding. Regardless of how useful the conversation may seem to some students in discovering knowledge and becoming more articulate, to others it is a waste of time. Even how valuable an asset conversation really is will vary from culture to culture. In researching speech patterns of students and teachers in American and British classrooms, Jurate Ruzaite remarks that British students typically do not use conversation to discover information from others or define their own positions in the classrooms and, therefore, speak in short fragmented responses very different from their teachers' speech. However, she discovers that "American students are very active participants in academic discourse" (2004, 21), use class discussion as a means of formulating their own views, and speak in longer, more fully articulated sentences similar to those of their teachers.[3] The value that each group places upon the experience helps to determine their speech patterns.

The social value of the teacher's prominence and the importance of student participation in classroom discussion should be taken into account when organizing classes because these predispositions are often unconscious and run deep, influence interaction within class and attitudes outside class, and, ultimately, if they are not taken into consideration, could

---

3 Ruzaite made these comments in a discussion following her conference paper on "Cross-Cultural Differences in Professional Settings: Vagueness in British and American Academic Discourse."

jeopardize learning activities in a cross-cultural classroom. Knowing the expected function and authority of the teacher and the kind of student relationships anticipated in the conventional classroom is of utmost importance in organizing the content and activities of classes. In classrooms with dispositions likely to run counter to new ideas about effective cross-cultural learning, teachers would do well to talk with colleagues and raise this issue with various groups, so that they can consider the differences and incorporate that thinking into group dynamics.

Stereotypes about the function of teachers and students or about students from different kinds of cultures can sometimes jeopardize the best intentions for a classroom. This concern can exist equally whether internationalizing education at home or abroad. William Gabrenya, Jr., for example, notes that "international students in America complain of their American peers' shallow friendliness, sexual free-for-all, alcohol addiction, and disrespect for teachers, whereas Americans in China are disgusted by their hosts' hostility toward strangers, sexual double standards, nicotine addiction, and submissiveness to teachers" (1998, 58). Should these stereotypical differences between social and classroom cultures of East and West lead to disrespect for other students and teachers, this can damage the classroom environment. Those who teach in a cross-cultural classroom need to be aware of these cultural perceptions and values, in order to deal with personal prejudices and expectations and forge them into a positive learning environment, but it is also important not to assume that these attitudes are inflexible and unchanging.

Classroom relationships focused more on the individual or on the group may seem worlds apart, but in the globalized world and international classroom they can collide. When they do, urgent accommodation must be reached, and the process might lead to negotiation, and, as Jeffrey Ady remarks, "negotiations are often conflictual, especially when parties to the negotiation do not enjoy great flexibility in positions they represent. Negotiations across cultural boundaries can be much more conflictual because there are frequent clashes between parties regarding culturally defined roles for negotiation" (1998, 111). If there are conflicts arising from discrepant cultural orientations, for example between the pedagogies of East and West or stereotypes about students, the individual classroom is not so likely to have structures for fruitful negotiation, and, if it is a sensitive issue that has escalated, the steps of negotiation have to be carefully articulated and rehearsed. Where there are no established roles and rules, teachers and students will have to be cautious so that an accommodation can be reached.

Knowing whether society gives primacy to the individual or the group in any relationship is an important starting point in constructing a positive international cross-cultural classroom and learning environment. Certainly, people can and do learn to adapt to different learning situations and contexts, and students that I have taught in Hong Kong, China, and Denmark have adapted well to the American style of teaching and respond well to discussion — as long as they are assured that they are not short-changed on my lecturing to them on important materials. Preferred modes can lie deep within a culture and need to be taken into account for the most harmonious and best learning environment. These attitudes manifest themselves in many ways within the society, and teachers need to be aware of how to deal with them within the physical environment and the organizational structures of schools and universities as well as the "mental spaces" of the students and their families.

3

The Classroom Environment: Physical, Emotional, and Intellectual Spaces

Education is the process of cultural transmission in which children learn what their society considers most important for them to understand in order to succeed as adults. As Kathleen Wilcox writes, "schools are not set up to socialize children for membership in some ideal society; they are set up to socialize children for membership in their own society as it currently exists and as it is likely to exist in the near future" (1982, 271). There is no international standard of classroom education and probably not even a single one within a particular culture or nation, although there may be only a limited number of options in a given society. These options arise out of the ideologies of the culture, as Elliot Eisner (1994, 47) observes, and give rise to curriculum ideologies:

> Values, particularly in America, proliferate, and these values find their educational expression in the ways in which schooling, curriculum, teaching, and evaluation are to occur. Curriculum ideologies are defined as beliefs about what schools should teach, for what ends, and for what reasons. Insofar as an ideology can be tacit rather than explicit, it is fair to say that all schools have at least one ideology — and usually more than one — that provides direction to their functions.

Because values are deeply imbedded in individual cultures and shape everyone's perception and behavior, they change slowly, but globalization necessitates that societies learn to respect one another and work harmoniously. In view of these contemporary transnational requirements, Robert Malone urges profound changes to our ideologies, mythologies, and perceptions so that we can talk across cultures: "It is precisely the ideological approaches that scientists and the rest of us adopt that are a part of the problem. Until we understand that the 'unbiased' reporting of 'facts' in 'common-sense' terms is but a product of our ideological and mythological categories, our doors of perception cannot be cleared to allow for the new insights we so desperately need" (1990, 174).

Some thinkers are critical of educational systems because they do little more than perpetuate what Philip Jackson calls the "hidden curriculum" (1990, 33) — that is, required behavior, rewards, and disciplinary actions within schools and universities and, beyond that, society's prejudices, habits, manners, patterns of thought, modes of governance, and fundamental ideologies — without coming up with anything innovative on teaching students how to think beyond their system. While there is truth in Jackson's claims, many educators believe schools and universities must strive to change behavior patterns (Tyler 1949, 6) and prevent people from becoming mere "technicians of the state" (Wong 2001, 55). Whether participating in critical discourse and reforming curriculum can change deep-seated ideological ways of behaving and thinking in society is uncertain, but it is important to try.

Critiquing society's patterns of thought and modes of governance is a lofty goal for education, but the process takes place in more humble spaces, whether physical or mental, and this is where I wish to begin because the space we inhabit is central to our educational system and reflects our "beliefs about knowledge and the nature of learning" (Toohey 1999, 45). All students need physical places where they can learn: a child who studies alone or who is home-schooled needs a certain desk or table in a particular room as a place of her/his own; an institutionally schooled child must also have a particular space to facilitate learning, although this space is shared with other children. There must also be a mental space, an assurance that society supports learning and that teachers and classmates will maintain an educational level playing field. Students need to believe that teachers will facilitate the learning process without prejudice and help to develop a personal and community identity, whether based on family and gender, race, class, religion, or age. Without that equality, the best physical spaces in the world will not empower students, further their education, or change their perceptions.

Physical Spaces

The personal space required for physical well-being is culturally embedded, and, to some extent, so are classroom needs and habits. On a personal level, societies develop zones of proximity and patterns of contact that they tolerate. In some, people stand comfortably close together when talking; touching each other on the shoulder as part of the conversation is a sign of friendliness; and men kissing women on the side of the cheek is considered a welcome greeting among friends. In others, men shake hands or kiss each other on the side of the face as a sign of respect, though those gestures cannot be extended from men to women. Space is never neutral, and the use of personal space in greetings and conversation are among the first things of importance in intercultural communication and the cross-cultural classroom.

Lectures, study, and discussion spaces have similar implications for the cross-cultural classroom. Every teacher knows intuitively that the configuration of space in a classroom can influence the success of a class. In my first semester of university teaching in the USA, my class met at 7:30 a.m. in an old building in which the desks were bolted to the floor at four-to five-foot intervals in each direction. The spacing of the teacher's desk and student chairs (to say nothing of the early morning hour) worked against discussion and effectively precluded group work in class, unless students were willing to stand together, which was inconvenient and uncomfortable.

Teachers cannot always choose their classrooms, but, after that first teaching experience, I check out rooms in advance of the first meeting of classes to see if there are problems with classroom provisions and space; and, if needed, I change to more pedagogically friendly classrooms, or, if not, think about my activities in terms of the available space. Some basic questions are:

- Does the classroom have appropriate lighting?
- Does it have windows?
- Can the windows be covered to show films, PowerPoint presentations, or the Internet?
- Is there a desk or podium to deliver presentations?
- Is there a space beside the podium to hold lecture notes?
- Does the room have blackboards and chalk or whiteboards and colored markers?
- Is there an overhead projector, a slide projector, a CD player, a VHS or VCD or DVD player and a television monitor, or multi-current connections for computers and PowerPoint presentations?
- Is there an adequate sound system so that students can listen to the lecturer or any of the electronic presentations?

All of these are basic questions, and the answers will determine how to carry out teaching.

On several occasions, I have gone into classrooms in various countries to give a lecture to hundreds of students and have had no blackboard, chalk, or overhead projector. In fact, because I experienced a lack of chalk so often, I routinely carry some with me. Similarly, there may not be a desk on which to put lecture notes and discussion materials. I also have gone into classrooms in the USA, Asia, and Europe, assured of VHS and DVD players, only to discover that they do not have the capacity to show tapes or disks from outside the country: domain-specific tapes and DVDs are often useless in different locations unless the equipment can override the constraints imposed by domain specificity. Similarly, I have taken slides with me to use in presentations, only to discover that no slide projectors can be found because slide technology has been superseded by PowerPoint software or that the classroom is too bright for anything on the screen to show up adequately. Also, in many cases, rooms are not wired for computer equipment, so that option, too, is sometimes unavailable. These are the hazards of teaching internationally, and those who plan to do so need to enquire in advance about the facilities and/or bring their own materials with them to lessen those problems. Those who are teaching abroad for only a short period of time (such as American Fulbright scholars) may have to go the extra mile in bringing essential classroom tools (chalk, lecture handouts, overhead transparencies, and course readings) with them. Sometimes, instructors even need to provide books for their students. Everyone teaching abroad needs to anticipate and adjust to differences in classroom resources.

Few classrooms — whether in tertiary, secondary, or primary education — suit every group of teachers and students, though, oddly, more thought is often given to the classroom spaces in secondary and primary schools than in universities. Too often in universities, those who plan interiors assume that lecturing is the basic mode of instruction, that chairs will be arranged in straight rows directly in front of the professor, and that as many chairs as possible can provide maximum efficiency in a room. Unless a professor does lecture all the time, such rigidly structured classrooms pose an impediment. Frequently, secondary schools also have regularized classroom spaces with desks configured in front of a centrally located teacher, but some have tables and chairs that can be moved in order to respond to particular tasks. If group work is the primary mode, tables can be randomly distributed. If the teacher wishes to speak, screen films and show transparencies, and still encourage discussion, tables can be put into a horseshoe, with the teacher in the center, creating a space that will allow for all of these tasks. In fact, tables and chairs generally allow more flexibility than do desks and chairs. At the elementary level, administrators are more likely to create spaces designed for maximum flexibility because teachers know that a young child has a short attention span and needs variety. Teachers can arrange the chairs formally to listen to some speakers, cluster them in groups around tables for group work, or remove chairs and desks entirely to accommodate other kinds of activities. That pattern, however, is not typical of elementary or secondary education in East Asia where the young in the classroom are treated as they would be in classrooms for older students. As Sam Winter (1995, 35) remarks:

> The traditional view is perhaps the dominant one in Hong Kong. The typical arrangement of furniture and equipment reflects the idea that the teacher is the most important member of the group. The teacher stands at the front of the class, beside the blackboard, and faces the students, lecturing them and setting individual 'seatwork' tasks. Students' tables and chairs are arranged in rows and columns so that all students face the teacher, rather than face each other. In some Hong Kong classrooms, the teacher finds it necessary (or simply prefers) to use a megaphone to address the students in the class. Under these conditions, student interaction is even more greatly discouraged.

All too often, at the university level, classrooms are based upon the notion that lecturers do not require tables, except in designated seminar rooms (which frequently have only one big table for under 20 members) or for the field of education and those practical subjects that aspire to have students working together and arriving at knowledge jointly in labs and projects — as a matter of course, these usually include architecture, engineering, and fine arts. Apart from seminars and practice-oriented subjects, if tables are used in larger rooms, they often function like linked desks. That is, long, narrow tables are placed in rows with students facing the instructor with little possibility of putting chairs on the other side of the tables so that, instead, students can face each other.

In fact, the international trajectory in education is probably from spatial flexibility for younger students to spatial inflexibility at the more advanced levels. This practice has an ideological basis: young children require free and unstructured space for socialization; adolescents need structure to prepare them for the adult world and, therefore, formally laid-out learning spaces and teacher-oriented classrooms; and university students look for structure and authoritative opinions in their chosen academic fields, and so need lecture halls. There are exceptions to this rule, both for underlying ideology, pedagogical practice, and classroom space, but, certainly, university rooms tend toward inflexibility in the use of space, and space often reflects the presentation of content and cultural ideology.

Three Spaces for Teaching: Lecture, Seminar, and Circle

Because the lecture model is internationally redolent of traditional education and authority, it offers comfort, security, and, for some, ease of expression. As one Hong Kong student remarked, "when we sit in the traditional way [in rows facing the teacher], students only can see their lecturers (and the backs of their classmates), and they may feel freer to express their feelings and opinions. And in this sitting mode, students are more active and relaxed in expressing themselves." Another student seconded that comment, but also wanted small-group discussion incorporated into the lecture time: "I think the best mode of instruction is a lecture with small group discussion. The discussion time should be around five or 10 minutes [out of 50] so as not to occupy too much time." Another preferred a standard classroom and a combination of lecture and student presentations that depend upon careful preparation:

> My favorite mode of instruction would be a combination of [the] instructor's lectures and students' presentations. If the instructor only talks in all the lectures in the course, students tend to jot down whatever the instructor says. However, if students are asked to do presentations based on their own research on the subject, it will be a great pressure on students. I think it is a good idea to ask students to do presentations on topics related to the subject, but at the same time the instructor should give more comment and advice to the presentation.

These various preferences indicate that, while students like lectures and strong leadership from the teacher, many also prefer that discussion and group work be an integral part of the education experience.

Others students are concerned that the traditional lecture model demands too little of them, regardless of whether discussion and presentations are incorporated. As an alternative, they prefer a less formal classroom with students sitting around a table with the professor. Some students find this "seminar model" comfortable because they can hear lecturers more clearly and interact more easily with other students and the teacher. Others believe that this modification in seating arrangement does not really change the basic structure and culture of the classroom —

lectures with students seated in rows or around tables follow the same teacher-oriented model for, in both instances, the instructor sits or stands at a distance from most of the students, tends to lecture or, at the very least, control the discussion. Students may have more space for writing when they sit in a classroom with tables, but teachers are generally removed from students, and, for those sitting at the far end of the table from the teacher or at her/his side, it differs little from the conventional lecture situation.

On the face of it, putting chairs in a large circle might seem to provide the most positive and significant alternative in classroom methodology, for "circling the wagons" proclaims the students' democratic equality with each other and implies that the power relations and distance between instructor and student are not important. In "Tips for Leading Discussions," Felisa Tibbitts promotes the circle as a basic learning model for human rights, saying, "If possible, have people sit in a circle, or at least facing one another" (1996), and Pamela George likes that idea as well, arguing, "Room arrangement sends out a symbolic message. Students need to be facing each other" (1995, 57). However, a Fulbright law professor who experimented with classroom groupings found that facing one another was uncomfortable for many Chinese students (ibid.).

As expected, some students are optimistic about a circle in which everyone shares opinions and, along with the teacher, contributes actively to the teaching process:

> Students' opinions are often impressive, and can inspire new understanding. The circle, then, can encourage shared learning and erase some of the formalities of a traditional, hierarchical classroom in which the teacher stands in front and dominates the class. In the "circle" style, students are supposedly equal with the teachers, can see each other, and voice their opinions, keeping everyone intellectually and physically awake. Students can get used to this face-to-face exchange, but the results are sometimes not as favorable as Westerners might hope.

As the student suggests, some students in a cross-cultural classroom are unsure that the circle accomplishes its intention, and Hong Kong, mainland Chinese, Japanese, and Korean students are often uncomfortable when having to sit in a large circle, finding that it discourages them from expressing themselves freely.

Sitting in a large circle may violate some of the fundamental aims of classroom communication. Min-Sun Kim (1998, 102) has identified five concerns that can influence the interaction of students and teachers:

1. Concern about lack of clarity
2. Concern about hurting students' feelings
3. Concern about negative perceptions and evaluations
4. Concern about imposing problematic attitudes and styles
5. Concern about lack of effectiveness.

In explaining these points, Kim argues that Koreans and other East Asians place less value on independent thinking and speech, directness, and clarity and greater value on collectivity, interdependence, and the wish to avoid "damage to the relationship or loss of face by the hearer" (1998, 102).

Face is a significant concern in the classroom, and face-to-face encounters can be part of the issue. In sociolinguistic parlance, "face is the negotiated public image, mutually granted each other by participants in a communicative event" (Scollon and Wong Scollon 2001, 45), and "face is lost when the individual, either through his action or that of people closely related to him, fails to meet essential requirements placed upon him by virtue of the social position he occupies" (Ho 1976, 881). The desire to save face may lead to indirectness and lack of clarity, but may promote harmony as well. As T. R. Reid notes of Japan, "good manners" and "polite" and "convoluted language" "maintain good feeling, to make everybody feel copacetic, so the overall group can continue to function in a state of harmony. And it works" (1999, 86). Craig Storti similarly observes that an Asian Indian person does not wish to "embarrass another person through any kind of overt confrontation" (1994, 3). Min-Sun Kim argues that, because of this East Asian wish to save face and avoid confrontation, Western attempts to establish face-to-face exchanges in the Asian classroom are not necessarily productive (1998, 103).

While sitting in a circle might seem an innocent arrangement and unlikely to embarrass anyone, some students do find it discomfiting, potentially humiliating because of possible confrontations, and stressful because they are "exposed." As one Hong Kong student remarked, "Students may feel pressure and be uncomfortable in the 'circle' style because everyone can see each other, and there is no privacy," and another corroborated that feeling, saying, "I feel pretty uncomfortable in the circle and I feel not only observed by the lecturer but also other classmates as well." This lack of privacy and feeling of visual assault arises from being "on display" to the entire class, leading to the view that a circle is counterproductive because students dislike being so visible and, as a result, may be reluctant to speak up. Although some students find that the circle can train them to be brave about voicing their opinions, others find it intimidating because they are expected to respond at a moment's notice with their response assessed by everyone in the class.

Sometimes students believe that the physical dimensions of the circle work against effective learning because, if they sit directly beside lecturers, they cannot hear or see them. In an English-speaking classroom, hearing and seeing an instructor is especially critical for students whose mother tongue is not English because they often depend upon seeing a teacher's face to decipher correct pronunciation, vocabulary, and meaning. Much information is conveyed through body language, and students who are unable to see the instructor may miss important physical messages. Also, students who sit too close to the teacher may think this an inappropriate informality. Equally importantly, although the purpose of the circle is to break down barriers between lecturer and student, students sometimes find that the circle works against equality and solidarity because it masks underlying power relations that continue to exist and undermine discussion. As one Hong Kong student noted:

> Although noble in theory, and occasionally successful in practice, this style has as many drawbacks as benefits. Although it does break up classroom monotony and physically manifests the idea of an open floor and democratic platform, the power inevitably shifts to the teacher because of the teacher's "airtime." It can also discourage and stifle shy students, or those who prefer the lecture style.

Some students see the circle in a more sinister way, as a mode of surveillance that undermines egalitarianism. From one student's point of view,

> When we are forced to make a circle in class at the university, it seems to me that making a circle becomes one of the "visible" rules, regulations, duties and responsibilities. In this regard, a circle provides an uncomfortable atmosphere for most [Asian] students. Tensions, anxieties and pressure are on their minds.

This student's notion of surveillance was self-consciously patterned after the French philosopher Michel Foucault, and she fully argued that the circle was a mode of interrogation and control rather than a democratic ideal:

> Foucault makes use of a circular prison as an example to illustrate his concept of discursive power, [and] the relationship between students and teachers sitting in a circle in class is the same as the relationship between the supervisor in the central tower and the prisoners. Foucault's

discursive power focuses not on the subjects of power but on power relations, the relations of force that operate within social practices and social systems. For instance, teachers are the reminders of the norms in the class. We realize what is the right thing to do under this situation. From Foucault's point of view, a society is structured like a prison in the way that we behave like prisoners in accordance with pre-given norms, and our identities are constructed within these norms.

This student continued that the circle is a difficult model because it introduces uncertainty, risk, and instructor capriciousness into the classroom, which may be unproductive and prevent students from attending class because they are frightened about participating or afraid they lack sufficient knowledge. The student said: "Before the lectures, students have to guess what the focus is in the lectures and the relationship of this and that particular subject . . . Even though I always sit in a circle, I always feel pressure. I do not know which questions I am going to answer in every lecture." There is a certain defensiveness in this comment for students always have to guess about the content of a lecture and how to prepare for it, but the opinion still deserves attention.

From years of experience, students know that teachers have power — and use it. That may be "soft power," to use Joseph Nye's political term (2004), but it is power nevertheless. Teachers may think that they are sharing power with students in organizing classroom space democratically, but students fully understand that it is the teacher who sets the agenda, monitors the students, and assigns the marks. Whether the power is soft or hard, it is still power, and many students are concerned that the circle is a duplicitous attempt to mask that power.

Still another student said that she feels pressure not so much from the instructors and the expectations implicit in the teaching of the subject matter, but from other students. The notion of surveillance thus extends to the students as well:

> Most of us may think that sitting in a circle can encourage people to speak up, and flourish students' participation in discussion, and there are several experiments testing this belief, [and] the results show that students feel more comfortable in rows and to speak up when compared with the circle mode . . . Some psychologists . . . explain that though eye [contact] can encourage people to speak up, that's only effective if individuals really want to say something, otherwise eye [contact] will become a source of pressure, and students may not speak up as there are so many students looking at them.

Another Hong Kong student remarked, "I agree that sitting in a circle is easy for people to communicate among themselves," though not for "different groups of people (target audiences) from various cultural backgrounds." This is an extremely important observation for the cross-cultural classroom and hints at an underlying problem: not all students participate equally, no matter how democratic and free the culture. Gender, training, language ability, personality, and other cultural differences, including culture of origin, are all potential factors enhancing or inhibiting the free exchange of information and ideas. When teachers from a Western culture want to introduce free-flowing discussion among all their students, some who come from a culture that does not find this of value may suffer considerably. Also, students who have been trained to participate readily may simply hijack the discussion process, leaving others out.

The heart of this issue is partly the conflict between group values and individualism, but another part in the international cross-cultural classroom is student hesitancy to expose uncertain language skills to other students. Those with confidence and bravado may still speak out, but many students participate cautiously, hoping not to have to answer questions directly at the risk of losing face in front of the teacher and other students. This is particularly the case when it is a second-language class for the students.

With different cultural perceptions and personal dispositions in the cross-cultural classroom, discussion and its space are never neutral. The circle may pressure students out of their passivity, and some will accept it readily, but it may continue to be uncomfortable because it is "foreign" to their social environment, disagreeable to their perception of classroom relationships and educational experience, and threatening to their identity. Given these reservations, the acceptance of discussion in general and the circle in particular may depend upon the attitude of the teacher, the manner of introducing the circle, and the number and kinds of students involved. It may be appropriate for a small group of six to ten students because they can listen to each other's opinion, but this method may not work in a class of more than fifteen students.

Comfort with each other and the issue of size, however, may be a problem for only certain kinds of students. Danish students, for instance, like the circle, regardless of the number of students involved, but still prefer to gather round a table instead of having completely open space. Danish students value their individuality and are trained to socialize in the classroom, so sitting in a circle and discussing topics together does not bother them, but in a traditional Chinese classroom that does not place so much value on independence in class discussion as part of education, students may perceive the circle as an obstacle to learning.

The traditional lecture takes advantage of space to provide students with useful and systematically organized information, and many believe that good discussion can come from this mode of learning as well. Most instructors and students, however, agree that exclusive dependence on the formal lecture leads to passivity among the students that can only be addressed by a seminar or circle. The circle is the most controversial form, with students having strong positions on its usefulness in promoting a positive and productive atmosphere for interaction.

Emotional and Intellectual Spaces: Ideology, Race, Ethnicity, Class, Family, Gender, Religion, and Age

Having adequate physical space is not all that students need to ensure the opportunity to excel; they have a right to expect equal treatment with reference to governing ideologies, race and ethnicity, class, family and gender, religion, and age. Most of today's international students are at ease with diverse experiences and want to be tolerant of different peoples and opinions; however, local students may not share the same experiences or opinions, and these issues should be self-consciously addressed in the cross-cultural classroom so that students understand the fundamental importance of respect, equity, and equality.

International cross-cultural classrooms in which teachers and students come from different countries are increasingly common in the globalized world. The University of Hong Kong (HKU) aims to have 25% of the students going abroad annually on exchange programs, meaning that, although classes might consist predominantly of local and mainland Chinese students, at least 25% of students in classes at HKU should be from other countries. It probably goes without saying that, because of their own wider experiences, students in the international classroom consider themselves more liberal and accepting than their nationally based counterparts. Westerners who live, work, and study with Hong Kong people share a vibrant multiculturalism, and the high percentage of interracial relationships throughout the region bears testimony to an acceptance of racial equality at the most fundamental social levels. It cannot be taken for granted, however, that interracial mingling and international backgrounds automatically lead to tolerance of different peoples and ideologies. The legacy of colonialism throughout Asia suggests that living in a foreign country does not guarantee equality and a liberal relationship with others.

The international cross-cultural classroom is a place that must enact civil and personal rights — teachers and students alike need to develop opportunities to learn about the cultures and values of the various races and ethnicities in the classroom, so that there is a growth of tolerance, acceptance, and understanding. Estelle Disch, for example, advocates the need for students "to learn enough about another culture to begin to know the history of a particular cultural group; to understand some of the common and not-so-common experiences of people in that culture; to understand the widely shared values of the culture; and to understand the place of the group within the wider context of U.S. society" (1998, 47). This "multicultural literacy," as she calls it, should be an especially important part of the transnational, cross-cultural classroom, and students also need the opportunity to face up to systemic cultural prejudices about themselves and others. De Vita notes that students from various countries and cultures "do not spontaneously mix" (2005, 75), so the teacher must ensure means for them to mix through various exercises and projects.

Still, as many are discovering in a globalized economy, nation, ethnicity, and race may matter less than class, especially since globalization is based on capitalism and a market economy, and class is often based on economics. Differences in economic wealth and related social status can thus complicate the cross-cultural environment and classroom. There are often discrepancies between the incomes of local and international staff, and these differences can show up in the workplace and classroom, creating perceived injustices. For example, American educators teaching abroad may be paid more than locals for the same work, but those paid by NGOs (non-government organizations) may receive less than locals. Sometimes, too, international staff receive housing superior to what local staff can afford. Issues of salary can affect the dynamics among students themselves when some carry more cash than others and can afford to buy more things. Indeed, in the cross-cultural classroom, "big" issues like race might be more readily accommodated than presumed "little" issues like economic and class relationships. Disparity of, and resentment over, wages can become resentment over nation, culture, and race.

In an international context, men and women and boys and girls probably think of themselves as tolerant of family and gender differences and want to do the right thing. Those who view tolerance as valuable are likely to see independent women as capable and courageous, but others may see them as overly assertive and dismissive of traditional roles and family values. Such cultural differences are deeply internalized and conflict with otherwise liberal opinions. The American acceptance of make-up and tight-fitting clothing for girls, the Middle-Eastern view that girls should cover their heads, the traditional Chinese view that the oldest male must speak for the family, the Japanese view that the family has primacy over the individual member — all of these might cause cross-cultural classroom difficulties if not handled intelligently by the teacher. What might seem positive, transformative, liberating, and empowering to some may seem regressive, negative, and socially destructive to others. The teacher in the cross-cultural classroom consequently has to be sensitive about race and class and discover the students' cultural attitudes about family, gender, and appropriate behavior in a mixed classroom.

Religion, like family and gender, can be a lightning rod and is often related to views of personal identity, family, social relationships, gender, and many other matters. In a secular space — whether classroom or workplace — issues of religious difference should not be relevant, but subconscious habits, religious obligations, and statutory or non-statutory holidays nevertheless intrude on that space. In a place such as Singapore, which is a meeting point for at least four great religions — Buddhism, Christianity, Hinduism, and Islam — many religious holidays are sanctioned and all religions have a cultural "voice," meaning that none of the followers of these religions feels left out or has to make special appeals for ritual observances.

In a non-secular place, such as an international school with a religious affiliation, those who follow a different faith or religion may feel under special scrutiny and, as a result, more pressure. Those who are responsible for that environment thus have to be especially sensitive about the needs and identity of those individuals and make sure that their special identity is taken into account, and that they are adequately included in every way. Asking students to talk about their religious views and to share their activities on special days of observance can go a long way to making everyone feel connected.

In an avowedly secular society like mainland China, a related issue can arise for the teacher abroad: although home to most of the major religions of the world, it gives no time off for religious holidays or festival days. It has three weeks of holiday, which everyone takes at the same time — Chinese (lunar) New Year and the two so-called Golden Weeks, one the first week in May and the other the first week in October. Otherwise, classes go on as usual, and because university terms are 18 weeks long, can cut across some of the major holidays that Westerners commonly celebrate.

For many, age is less important than issues of race, ethnicity, class, family, gender, and religion, but in a survey of students in my university classroom in Denmark, it emerged as one of the major considerations. At least half the students in this particular class did not come to university directly from high school and were concerned about being accepted, despite their age, previous education, or experience. This can also be an issue in societies where almost all the full-time students come directly from high school. In Hong Kong, for example, undergraduate programs are only for full-time students with few university places assigned to those who do not come directly from high school. As a result, older students who have worked for a few years are a rarity and are often ignored by the other, younger students. Consequently, age can be an issue, and, when there are discrepancies of age in the classroom, it is important to accommodate and incorporate everyone. The odd-person-out might just as well be someone younger or older, but the same cautionary note needs to be sounded — that ways must be found to make certain that students feel incorporated.

In brief, "space" is physical, emotional, and mental, and everyone needs to feel that it is possible to share equally in the learning environment, but it is also important to note that what works well back home may not work equally effectively abroad. Educators need to develop strategies of incorporation, and raising the issue with the group itself can be an effective way to deal with the situation. In Denmark, for example, most decisions are taken by consensus, and groups are used to having the opportunity to talk out significant issues. Procedures that are put in place without the incorporation of a group decision are much less likely to go down well than are those in which everyone has a voice — even if the decision of the group goes against that of a particular minority. In such cases, self-conscious reflection on these matters in public is an excellent way to move forward and ensure public support in general.

4

The Teacher-Oriented Classroom

Institutional culture perpetuates itself, and those trained in particular organizational, disciplinary, and pedagogical forms often repeat them. As Marilyn Amey and Dennis Brown note, faculties in universities "are organized by discipline, disseminate research through discipline-based journals and conferences, and are rewarded for contributing to and expanding the disciplinary knowledge base. The next generation of faculty are trained and enculturated into their specific disciplinary model during graduate school and early career experiences, thus perpetuating and scripting future faculty in the disciplinary lens" (2004, ix). Even when new areas of study, disciplines, programs, and centers of learning develop, because of the power of tradition, the actual teaching within them resembles that of their predecessors. Also, because, broadly speaking, teaching is contextual, conceptions of teaching are simultaneously familial, local (dependent upon particular experiences and institutional needs), regional, national, and even broadly hemispheric. Traditionally, East Asia, Southern Europe, and Africa have supported the teacher-centered classroom, in which the single classroom teacher takes the initiative in imparting knowledge to students, while North American education circles — whether scientific, technical, liberal arts, or professional — claim to value the student-centered classroom, in which there is more equality and sharing between teacher and student.

These teaching preferences are often deeply entrenched, and Geert Hofstede speculates that such attitudes to learning go beyond mere cultural preferences. Although he focuses on language-based preferences — for instance, with Germanic-speaking cultures valuing equality and Romance language-based cultures valuing greater hierarchy (1997, 42) — there are implications for attitudes to learning as well.

Despite the mechanistic implications of Hofstede's argument, these values are never absolute over time, even within homogeneous cultures. Thus, while it may be true that the teacher-oriented classroom continues to dominate culture in Hong Kong and mainland China,[4] it is equally true that many universities in these places have set their sights on educational methodologies that value classroom discussion. Also, despite strong public statements in support of discussion-oriented classrooms, most Western cultures still depend overwhelmingly on the primacy of the lecture. According to Lion Gardiner in 1999, 73% to 83% of university professors responding to his questionnaire in North America actually prefer lecturing to discussion, student presentations, and one-on-one instruction. In short, traditional regional- or national-based agendas for, and statements about, pedagogy cannot be taken as absolute. The USA and China are two cultural behemoths coming together and exchanging values and techniques that will influence the twenty-first century, and these will undoubtedly include assessments of teacher- and student-based classrooms.

Part of the dialogue about the teacher's role concerns the on-going debate about one-person classrooms and single-discipline approaches, as opposed to team teaching and interdisciplinarity. These seemingly disparate issues are joined at the hip because, when more than one teacher is involved in a class, it is usually to offer perspectives from another discipline. According to Amey and Brown (2004, 2), interdisciplinary collaboration that results in integration of ideas can be defined as:

> faculty and staff from various disciplinary backgrounds (paradigms) often within a single university, organized to address a predetermined task. The starting place of this multiple disciplinary effort is to purposely bring together members from various fields to apply their expertise in successfully resolving complex problems. Unlike traditional faculty work, the intent is to have the faculty come together intellectually [and] . . . to think collectively. (2004, 2)

---

4   Countries that were part of the British Commonwealth supplemented the formal lecture methods with informal tutorials of about four to eight students who were asked to respond to questions about the lectures, readings, and other texts. This tutorial system allowed for some relaxation of the reserved and respectful professor-student relationship that characterizes Asian lecture halls. Unfortunately, as a result of global financial cuts to education within the past few years, tutorials and seminars are fast disappearing, leaving the traditional lecture mode intact, despite the desires of some teachers and administrators to create alternative learning.

Whether collaboration is interdisciplinary, multidisciplinary, pluridisciplinary, or transdisciplinary depends on how it is approached. As Julie Klein (1990, 56) writes,

> "Multidisciplinary" [and "pluridisciplinary"] signifies the juxtaposition of disciplines. It is essentially additive, not integrative. Even in a common environment, educators, researchers and practitioners still behave as disciplinarians with different perspectives. Their relationship may be mutual and cumulative but not interactive, for there is "no apparent connection," no real cooperation, or "explicit" relationship, and even perhaps a "questionable eclecticism." The participating disciplines are neither changed nor enriched, and the lack of a "well defined matrix" of interactions means disciplinary relationships are likely to be limited and transitory.

Interdisciplinary collaboration puts disciplines together so that, over the short and long terms, the work is integrative, while transdisciplinary collaboration goes beyond that to create a synthesis. Robert Costanza says, "Inter- and transdisciplinary research differs from typical disciplinary research in its basic focus and goals. Disciplinary research seeks to increase knowledge and techniques within a limited intellectual sphere while inter- and transdisciplinary research are multiskilled and problem focused" (1990, 95).

Some educators argue that multidisciplinarity is good enough as one person can only know one discipline well, and putting different disciplines together in conversation is as far as education should go; anything else will result in shallow knowledge and disciplinary poaching. Other educators decry traditional disciplinarity, believing that disciplinary fields are arbitrarily defined and that students are not being well served by submitting to narrow definitions and fields. William Reckmeyer argues that "the culprit seems to be overspecialization and our predilection for parochial modes of inquiry that prevent people from seeing the connections common to different situations" (1990, 54). His concern reflects that of Julie Thompson Klein who favors interdisciplinarity to achieve integrative views, although she has reservations about the synthesis or "convergence" (Nowotny 2003, 2) promised by transdisciplinary inquiry. She prefers a self-critical and self-reflexive approach and notes the critical vocabulary that has crept into interdisciplinary studies as a kind of self-critique: "a new rhetoric of interdisciplinarity developed in turn. 'Plurality' and 'heterogeneity' replaced 'unity' and 'universality.' 'Interrogation' and 'intervention' supplanted 'synthesis' and 'holism.' And, older forms of 'interdisciplinarity' were challenged by 'anti,' 'post,' 'non,' and 'de-disciplinary' formulations" (2005, 5). In short, Klein feels that it is necessary to critique the interdisciplinary process while engaging it and does not favor the preservationist agenda of maintaining strict disciplinary boundaries.

Interdisciplinary inquiry is especially valid in the international cross-cultural classroom because students of various ethnic and national backgrounds do not have identical background knowledge bases. When I first began to teach university-level American literature in Canada, I found that literary theories per se went only so far in helping the students grasp content and approach because, at that time, they were generally focused on the piece of literature itself. Most of the students in the class were from Canada, had never been to the USA, and knew little of the historical and philosophical context of the literature, and so American literature for them consisted of deculturated artifacts. That mattered less with respect to contemporary materials because they shared in cultural background and values through the mediation of the media, but it mattered considerably when teaching students about the Puritan poet Edward Taylor or the Transcendentalist Henry David Thoreau. I quickly realized that I had to imbed these works within the general culture, history, philosophy, and religion of the periods, or they made little sense to the students. I also realized that in Thoreau's case, drawing upon the art from the Hudson River School helped to demonstrate his links to American Romantic ideology as part of the cultural configuration.

As I moved to Hong Kong, mainland China, and Denmark, making interdisciplinary links and giving multiple perspectives became more critical in presenting cultural complexity because students were physically and intellectually further removed from the American context.

One Teacher/One Classroom

The most pervasive form of teaching across the entire globe is doubtlessly based upon a single instructor in a classroom, and solo-lecturing is one of the most efficient means of delivering information and cultivating knowledge. As Sam Winter remarks of teaching in Asia, "it is normally assumed that the teacher is the most influential participant in [the classroom]. After all, he/she is professionally qualified and is paid to teach and to manage the students in his/her care. This view has encouraged the viewpoint that student interaction is a bad thing, generally encouraging . . . disruptive behaviour, and interfering with learning" (1995, 35). Lecturing by itself, however, does not ensure that students will grasp or be able to remember the points any better than in discussions. In fact, the length of the lecture has a great deal to do with students' ability to recall material: more than 50 years ago Joseph Trenaman discovered that "assimilation diminished seriously after fifteen minutes," and a few years later studies by James Hartley and A. Cameron showed that, in a lecture of 10 minutes with "ideal notes," students could recall 70% of the main points, but, if it were 45 minutes, they could recall only 20% (McLeish 1976, 270, 272). These statistics are disturbing, especially when supported by other research suggesting that, among other things, students retain information better from reading or discussing it. Lectures need to be very good, cogent — and quite condensed — to be effective.

Lecturing can cover a multitude of situations and a broad range of classroom sizes, and these variables can contribute to the students' ability to remember materials. The number of students listening to an instructor can vary considerably. In the USA, kindergarten classes are usually small because of the short attention span and particular emotional needs of the youngsters and their demands on the teacher. Secondary school classes hover around 25 to 30 students, as mandated by the education departments, usually on the basis of budget rather than educational merit. University classes vary from small seminars of a few students to large lectures numbering several hundred students, depending on the year of study, the discipline, and the kind of institution. These numbers and assumptions do not hold true, however, in other countries. As T. R. Reid remarks of primary education in Japan, "On the average, Japanese schools have thirty-five to forty students per teacher; the ratio is largest in the lowest grades, and gets smaller as classes become more specialized in high school." He adds that a Japanese teacher told him this number was required "so the teacher can build a lot of groups and the various groups can work with each other" (1999, 149). Up to a point, the larger the class, the better, so that harmony can be achieved through the formation and interaction of groups.

Student numbers are one concern in a classroom, and academic specialty and specialization is another. Teachers at all levels research a vast range of materials, and only a few have the advantage of always teaching within their specialty, even at the university level, where almost everyone is responsible for survey courses. Many teachers can readily gather information and undertake research, and many are able to impart knowledge effectively, but to have both at once in a single classroom is not as easy as it seems.

Still, even with research demands and restricted time, many teachers prefer to gather their own materials and be responsible for presenting them individually rather than working with a team. Unless members of a team actually do work together effectively, it is often easier for one person to manage the various demands of the classroom. This observation should remind us that, although learning has become increasingly group-oriented, the act of teaching itself has not and still depends heavily upon individual responsibility.

It is fair to say that many students in the international cross-cultural classroom prefer it this way. Providing the teacher is effective, students often like having one authority in the classroom. In that way, they can become attuned to the teacher's patterns of thought and expression, the nuances of style, and facial expressions and body language. Students understand that, if they develop a good rapport with the teacher, the classroom environment will be a comfortable and efficient place for learning. By contrast, when students do not know presenters well or at all, they may feel that they get only the broad brushstrokes of the ideas and presentations, and may not know enough about each presenter to capture the subtleties of speech, facial expression, and body language.

Both the desire to be taught by one particular teacher and concern about not being able to gauge guest speakers may be extremely relevant in the cross-cultural classroom. It is probably a truism, but necessary to emphasize, that effective classroom techniques depend upon the teacher's overall attitude, sense of compassion and helpfulness, ability to speak clearly and articulately, positive body language, and unfailing sense of humor. (Students in the cross-cultural classroom, however, sometimes find humor problematic. Danes, for example, acknowledge their sarcastic sense of humor and believe that foreigners find it difficult to understand or appreciate. In the cross-cultural classroom, while it is important to have a positive attitude and to be good-natured, it is also important to recognize that humor can be misunderstood, divisive, and even alienating.)

When the one-person classroom goes well, it can be very, very good, and many students like that. For some students in Asia, the performance- or instructor-based classroom model provides the most efficient means to convey the maximum amount of information in a short period — information they require before feeling comfortable in discussing a topic. One Hong Kong student confessed that the lecture was her favorite mode of teaching:

> In a lecture, students should focus on listening to and writing down the important points that a lecturer is going to talk about. I do not think

that it is a time for discussion without knowing any background. Also, I need more time to digest what I have learned. . . . I really hope that the instructor can present his/her own arguments in clear, systematic, and coherent ways. Discussion is important but learning certain knowledge from instructors in lectures is also important.

Another student reinforced this point, arguing for a "formal" classroom in which teachers "prepare some outlines/handouts of the lecture and students have some time to discuss questions with lecturers at the end of the class."

First and most importantly for the international cross-cultural classroom, teachers need carefully articulated syllabi to ascertain that the students understand the goals and requirements of the course. Conveying this sense of grounding and thoughtful presentation helps build the students' confidence in the study and teacher. Course outlines should be as specific as possible with goals, required reading materials, and weekly assignments carefully planned and documented. In addition, they should provide particular details of examinations and oral and written assignments, including their relative weighting and due dates. When students have these course outlines, they can plan their work and are less likely to run the risk of not being prepared. Preparing syllabi is not the custom in every country, however, and students can feel quite daunted if they have never had a syllabus that lays out the term's work in advance, so consultation with local staff is absolutely necessary at the outset. In some countries, for instance Canada and the USA, course syllabi at secondary and university levels are considered legally binding documents, making promises about what will happen in the classroom. While other countries might not view them as legally binding agreements between teacher and student, these syllabi define the course and give a sense of professional expectations. However, it was my experience in mainland China that teachers did not draw up syllabi, so that students only found out their work on a weekly basis. Consequently, in first handing out my syllabus, I frightened many of the students who thought the workload unmanageable because they were seeing all the weekly requirements at once.

Second, teachers need to pay special attention to, and give as much information as possible about, the required and optional reading materials. In detailing her experiences with international students, Janette Ryan (2005, 94) lists these essential points for teachers in providing reference/reading lists:

- The selective use of references/readings
- Providing annotated bibliographies

- Marking key texts
- Identifying relevant chapters or excerpts
- Using electronic materials (for faster searching of relevant information)
- Checking the accessibility of texts or websites used (for Plain English and straightforward and pertinent information)
- Checking the relevance of the language used and making sure it is appropriate for the target audience
- Including foundational or definitive texts
- Providing reading lists early
- Making unit or module descriptions available electronically
- Providing a glossary of key terms and concepts.

This list indicates that teachers can take nothing for granted in international teaching and have to go the extra mile in referencing important texts.

Third, teachers must also give as much information as possible about the organization and content of each presentation or lecture. It is extremely helpful to students in the cross-cultural classroom for the teacher to introduce the lecture with an indication of the important points to be covered or the direction the lecture will take. Similarly, it is a good idea to sum up the presentation at the end. It often happens that, as a result of questions and comments, a lecture may stray creatively from the announced format, so summing up is useful for both teacher and students.

Fourth, teachers should give a handout for each lecture, taking into account the needs of the particular audience. Normally, an outline of the presentation, critical concepts and key terms, and important quotations can help students to follow the lecture. Students who are not native English speakers — and even those who are — can spend an enormous amount of time trying to figure out what the teacher is saying, attempting to take notes, and, as a result, not following the presentation. Having the major points on a transparency shown on an overhead projector or in a PowerPoint presentation can certainly help, but good written back-up materials — including copies of PowerPoint slides — allow students to focus on the progression of the lecture and discussion and give them material to take away from the lecture and think about more carefully later.

One critical point here is that transnational students often believe that they need a comprehensive view of the material so they can sense where the lecture is going. Another critical point is that many non-native English speakers require a written handout in order to see and understand important terms and central ideas. The elaborateness of these handouts will vary with the age and sophistication of the students as well as level of instruction, but the cross-cultural classroom might require at least one carefully conceptualized page. I can still remember alluding to Plato in a first-year English course at the University of Hong Kong and having some students ask me who this man was and other students wanting to know exactly what was "play-dough."

The anxiety of students wanting to get the information right and not having handouts to help inevitably resulted in a significant classroom problem: guest speakers — and local lecturers — in Hong Kong were often disturbed by students talking among themselves during the lectures. "Talking loudly in lectures" is one of the issues that Jude Carroll denotes as a behavioral pattern unacceptable to Westerners but taken for granted by many other groups (2005a, 29). Some of this chatter in the classroom, theaters, and conferences represents a cultural difference in what people find acceptable, but much of the ambient noise results from their attempt to clarify words or terms, which the audience did not hear properly or did not understand. Teachers in a cross-cultural classroom cannot take for granted the background of the students in particular subject areas, and they cannot always be sure the student is hearing the same words teachers think they are saying. For this reason, too, teachers need to repeat and rephrase key terms and ideas frequently so that students hear it in different ways.

I cannot stress too much the importance of written assistance and verbal repetition in a cross-cultural situation because, unless all of the students are native speakers in an English-language classroom, there is a heightened chance for misunderstanding. Also, differences in accent and pronunciation can disadvantage students, and written materials alleviate the problems of pronunciation and reduce misunderstanding. In addition, because some students learn better by reading material and some by hearing it, everyone can have basic written materials in front of them and then concentrate on the fine points of the oral presentation.

As Asian and European students often express the need to have sufficient information and understanding before opening themselves to discussion, these handouts enhance discussion. Whereas North Americans can be comfortable in discussing an issue as a first step in acquiring information, students from other cultures want information before entering into discussion. Again, sufficient written handouts provide basic concepts, so that the students can respond to these intelligently.

To be effective in a cross-cultural classroom, teachers who single-handedly manage their own class have a great deal of personal freedom as well as responsibility, but they can take some initial positive steps to foster the best learning environment by:

- providing course syllabi or outlines for the term;
- going over these outlines in detail on the first day of class;
- reviewing the key points at the beginning of each presentation or lecture;
- using PowerPoint or overhead transparencies to organize the key lecture points and pertinent illustrations;
- distributing a written handout of important points, concepts, and terms for each lecture;
- repeating and rephrasing these concepts in different ways during the presentation; and
- summing up the important points at the end of each presentation.

Articulating carefully and speaking slowly are also essential characteristics in presenting to a cross-cultural class. Addressing different cultural expectations about learning in the classroom is potentially a difficult issue, but, when handled responsibly and professionally through carefully structured presentations and handouts, can provide excellent learning experiences for everyone.

Team Teaching and Interdisciplinarity: Many Teachers/One Classroom

Several issues — respect for authority, emphasis on individual responsibility (or, in some cases, the responsibility of the entire group in moving forward), and understanding material before having to comment on it — need to be recognized before deciding on the best approach to a particular classroom, but one approach that should be considered is that of team teaching.

Team teaching is a natural extension of our wish to share knowledge, put different disciplines together for better understanding, continue learning, and form networks, and this is especially critical when moving to foreign countries. Most of the time, people are happy in a new country if they find a group of friends and like-minded associates, and they are often unhappy when they do not. This is equally true in the classroom: the more isolated and friendless we feel, the more likely it is that our attitude to work will suffer, as will our ability to adapt to a new culture and country. This network is important for even the most basic essentials of our new life; we need to know where to shop, locate places to relax, and access the entire social network — good doctors, dentists, churches, clubs, and volunteer opportunities, to name a few.

If two teachers are new to the classroom, team teaching can provide opportunities to assess the material and the students as well as focus on approaches that draw on each other's strengths, creating a new understanding and integration of different disciplines. It develops the core of an intellectual and social community. Also, more than one perspective on the same issue can resolve a particular problem and shed light on a complex issue, confirm its difficulties, or show how a particular attitude might be an overreaction. Having at least two instructors is also useful as a check on marking practices. Because, as discussed later, grades are context-specific, it is useful to have two perspectives in that most sensitive of tasks. If one of the pair is familiar with the school or university and native to the country, that, of course, can help the new person negotiate the demands of a new culture and, if English happens not to be the native language, then can help with issues of translation and cultural adaptation.

Team teaching is also a useful step on the path to interdisciplinary collaboration. William Newell says that team teaching is a first step in the interdisciplinary process, and he qualifies this by noting that "the main difference between interdisciplinary teams that prepare faculty for team teaching and interdisciplinary teams that prepare faculty for separately taught sections of the same course is the command required of the perspectives of other disciplines represented in the course" (1994, 36–37). By this estimate, team teaching puts disciplines together so that the real work of interdisciplinary integration can follow and so that "with experience, a single faculty member can design an interdisciplinary course . . . after developing sufficient feel for the worldviews, concepts, theories, and methods of relevant disciplines to be able to shift with ease from one perspective to another" (Newell 1994, 37).

It is fair to say that not every subject requires team teaching and interdisciplinary collaboration, with mathematics as one of the most resistant (Siskin 2000, 183), but certain subjects benefit from it, particularly ethnic studies, women's studies, and area studies — American studies, Asian studies, Canadian studies, Chinese studies, European studies, Scandinavian studies, and so on. In these subjects, particular interests, geography, and/or uniform culture define the area, so that anything within a given geographical area and cultural spectrum can be included readily. Culture, film, history, literature, music, sports, and geography are only a few of the contributing specializations, and the convergence of these disciplines in the same classroom can be informative and liberating. John Stephens notes:

In pursuing interdisciplinary ways of knowing, American studies seeks to integrate into its own work the newest research of other fields and to develop links among disciplines. In recent years, for example, feminist studies, communication studies, critical historicism, political cultural studies, international comparative studies, and other new fields have been incorporated into dynamic American studies programs and scholarship. In alliance with colleagues in newer interdisciplinary fields, such as ethnic and minority studies, American studies scholars are critically examining the myths and realities of US society and seeking answers to complex questions about US history and culture that cannot be adequately addressed within established disciplinary boundaries. (1996, 5)

Teaching area studies can thus become an interesting educational experiment, for not only can interdisciplinary perspectives be unique in a discipline-oriented environment, but the teaching styles can be more student- than lecture-centered. Some of those so-called "American-style" characteristics (which are considered in the next chapter) can, therefore, be usefully employed, including an informal, interactive classroom with ample discussion, teachers and students on a first-name basis, and an invitation to query instructors' attitudes as well as those of other students.

Area studies, however, generally fall outside normal administrative departmental and disciplinary arrangements, and this tendency has an impact on teaching as well. With few exceptions, universities in the USA and abroad consist of departments situated in Colleges or Faculties (generally, these are interchangeable terms, depending on American or European influences), typically those of Science, Social Sciences, and Arts, and of professional schools such as Education, Medicine, Dentistry, Engineering, and Business. Professional schools are drawn together by internal academic and external professional requirements, and departments of Science, Social Sciences, and Arts are diverse with different requirements, specializations, and methodologies. Although courses in various departments may resemble each other and even use similar texts (for example, those of Cultural Studies, English, and Linguistics), there is often little opportunity for inter-departmental teaching because departments are well-guarded fiefdoms, and faculty members do not usually teach across their boundaries. This practice is slowly changing in the USA, but it is still rare for an instructor of one department in Asia, Europe, or North America to lecture in a classroom of a competing department.

There are many reasons for professors not sharing classrooms with other departments. Different kinds of disciplinary training and foci are important considerations, but so is the financial bottom line. As financial and human resources for academic units are often based upon enrollment, departments may not take kindly to faculty members assisting sister departments. This department-based model is well entrenched intellectually and financially, and sometimes remains resistant to change, regardless of country, and can present barriers to interdisciplinary study and team teaching.

Practically speaking, programs in area studies can be either disciplinary or interdisciplinary based, and this can determine the possibilities of team teaching. In many instances, area programs require students to take courses from a variety of disciplines such as history, geography, and English, with each course protecting its disciplinary function, and only the students themselves draw these subjects together in their minds. In these cases, universities provide little incentive or reason for teachers to consider working together on courses.

In other cases, programs can be administratively and ideologically interdisciplinary, self-consciously fostering an ongoing integration of different subject materials by core faculty members. Sometimes these latter integrative interdisciplinary programs hire their own staff, but it has often been a practice — at least in starting them — to depend upon faculty members from various departments volunteering to give particular lectures. Logistically, this practice can be a nightmare over time because volunteers may not always be available or able to maintain their commitment. Because of difficulties in obtaining funding for such programs and systemic difficulties of an institutional culture dependent upon volunteerism, there are many instances in the USA and Europe of area studies becoming departments to gain autonomy, gather badly needed resources, and develop rich and varied programs that can utilize team teaching.

Area cultural studies often go against the institutional grain in their structures, sometimes creating interesting opportunities and perils, or both at once. Area studies in general and American studies in particular both arose in the 1930s and 1940s, and both have been linked to the rise of interdisciplinary inquiry (Klein 2005, 2). Area studies have grown rapidly in many places, especially in international settings, because students appreciate their breadth of subject matter, the focus on one culture or geographical area, and, above all, the distinctiveness of their teaching when based on a team effort. That is the opportunity, and area programs in China, Denmark, Germany, Japan, and Korea have seen explosive growth because of it.

Despite their popularity and growth, there is a particular danger that universities allocate inadequate funding for the operation of area studies, so that they are always the poor administrative stepchildren, unable to offer little more than part-time contracts. Another peril can be the dominant form of pedagogical training for the students and their role in classroom practices. In Asia, for example, local students, who at this time constitute about 95% of any given university, have most likely been trained in a traditional way by a single teacher, whereas in a team-teaching, interdisciplinary environment, students are often asked to contribute more than in a single-teacher classroom. From the point of view of the students, the traditional classroom permits them to gather required information and perspectives and allows the entire group to move forward rather than a few individuals standing out prominently. In this traditional classroom, the students often argue that regularly volunteering information and opinion and entering into discussions in too obvious a way might jeopardize their relationships with other students. From the point of view of many Western faculty members, however, this style prevents active classroom discussion and limits teaching to lecture-based, rather than student-based, activities.

Given these cultural constraints, developers of interdisciplinary programs have to think outside the institutional box and put together grass-roots programs. By gaining the commitment of core full-time and part-time teachers from various departments who present occasional lectures in area studies courses, programs might be able to put together enough human resources to create a truly interdisciplinary approach. If the personalities and skills of the core teachers blend, the teaching might grow to be admired and widely known for its special pedagogical characteristics. As Amey and Brown note, however, participation in the interdisciplinary process cannot be taken for granted because professors generally follow individualistic models, come out of multiple disciplines and perspectives formulated during graduate work, and have varying "viewpoints, orientations, ideologies, and language" (2004, 98) that can conflict. For faculty members to work together is thus part of "transformative learning."

If faculty members intend to put together an interdisciplinary curriculum, they have to follow a team building process to make "connections" (Boyer 1990, 13) and avoid "paradigmatic frictions" (Amey and Brown 2004, 100). As a first step, they might talk about offering key introductory courses and later consider other foundational and theme courses based upon the interests, strengths, and available time of participating volunteers. In the team's initial meetings and those that follow, "a variety of essentials get worked out: the disciplinary perspective underlying each reading; the key points that need to be made and the questions that need to be raised about them in the next week's seminar discussions; and paper topics, examination questions, and 'right' answers" (Newell 1994, 36–37). The first of these courses might well be based upon history, literature, politics, and current events. Guided by a core leader, faculty members from a few departments can begin to assist by offering lectures in those courses.

However, some might begin to volunteer to offer additional theme courses as well. I stress volunteering because that is often essential for a developing program, but inevitably volunteerism must give way to ongoing paid positions if a program hopes to protect its integrity and develop in a professional manner. Various faculty members may begin by participating in the planning of these courses, and, through initial consultation by e-mail exchanges, identify various issues to establish such foci as:

- the treatment of the subject historically;
- current cultural considerations;
- regional perceptions related to the theme;
- the theme as manifested in various forms, such as music, art, literature, and film; and
- gender in relation to the theme.

After the participants agree upon topics through e-mail communication, they can identify texts drawn from the relevant disciplines, and can develop a syllabus, taking into consideration the participants' viewpoints to provide a manageable workload for the students. If the participants in this course were experts in film, history, literature, fine arts, and music, they might tend to focus on historical, cultural, and artistic considerations; and, if the participants were drawn from other academic areas, then the characteristics of the course would obviously follow another pattern.

Once the group establishes a workable model of collaboration in one course, the pattern can be followed in other courses, and various individuals can take their turns in developing unique and interesting interdisciplinary, team-taught courses. These courses should be reviewed annually to see if their aims are achieved and if revisions are required. That way, fine-tuning can become an on-going part of the process.

The collaboration of representatives from various departments can, in itself, be a milestone at any teaching institution, and the participants can establish strong and lasting friendships as well as interdisciplinary research projects on the basis of it. The glue that cements this relationship can support the actual classroom experience. A parade of faculty members into a given classroom week after week certainly could allow students to receive different disciplinary perspectives on the same topic, but it is necessary to go beyond that to integrate the fields of knowledge and create a positive learning environment.

To a great extent, the integration of the fields of knowledge must be the role of a coordinator because teachers volunteering their time for such a program usually do so in addition to regular commitments and are often unable or unwilling to commit too much additional time to the endeavor. Three or four lectures per course is common, meaning that the role of the course coordinator is critical to the proper functioning of the course. Because most academic institutions follow the familiar academic tradition of one teacher/one classroom, students are not used to having a number of different presenters in a given course, and they prefer the coordinator to become the central figure with whom to identify. That coordinator can schedule the presentations, introduce the topics, provide lectures that bridge other people's materials, present at least half the lectures on her/his own, and undertake the marking. Faculty members are generally willing to give guest lectures if they do not have to do marking because, otherwise, their commitment of time is more than they can manage. The coordinator must be a neutral leader (Amey and Brown 2004, 133), ensure the course's intellectual integrity and positive classroom environment, bring the disparate materials together, provide links and assure continuity, do the marking, and become the beating heart of the course.

Without the coordinator's active integration, there is always the possibility that a course might simply become a series of disconnected modules. While such a series might be effective under particular circumstances, there is usually a critical need for the coordinators to bridge the various presentations and ensure that interdisciplinary methodology is applied at every turn. If a course in European Studies happens to deal with London as an exemplary European city, the coordinator must provide links between the domestic spaces, business, and entertainment that team member presenters talk about. At the end of the day, even in team teaching with a model of decision-making based upon consensus, one person must take primary responsibility.

It is important that the coordinator also creates a non-threatening space for the various presenters and students (Amey and Brown 2004, 100). Those who lecture need to be assured that they will be welcome and their ideas given respectful consideration. If instructors only present their lectures to the students, and colleagues only come to class on the dates of their presentations, the issue of classroom dynamics for instructors may not arise. However, if instructors feel comfortable with one another and share an interest in the subjects, they may well want to sit in on each other's lectures. This building of a team can be a means of sharing information and expertise, so that lecturers develop basic competence in others' materials and try to pitch their own presentations in such a way as to integrate other teachers' materials. It can also serve a mentoring function, with experienced teachers guiding and directing less experienced ones. Two or three lecturers might well be in the audience with the students, listening respectfully and sharing insights with the presenter, leaving time at the conclusion of the presentations for instructors and students alike to share observations and ask questions. Those who are lecturing can often design their lectures to include, at selected critical junctures, the colleagues who are listening.

Students initially bemused by this framework will begin to look forward to it and become pleasantly surprised by the instructors' interactions with each other and ease of incorporating different perspectives and opinions. As a result, respectful and dynamic interaction between faculty members and students can become a model for students to see how dissenting voices and differing perspectives can be incorporated in a non-competitive space. Effective use of team teaching can do a great deal to allay student concerns about the so-called culture of questioning in the classroom in which they are expected to ask questions of the instructor and fellow students. For those who come from cultures that do not confirm the value of questioning in class, seeing polite and respectful differences of opinion among instructors can go a long way to making them feel comfortable with the process.

Team teaching is also an excellent way for faculty members to gain understanding and respect for their colleagues. Initially, some instructors may not understand the process or feel secure with it, but most will feel increasingly comfortable with the dynamics of interdisciplinary team teaching. It is important to pay special attention to the development of team teaching because people do have different conceptions of it. Some seem to think team teaching is either a series of guest lectures or panel discussions; but, while these are both useful parts of team teaching, that is mainly a multidisciplinary, rather than an interdisciplinary, approach. On most occasions, interdisciplinary team teaching is less formal, more interactive, and with shared responsibility. Ideally, a number of people should be involved in each course, and, while they do not have to attend every class, they need to be involved in conceptualizing the course and building the syllabus. They also need to be enough a part of the course to develop collegiality in the classroom, giving each an opportunity to learn from the other and the students an opportunity to become comfortable in sharing ideas. In addition to formal responsibilities — a lecture or two and a couple of times on panels — the team should meet periodically to discuss the direction of the project, in terms of content, interdisciplinary work, and teaching directions. Participating faculty members should present themselves as a group early in the semester to introduce the students to the team concept.

Faculty members who share common experiences in the classroom should discuss classroom pedagogy on a regular basis. As a group, they can try different models, mixing lecture and discussion in classes of all sizes, putting students in a large discussion circle for classes of under 30, and breaking modest-sized classes into small discussion groups of four or five students, and larger-sized classes into groups of around 12 students. They can try these various approaches and meet over coffee or lunch to discuss how they have worked. In certain courses, they can also involve students in thinking out pedagogical strategies, so that they know the teachers' aims, reflect on their appropriateness, and comment on how well they were achieved. By faculty members' talking about these ideas with each other and including the students as well, they can all share responsibility for the classroom success. What the team chooses to use, however, will depend upon the nature of the teachers, the students, and the classroom context as such. Because interdisciplinary work and team teaching are still relatively untried concepts, teachers need to figure out ways to make it work especially well with real situations. They cannot assume that their previous experiences in the USA or another foreign location will be the same as their current teaching situation, and therefore need to work hard at making the right connections as they go along. Of course, there is nothing like the right classroom synergy, and part of a positive teaching experience can be the luck of discovering that synergy. In Newell's terms, "collaboration on an interdisciplinary team is a lot like marriage. One must ask whether the particular mix of personalities proposing a course will work together appropriately" (1994, 37–38).

Talking about teaching between teachers and students can also make students more aware of their responsibility in creating goals and mechanisms for a good learning environment. The learning goals that teachers and students together identify in an interdisciplinary classroom might well include the importance of knowledge transfer, the ease of expressing thoughts in class, the ability to give presentations and write essays in English, and the development of critical thinking. Although students all over the world would probably say that knowledge is an important aspect of any course, they might have very different views about the fundamental acquisition of that knowledge, and an open discussion of that topic on a regular basis can assist in an acceptance of the basic classroom strategies. This is all part of critical thinking.

Another significant aspect of team teaching in an interdisciplinary classroom is the teaching of critical thinking. With television and films as their highly mediated sources of information, students sometimes lack critical perspectives on certain basic issues. One purpose of team-taught, interdisciplinary area studies courses is the dissemination of information and presentation of diverse insights and contrary perceptions of particular cultures to help students become critical of all information. Although they must understand basic social and intellectual constructs, they need to query sources of knowledge and kinds of information.

One way to help with critical thinking in the cross-cultural classroom is to encourage students to compare the global with the local — especially when the focus of the area studies is on a country other than their own. This "engagement with local contexts and processes increasingly raises the issue of how these relate to the wider context and to the major, global issues that are shaping the world" (Webb 2005, 110). For example, German students who are comparing the USA and Germany can often bring new personal perspectives to the material and learn a great deal about their own national identity and that of the Americans and the way this plays out on the international stage. This, after all, is a customary strategy of interdisciplinary inquiry — by comparing disciplinary perspectives, students can better understand the complexity of the issues and learn to critique them; and by comparing national perspectives, students can better understand the complexity of the global environment and learn to critique the actions, results, and motivations of various countries.

Closely related to critical thinking is the students' ability to become better writers and speakers. The speaking and writing abilities of students vary considerably, but, in cultures that place a high importance on examinations, writing essays during the term is sometimes not so important. As discussed more fully in Chapter 7, "Assignments and Assessments," many universities throughout the world still require final examinations worth 60–100% of the course grade, giving students little reason to value on-going assessment of essays and other projects during the term. Where this tradition is alive, teachers might consider reducing the final-examination requirement if it is negotiable, giving students a greater opportunity to write journals and short reports on a regular basis and longer essay assignments at the middle and end of term. While most courses still favor an end-of-term examination or in-class test, they can settle for a less significant weighting, perhaps only 20%. This reduction in the examination component and increase in the essay writing component might allow students to recognize the importance of on-going practice in speaking and writing English and, consequently, be more appreciative of cultivating those skills.

In my experience, students are enthusiastic about an academic program that stresses team-teaching and interdisciplinary inquiry among its staff and students. When like-minded, intelligent teachers work together and when students are involved in the process of learning at every level, rewarding academic experiences can happen. When they work together like this, the walls that are so carefully constructed between academic units begin to crumble, allowing a new kind of complex understanding and human synergy. This is what a teaching team which dares to be interdisciplinary and pedagogically innovative can accomplish.

Classroom Tools for Lecturing

Whether with a single instructor or a team, there are important aids and tools to enhance lecturing in the classroom. These include overhead projectors, CD players, PowerPoint, and the Internet. Omitted from this list is the slide projector because that piece of equipment is outdated and impossible to find in almost any location — whether the most or least technologically innovative classroom and country.

Overhead projectors

Overhead projectors have been a part of classroom presentations for many years, are inexpensive and readily available, and are effective in presenting uncomplicated outlines and simple illustrations on plastic transparencies or "overheads." Available in black and white as well as color, overheads can be seen in almost any kind of light, but colored ones do fade out on the screen even with controlled lighting. Moreover, teachers sometimes try to use too many transparencies, mixing them up and losing their place, and the machines do not always focus properly, making print and pictures difficult to see. Older projectors used only transparent overheads, but recent projectors are much improved and can show anything placed directly on the mat under the light, without requiring the production of transparencies. The problem of getting them focused adequately, however, still exists. This medium is especially useful as the teacher can write directly on the transparency while showing it and thereby alter the information, responding to and recording student comments.

CD players

Another easy and inexpensive piece of technology for the classroom is the "boom box" or CD player. For those in the humanities, social sciences, or area studies, the ability to play music in aid of history, literature, and culture is important, and public and university libraries often have good collections of CDs that can be used for teaching purposes. Illustrating the development of railroads and related movements of American people in the nineteenth and early twentieth centuries by playing "Hallelujah, I'm a Bum," "John Henry," and "I've Been Workin' on the Railroad"; exemplifying the evolution of popular culture during the Harlem Renaissance by playing Duke Ellington; or demonstrating what Jack Kerouac means by "be-bop" in *On the Road* by playing Charlie Parker — all of these interdisciplinary aids can make important differences in the students' appreciation, understanding, and integration of important concepts and cultural relationships.

The Internet

One of the great equalizers in cultures, the Internet makes first-world knowledge and expertise available around the world to students and faculty members who need its capabilities. Although poor countries may not be able to provide computers and Internet access for all schools and universities, many philanthropic foundations provide funding so that access is available in most universities, even in the poorest Third World countries. Many universities in Japan, South Korea, Hong Kong, and mainland China have policies that all students should own laptops and have worked out agreements with large corporations such as Lenovo (formerly IBM) to assist their purchase, so students have them and are used to exploring a wide range of materials, often know how to operate them better than their instructors, and have become quite sophisticated in using them to make presentations.

At the moment, the most advanced form of technology available to the classroom lecturer is the Internet with its endless parade of sounds, images, and critical documents. When this technology is available in the classroom and when it works, connections on the Internet are very effective. Teachers wanting to talk about contemporary art can go online and use pictures drawn from various websites such as Google.image to provide illustrations. Those who want to talk about Elizabethan plays can go to the University of Pennsylvania website and compare historical editions of Shakespeare's *King Lear*, listen to the actual language of the play, and show different theatrical interpretations. And geographers can go to Google.maps and find numerous national and world maps as well as those of small streets in New York City. These are just a few of the possibilities, and new resources appear almost daily on the Internet.

Although classrooms increasingly have ports available for teachers and students to plug in laptop computers, the use of the Internet does sometimes pose a problem. Different countries and individual classrooms have different requirements and electrical power capabilities, so the easy use of this technology is never assured, even in the most advanced technological locations. Teachers going to countries with different electrical voltage and plug sizes will need to make certain they have power adapters so that they can plug in their computers. In any case, a minimum of 15 minutes is often required to make an Internet connection or set up PowerPoint, and sometimes the technology fails entirely at the outset or during the presentation itself. Presenters need to have overhead transparencies to use as a backup when computer technology is inaccessible or fails. An added frustration in using the Internet for music or voice is that the sound is often unpredictable, and many well-intended presentations have gone awry because students cannot hear the sound or the images cannot be transferred from the computer to the large screen.

PowerPoint presentations

PowerPoint is perhaps the most effective and dependable of the computer technologies for the classroom, but it is not for all faculty members: many do not like having to organize their lectures far in advance, make detailed slides, have those slides control the sequence of the lecture, and be obliged to give copies of the electronic PowerPoint to those who ask. Moreover, with this technology, it can be difficult for discussions to arise spontaneously in class.

PowerPoint can function effectively in the international cross-cultural classroom for very important reasons. First, creating PowerPoint presentations helps ensure organized lectures that students can follow with ease. Second, students can apprehend the important ideas and terms on the screen and focus better on what the teacher has to say, reduce the chances for misunderstanding, and be secure in a basis of knowledge for discussion.

Finally, PowerPoint can incorporate pictures and video clips along with the main lecture points, thus creating livelier, more graphic presentations and avoiding the hazards of trying to access them through the Internet while class is in progress.

Yet, there are pitfalls. Presenters are not always aware how many slides can realistically be included to fill the time in a productive and interesting fashion. It is all too common that lecturers drag out their lectures because they have too few slides and too little information, or talk too quickly because they have compressed too much material into too many slides, and include statements that cover the entire screen and are too difficult for the audience to read and comprehend in a short time. Time management is consequently a major consideration as is the amount of written material and bullet points on each slide.

Other problems with PowerPoint presentations include the presenter not having chosen an effective design template to highlight the print, the room having too much light for the slides to show up, or the technology not working as anticipated — the power fails and the files cannot be loaded or get lost. In addition, attempting to access a film clip can sometimes cause considerable delays and often does not work at all.

To ensure the best results for students in an international cross-cultural classroom, the instructor should make copies of the PowerPoint slides, with six to a page and hand them out to the students to accompany the presentation. Some teachers are reluctant to do this because it means that their lectures are no longer in their own possession and become part of the public domain, but the benefit to the students is significant. They have the slides in front of them and do not have to scramble to write down the basic thoughts of the presenter but can add to them as they see fit. Moreover, students whose first language is not English can look up the words that they do not know and thereby enlarge their vocabulary and ensure their comprehension of the lecture. In fact, students in mainland China ask if I can e-mail the slides to all of them the day before class, so that they can look up all the words in advance and be fully ready to listen and understand the presentation. Their intention is not to skip class as a result but to understand the vocabulary and argument well enough to get more out of the lecture and participate readily in discussion. In fact, many university courses now allow instructors to manage their courses electronically, which includes posting the syllabus and PowerPoint lectures and having all of the readings electronically scanned and posted as well.

PowerPoint does much to ensure logical and coherent presentations. What it cannot ensure is that the lecturer will engage this technology and students themselves in a creative manner. Too often, the lecturer only reads the basic points without expanding or clarifying them or without engaging the class. In some cases, lecturers only look at the monitor in front of them or look entirely at the screen so that eye contact with the students, classroom rapport, and creative vitality are lost.

Despite the many virtues of the classroom lecture style — with a single presenter or a daring team or with the aid of interesting technology, lecturing alone can almost never accomplish everything that needs to be done in the classroom. Students whose first language is not English might not be able to follow all the material in an English-based lecture, even with overheads, PowerPoint, and copious handouts. In addition, attention spans are limited, and even with the variety added by team teaching or with the assistance of technological aids, students might not be able to sustain their concentration at all times, losing their focus, failing to understand or remember salient points, and missing some of the basic building blocks of information and knowledge. Lecturing may not help students to "analyze, synthesize, or integrate knowledge," especially "when material is complex or abstract" (George 1995, 70). Consequently, even though the lecture method is still the most significant part of any classroom, other means have to be considered as well to make the learning experience stimulating, complex, and well rounded.

5

The Student-Oriented Classroom

Although lecturing is the foundation of the classroom and the preferred pedagogy for most teachers internationally, American educators and students state a strong preference for discussion, either as a supplement to, or a replacement of, the lecture, and think of this as the modern approach. Surveys show that American students favor seminars and discussions over lectures by a ratio of 3 to 1 (McLeish 1976, 293). It is well known that many Asian communitarian societies traditionally support thoughtful, well-prepared lectures over class discussion (Morris and Marsh 1991, 259), and it can be frustrating for transplanted teachers to discover that the discussion prized in the American classroom is not so highly regarded in other societies. Fulbright Professors going abroad to other English-speaking countries (Australia, New Zealand, and Singapore), South East Asian countries (Malaysia, Pakistan, and Thailand), diverse liberal countries from all over Europe (Czechoslovakia, Hungary, Ireland and Norway), and other countries well known for their casual style and Western orientation (Israel) all commented that they had a difficult — and in some cases an impossible — time getting students involved in discussion, and that this was a handicap to their teaching (George 1995, 150–51).

Students in the international cross-cultural classroom may resist some aspects of a foreign-imposed curriculum, and, as Graham Pike notes, it is axiomatic for global education that teachers "recognize that they have a view of the world that is not universally shared," that they need to be aware of the local context in which they teach, and that they need to develop in the students "an awareness and understanding of the global condition and of global developments and trends" (1990, 134, 135). The first step, then, is to explore national and local attitudes toward the classroom without assuming that a one-teacher/one-classroom, team-taught and interdisciplinary classroom, or a student-centered classroom is the answer to pedagogical problems and learning issues. It would be a serious mistake for teachers to move to a different culture and immediately impose particular classroom practices without trying to investigate possible problems and solutions in advance. Provided that is done and that teachers give adequate information and knowledge, assist individual academic growth, and ensure that the cross-cultural classroom fosters group solidarity (Slethaug 2001), students should find discussion enjoyable in itself, an important learning tool, and invaluable preparation for the give-and-take global economy.

Problem Solving, Group Work, and Presentations

In general, a student-centered classroom is one that tries to make students comfortable and cooperative with each other, responsive to teachers, and personally responsible for the learning environment. In a completely student-centered classroom, the teacher might not give lectures or presentations and would serve solely as a resource person, guide, and cultural interpreter. Some American students thrive on this approach, which Dr. Maria Montessori made famous in schools that focus on "learning through discovery" and on teaching children to discover their own potential. In these schools, the teacher's function is to stimulate the children's imagination and facilitate the development of their interests. As the Montessori website notes: "We are here to nurture your child and to help you with the important work of guiding . . . intellectual, emotional and physical development, . . . enabling him or her to develop the habits, attitudes, skills and ideas that lead to a lifetime of creative thinking and learning" (2006). This unstructured schooling in the Montessori schools is mainly for children under the age of 12, and educators generally assume that more mature students require more direction, if not formality, so that instructors are almost never just resource people. Teachers most likely to serve primarily as resources do so in classrooms with highly developed practices of cooperative learning that "not only produce higher levels of 'on task' behaviour and achievement, but also promote higher student self-esteem, better student relationships, the ability to take the perspective of others, and more positive attitudes towards teachers and school" (Winter 1995, 37).

A particularly interesting form of classroom cooperation is problem-based learning (PBL), which "challenges students to 'learn to learn,' working cooperatively in groups to seek solutions to real world problems. These problems are used to engage students' curiosity and initiate learning the subject matter. PBL prepares students to think critically and analytically, and to find and use appropriate learning resources" (Duch 2006). As part of the process, students are given problems to work on, either individually or in groups, and can use textbooks, the library, the Internet, the media, knowledgeable individuals, and other relevant resources to help solve them.

Students generally agree that individual problem solving is useful, but not all students think group work is "worth the effort" (Carroll 2005b, 85) because it is "a poor reflector of individual abilities" (De Vita 2005, 77). In North America, cooperative PBL at the university level often goes against the "competition model" that students have used to gain college admittance, based, as Kris Bosworth remarks, on "one's own work, the sometimes destructive criticism of the work of others . . . the sharing of ideas only with power figures, manipulation of the system to one's own benefit where possible, and a general lack of trust" (1994, 26). Consequently, many of these groups and projects run into some level of difficulty and resistance because students do not have a good pattern of working together. De Vita argues that this resistance is more acutely experienced when international students are involved because the various national groups tend not to mix (2005, 75).

Students abroad, however, may have a better pattern of working together from early in their schooling than do North American schools. In countries such as Japan, group work is the basis of all education. According to T. R. Reid (1999, 149):

> Schooling in Japan, like everything else in Japan, is a group endeavor. The small group of four or five children is the basic unit of learning, in every subject, in every classroom. For Japanese educators, this methodology is a two-birds-with-one-stone kind of thing. Group learning is considered the pre-eminent strategy for academic topics, and, of course, the constant small-group interaction also teaches the children the essential Confucian skills of cooperative group membership.

Students may enjoy coming up with individual insights as part of group work, but in some places only the collective response and voice of the group is important. As the Lingenfelters remark of one of the western Pacific islands close to the Philippines: "Students helped one another with everything and almost never worked alone. They were personally self-sufficient, yet they tended to answer my questions as a group" (2003, 14).

Many university students in Europe and Asia find that, under the right conditions, working in groups to solve problems and discuss issues is a preferred mode of learning. Almost to a person, my students in Denmark, Hong Kong, and mainland China were enthusiastic and inspired in working with classmates, and discovered that the intimacy of a group led to intense discussions and productive exchanges of ideas — although they still did not always like to be assessed on it, a phenomenon that Carroll finds quite common (2005b, 85).

Frequently, group discussions discover different perspectives and angles of vision when students are candid and relaxed in this small setting. These opportunities broaden students' horizons, enable them to know and respect each other, and confront some of the politics of learning because they learn to be committed to their ideas, articulate them clearly, and try to persuade others, and also discover the art of negotiation and compromise in order that members can work together and achieve common results.

Sooner or later, however, students in groups can experience varying degrees of conflict in their academic relationships and need to know how to address and resolve it (Carroll 2005b, 90). Bosworth argues that this is frequently the case in cultures where students are schooled in competition (1994, 26), but, in fact, it probably happens everywhere. Conflict arises for various reasons, but it commonly involves personalities rather than ideas, perhaps because someone talks too little or too much, is too quiet or too loud, or is too passive or too aggressive — that is, falling short of the ideal. De Vita remarks that in some cultures the ideal classmate is the one "who is intense, talkative, employs direct communication and doesn't miss an opportunity to subject ideas to critical scrutiny," but in other cultures the one with "diplomacy, tactfulness and a certain degree of inhibition" is preferred (2005, 78). Jeffrey Ady confirms that tension arises because some want — and act out — the ethos of individualism as a core cultural value and others collectivism (1998, 111). As a result, those who do not live up to cultural expectations and norms can be perceived as problematic. Others, including Gerald Graff (1992), have written about the importance of addressing conflict in the university context and using it as an educational tool, but in certain cultures engaging conflict directly would intensify the problem rather than defuse it.

Supervised group activities can certainly provide a good basis for experience in articulating informed positions and resolving personal and intellectual conflict, but many cultures, including China, Japan, and the Scandinavian countries, go to great lengths to avoid even the appearance of conflict in the first place, especially in the classroom. The use of consensus in Dutch and Scandinavian classrooms and the importance of "face" in Chinese culture are means of preventing or dissipating conflict

— whether that conflict is based on personal disagreements or intellectual questioning — because these cultures place high value on interdependency. Ady's description (1998, 112) of individualistic and independent people versus those who are interdependent indicates their differing contributions to classroom behavior:

> A dominant independent self-construal, reflecting cultural individualism, leads one to be unique, strive for one's own goals, express one's self, and communicate directly . . . A dominant interdependent self-construal, on the other hand, reflects cultural collectivism's imperatives in that the individual must mesh with his or her in-group, act appropriately, promote in-group goals, communicate indirectly, and understand what others are thinking.

Each of these can contribute positively to group work, but these two kinds of cultural constructions in the same classroom may pose a challenge for the teacher unless carefully negotiated.

In respect to classroom dialogue, questioning those in authority is seen as disrespectful in some cultures, so, in teaching abroad, Westerners must consider whether a "culture of questioning" goes against respectful treatment of the teacher (Heath 1982). In my first lecture to a group of 250 first-year students in Hong Kong, I asked students to come to me after class if they had questions. One of the tutors informed me that no one would do so because asking questions would be considered disrespectful to my education, age, and authority; and, possibly, because English was not their first language, it might lower my respect for them and their linguistic errors would compromise the "hierarchical role differentiation" (De Vita 2005, 78). To question me might also indicate that they had not listened carefully to the presentation and so failed to understand the material, again lowering my respect for them and those of their peers as well. The tutor was partly correct: at the end of the first class, only a few students came up to ask me a question. At the end of the second class, however, I asked students to write out any requests for clarification or additional information on pieces of paper and put them in my mailbox. I received nearly 40 responses. The tutor was quite wrong about it this time because the students were more familiar with me, I gave them an indirect way to ask questions, no one lost face, and I got the feedback that I wanted. Raising questions directly and engaging in discussions are not always viewed as positive forms of learning, especially in a large class. According to McLean and Ransom, many "students face a cultural dilemma when they don't understand something explained by a lecturer. The student is concerned about losing face because they have less than perfect knowledge and there is also the implication that the teacher didn't explain properly (and the student may therefore be concerned about the teacher 'losing face')" (2005, 49). When this is the case, teachers need to think of alternatives.

Another difficulty for discussion groups in the cross-cultural classroom is that of students who do not engage actively with the group or fulfill their responsibilities. Students are sometimes wary of group projects and discussion because of teammates who have abused a working relationship, broken promises, and generally not pulled their weight in a task — but have shared the credit for the assignment. In group-work, "if someone goofs," one Danish student told me, "you pay the price." Students do not like it when they are asked to be independent, responsible, and hard-working, while one of the members of their group is lazy, intellectually dependent, and personally irresponsible. Moreover, in education, there is an unstated code which suggests that students should not disclose other students' lack of participation, and that can build resentment. When the group works well, students find the personal independence invigorating, and, when it works poorly, others' dependency drags down their own time and effort.

PBL puts responsibility squarely on the shoulders of each student and group, but to start the process teachers must phrase the assignments carefully, with all — not just one — of the class's cultures in mind. Students from different cultural backgrounds have different expectations about the specificity of the assignments and different interpretations of the terminology and tasks. Also, the instructor needs to consider carefully how much time solutions to problems will take. This question of the right length of time for assignments is critical in a cross-cultural classroom in which students from different nations, cultures, and native languages may require varying amounts of time to undertake complex tasks. It takes considerable thoughtfulness about the requirements of the assignment and experience with the group to assess the abilities of students in a class and their cultural adaptation well enough to estimate the right amount of time to complete work on materials. The teacher must pitch the problem at just the right level for each student or group, giving more or less time for it depending upon the language abilities of the students and their level of achievement.

A cross-cultural class should certainly consider implementing PBL as one of the basic strategies, but some international students have reservations about its too-pervasive use because their own countries require formal examinations for almost every stage of education — admission to primary and secondary schools and universities; progress through university programs; and even work, in the case of the civil service. If students are accustomed to a set curriculum and particular kinds of examinations and believe that their chances for further education and work opportunities will be jeopardized by a departure from those, they will not appreciate a class based entirely upon problem solving. Consequently, although problem solving can be an extremely important learning tool, it may need to be integrated with other approaches so that all students can prepare for other eventualities without penalty.

If problem solving is part of group activities, those must be planned carefully, both in terms of the larger class and composition of groups. I previously discussed the formation of discussion groups when considering the actual space in the classroom, but need to take this issue one step further. As noted in Chapter 3, students often have a mixed attitude towards sitting in a full circle, but most willingly accept variations of that, such as sitting around a table or in an open semi-circle. Each of these alternatives promotes the personal responsibility of students, and students often find that gathering around a table or a semi-circle allows them to see and hear the lecturer better, feel less pressure because they do not have to sit beside the teacher, and escape being the object of the gaze of the class. They have also remarked that a semi-circle, with the instructor seated at the front, does not create the false impression that the instructor and students are equals. Americans especially like to suggest that teachers and students should be on a relatively equal footing in the classrooms, but students from abroad, who often have great respect for teachers, realize that they — and not the students themselves — do have the final say in creating a particular learning environment, giving out assignments, and awarding marks.

One of the students' favorite models, regardless of their national origin or culture, is a small group of four or five students. With that number, enough viewpoints are represented to make for a good discussion, no single person has to carry the burden of discussion, and students become tutors of their peers. As Hofstede remarks (1997, 62):

> Collectivist culture students will also hesitate to speak up in larger groups without a teacher present, especially if these are partly composed of relative strangers: outgroup members. This hesitation decreases in smaller groups. Personally I obtained broad participation when teaching a collectivist class by asking students to turn around in their seats so that groups of three were formed. I asked the students to discuss a question for five minutes, and to decide who would report their joint answer to the class. Through this device students had an opportunity to develop a group answer and felt comfortable when speaking up before the class because they acted as the small group's representative.

Hofstede's comments resonate with T. R. Reid's assessment of the primacy of small groups in Japanese education (1999, 149), as well as my own experiences in Europe and Asia. For short-term discussions, giving students a fixed period of time to discuss a topic and then having a spokesperson (or the entire group) report back to the class creates a sense of responsibility, establishes workable limits, and allows a comfort zone. Frequently, the instructor can effectively lead a discussion and interweave a lecture based upon the opinions of the various groups.

A further refinement of this classroom strategy is the jigsaw approach. First described by Elliot Aronson, this approach involves several small groups, each responsible for one aspect of a problem or topic, so that when all the groups report to one another and/or the entire class, the solution becomes clear to everyone. This variation of the small group has the advantage of covering more issues and with greater complexity than having each group addressing the same problem (Winter 1995, 38).

An individual or group presentation is another excellent way to encourage and highlight class participation on a more formal level. Students working in small groups can report back to larger groups, which can be very valuable, but presentations can be to the entire class as well. They can develop short, creative oral presentations for class, demonstrating their knowledge of the material, ability to organize and focus, and skill with available visuals. As a result of discussing topics in class, reporting on the findings of a small group, or making formal presentations, students gain confidence in voicing their opinions. Many quiet students discover, and learn to celebrate, their courage in articulating perceptions and viewpoints in class. It is an extremely important moment in any classroom, but particularly in the cross-cultural one, when students discover that they have opinions to share, that differing opinions are really valued, and that teachers and students can work together to foster a positive environment in which they share these insights.

With about six members to a group and a 20-minute limit, students have proven able presenters in my classroom. If they have personal computers, they can also organize and illustrate their presentations on PowerPoint, developing another valuable skill that will help them in the future. However, because PowerPoint takes time to set up, if students link up their own computers, a great deal of time is wasted. Generally, it is better to use one computer and have each student put in a memory stick (USB flash drive/thumb drive) at the appropriate time. Although it can be good pedagogy to include these presentations during the term, by the end of term, the students should have a strong mastery of the coursework material and can be more creative and knowledgeable in their presentations. I have found this approach effective in Denmark, Hong Kong, and mainland China, and it has some special benefits when students are expecting an oral component in their program examinations. In Denmark, for example, undergraduates are expected to complete a Bachelor's project that they will have to present and defend orally. Generally, as students do not make oral presentations in courses, providing an opportunity to do so can give much needed experience, confidence, and ways of judging a good oral from a mediocre one.

A word of caution, however, needs to accompany this celebration of presentations: many students and faculty members find them a waste of time, and some teachers who have experimented with them have abandoned them as a classroom tool. The strongest objection comes from both students and teachers who think that professionals need to impart their knowledge directly through lectures. Those who follow this line generally have no confidence that students will have the depth of knowledge or experience required to explore a subject adequately. This question about the authority and limited value of student presentations is accompanied by a view that most of them are low-level and boring. Perhaps, then, especially in the cross-cultural classroom, students need to be assured that teachers impart sufficient information and that adequate help is given to them so that presentations are sufficiently informed and lively. Students clearly need practice, and, with adequate supervision, their presentations will have substance and interest.

Shared Responsibilities for Groups and Teams

Every classroom and institution has its own personality, and some classes come together easily and function well because of the special mix of staff and students. When that is the case, it is inspiring and invigorating, but others take hard work. Most courses and classrooms are assembled at random, bringing together students who might otherwise not have a chance to know one another, allowing them to discover shared interests, and giving them an opportunity to develop firm relationships with those partners. It can be problematic, however, when there seem to be no "natural" alliances within a class, resulting in conflicting personalities, abilities, and work habits. Consequently, teachers may want to structure groups in classes less randomly and more formally to ensure that personalities blend and students work together toward common goals with high levels of achievement.

In creating groups which function well, teachers in cross-cultural classrooms can take advantage of basic team-building concepts as well as studies on group formations carried out by various universities, such as the

Institute for Interactive Media and Learning at the University of Technology, Sydney, Australia, the Center for Teaching Excellence at the University of Kansas, or the Cooperative Extension at the University of Nebraska-Lincoln. Most educators do not think automatically about classes or groups as teams — though those in physical education, business schools, or schools of nursing undoubtedly prove exceptions here — but if they do, then teachers and students alike can be more responsible and effective in their efforts.

It is useful to look at the entire classroom as a team but this is particularly critical in small groups that are expected to work together over an extended period. *Very simply, a team is a group of individuals organized to work together to accomplish a set of objectives and goals that generally cannot be achieved as effectively by working alone.* Setting up these groups can be a team effort in itself if decisions about goals, equity, balance, and representation are taken together by teachers and students. Moreover, students themselves can help make certain decisions about the functions and responsibilities of the group or team, including assistance with assessment.

The participatory process of group work typically goes through five stages — *formation, self-definition, integration, performance,* and *evaluation and assessment:*

- *formation* — The teacher articulates goals, establishes general guidelines, and (with or without student input) selects group members.
- *self-definition* — The students take those goals, create their own targets and strategies, and choose teammates for particular purposes.
- *integration* — The students undertake their individual tasks, further define and clarify the topic through their research, and begin the process of integrating perspectives.
- *performance* — The students present the materials to the teacher and the rest of the class as a written project and/or oral report.
- *evaluation and assessment* — The teacher and students evaluate the merit of the project and working relationships.

Formation

Getting the composition right in forming groups for a long-term project depends upon the individual characteristics of the classroom, but if mixed in gender, ethnicity, and age, then achieving balance across the spectrum is ideal. Levels of maturity and scholastic achievement must be taken into consideration as well: sometimes the teacher might want groups of students who are at the same level of accomplishment and at other times may prefer distributed levels of achievement.

In establishing groups, teachers need to identify firm goals so that students know the objectives of the project, how assignments meet those objectives, and what is required of them in the short term as well as the long term. It is important to remember that students from different cultural backgrounds may want to think about goals and objectives in different ways. East Asian students often like to work within clearly defined parameters and value specificity in defining goals, whereas American students are often happy with more general statements that allow them to choose their own focus and define exercises and topics as they move along. Students from some cultures may become annoyed if objectives and goals are too precise and prescriptive, but others may become frustrated if the assignments are fuzzy, unfocused, and lacking in detail and specificity. Teachers abroad will have to check with those experienced in the culture to ascertain what the local tendency is and what can reasonably be expected.

After establishing goals, the teacher needs to review the assignments and possible topics. Because what particularly interests one person may not interest others, students need a variety of topics to consider for their research. Different cultures value different things, and teachers need to understand that they may have to give special consideration to the range of choices, appealing to the various backgrounds and cultural interests of the students. In many cases, students in Asia have little experience in formulating their own topics and prefer to have a range of available options. Too many topics and choices, however, can frustrate students. (This latter problem is particularly true for examinations: reading a number of questions and thinking out the implications of each can take too much time — particularly when the language of instruction is not their first language — and diminish their ability to write solid answers.)

Because group members work closely together, it is important that they participate willingly and recognize their shared responsibility and interdependence. Students who come from a culture favoring individualism or who have had an unfortunate experience working in a group might well want individual assignments. Such students need assurances that this experience has value and that they will not be penalized for classmates who fail to participate adequately. If the teacher can create ways to ensure personal responsibility and provide a buffer for a group with an irresponsible member, then team members will be much happier throughout the entire experience of working together.

One way to begin the process of establishing working relationships and personal responsibility is to emphasize that a group has the opportunity to take a project further than any one individual can, and that all students need to share viewpoints, have something positive to offer, and are expected to work hard, contribute equally to a project, and respect their partners' work. Perhaps the key term here is *respect* — for the person, the integrity of the group, and the project itself. The integrity of the group is a direct result of respect and mutual trust. Students must also recognize that everyone's work can be improved, and part of the purpose of a group is that members learn by constructively criticizing their own work and that of their partners.

Students also need to develop a sense of personal security and trust in the group. This, of course, is closely related to the importance of respect considered above. Personal security is achieved, in part, through an acceptance of each teammate and a positive climate of communication; it is usually the teachers themselves who, by example and strong admonitions, set the tone for this kind of acceptance among the group members. In forming groups teachers therefore need to:

* base the composition of groups upon sound pedagogical principles and an awareness of the specific class;
* articulate the goals clearly;
* think of a sufficient number of topics for the group;
* emphasize respect as the foundational principle of collaboration; and
* set the tone for security and trust.

Self-definition

When students understand their group's goals and the available topics, they can choose wisely, decide on strategies to achieve the goals and implement plans, help ensure that everyone participates fully, and keep lines of communication open between themselves and their teacher. The group's first task is to discuss the overall goal and establish preliminary targets. Teachers may believe that they have given explicit instructions, but, especially in the cross-cultural classroom, students may not "hear" precisely what teachers think they have said — perhaps because they do not understand the language adequately or because it is, as Hong Kong students often say, "out of their expectation." When something is "out of expectation," it is beyond the normative rules or conditions of the culture — and this can be the culture of the classroom as well. Because of this chance for misunderstanding, each group needs to clarify, reflect on, and rephrase the goals in its own language. They then need to think out short-term and long-term targets to accomplish those goals.

In establishing targets, students should carefully consider and agree upon their own roles and responsibilities to achieve the best results.

Sometimes goals and responsibilities are simply "understood," but, more often, the teacher or the leader of the group (elected by consent or appointed) needs to make certain that the roles and responsibilities are evenly distributed and well defined. It is also important that students know when results are due, not only for the final stages of the process but at intermediary periods as well. It is perhaps a truism that classroom groups must be dedicated to results but it is necessary that they comprehend their ability to define the topic, influence the process, and contribute effectively.

The members' recognition that their contribution is essential and valued both by the group and the teacher will go a long way toward achieving positive results. Getting members to recognize everyone's value in a group helps them acknowledge their own personal responsibility in generating fresh ideas, taking risks in implementing those ideas, and contributing to the overall success of the group. This awareness of having a personal investment in the activities, in effect of being a stakeholder, should help equalize responsibility. Related to this is the need to emphasize the interrelationships and interdependence of the group and to avoid duplication of work, minimizing conflicts that can arise from unclear responsibilities. The building of team efforts must ensure the accomplishments of the group and the individual as well. In working as part of a cross-cultural group, then, students need to:

- be clear about goals and establish targets;
- care about achieving results;
- delineate their individual roles;
- know they can influence the agenda;
- cultivate a relaxed climate for communication;
- feel free to create new ideas;
- strive for a high level of interdependence and individual achievement; and
- be prepared to take risks.

Integration

To ensure that this integration of group members is working, the instructor might hand out an interim questionnaire, which has the advantage of making sure that the project is going well and anticipating any problems among members of the group. This step is particularly useful when a project is carried on throughout the term rather than in a short one- or two-week period. The following slightly modified questionnaire developed by Arnold Bateman (University of Nebraska, Lincoln 1990) enables team members to identify their attitudes towards the group at any time in the project, though a mid-project assessment can help to ensure that a project does not derail because of poor relationships among the participants:

Evaluate and Rate Your Group's Development

How do you feel about your group's progress? (Circle rating).
1. Group's purpose
— I'm uncertain   1 2 3 4 5 — I'm clear

2. Group membership
— I'm out   1 2 3 4 5 — I'm in

3. Communications
— Very guarded   1 2 3 4 5 — Very open

4. Group goals
— Set from above   1 2 3 4 5 — Emerged through team interaction

5. Use of members' skills
— Poor use   1 2 3 4 5 — Good use

6. Support
— Little help for individuals   1 2 3 4 5 — High level of support for individuals

7. Conflict
— Difficult issues are avoided   1 2 3 4 5 — Problems are discussed openly and directly

8. Influence on decisions
— By few members   1 2 3 4 5 — By all members

9. Risk taking
— Not encouraged   1 2 3 4 5 — Encouraged and supported

10. Working on relationships with others
— Little effort   1 2 3 4 5 — High level of effort

11. Distribution of leadership
— Limited   1 2 3 4 5 — Shared

12. Useful feedback
— Very little   1 2 3 4 5 — Considerable

Figure 5.1   Interim Evaluation Form

After the evaluation has been given and the results taken on board, the teacher needs to ascertain that students are working well together to focus and qualify their topic. As the members pursue their individual directions and share their research, they will need to be attentive, listen to everyone's viewpoints, and feel comfortable in sharing their own. The research itself, different information, and varying perceptions will help redefine and shape the topic, taking the group in directions that the teacher and the members themselves may not have anticipated at the beginning of the project. Students need to understand the importance of flexibility and creativity and feel that they do have choices in redefining the project as they discover and share new information.

Fundamental to any project is the need for accuracy in gathering information and drawing conclusions and the interim stage is a good point at which to stress that. All group members have a responsibility to be prepared and know facts for, without accuracy, no research project can proceed far or gain credibility; and, if the material is inaccurate, the conclusions will be mistaken and the project put at risk. Unless they are fully prepared and armed with absolutely accurate information, members will compromise the group's work and undermine their own and others' viewpoints.

If students have done their homework and researched the topic carefully, others will be inclined to listen to them and be attentive to their viewpoints — one of the primary functions of group projects. Everyone needs the opportunity to speak up and be heard, but only when they are fully prepared is this likely to be wholly positive. Students want to be articulate, and, when they have a firm grounding in facts, they will gain the confidence to share opinions and integrate other perspectives with their own. Tolerance, a fundamental value within the cross-cultural classroom, is fostered and enhanced by a standard of excellence in work habits, research methods, quality of information, and project results.

In this important part of the process of group work, students need to:
- participate in a mid-project group evaluation;
- undertake individual tasks in the context of the group;
- be attentive, listen, and share viewpoints;
- allow for diverse experiences and opinions;
- continue to shape and redefine the topic;
- ensure accuracy in their work; and
- begin integrating perspectives.

Performance

Students need to share their discoveries with the class on an informal or formal basis after they have read the key texts, worked together, and compiled reports. This is not necessarily the most important step in the process, but it is surely the one that confirms the topic's worth and group's value in everyone's mind. A final presentation can motivate students highly, make them feel that they are valued and respected members of the classroom, and give them an important lifetime skill. Professional schools of business, engineering, and law often base their entire curriculum on class presentations drawn from problem-based approaches, a tendency encouraged by graduate schools and potential employers alike who appreciate the independence, personal responsibility, and presentation skills required for these tasks. As an important part of the strategy of these presentations, teachers must be firm about their actual length, both with respect to the number of pages for a written project and the time allowed for an oral presentation. Students need to learn to limit or expand their ideas for a given amount of space and time.

Sometimes projects can be presented in written reports, and students will gain valuable experience in composing them as individuals and groups. It is often helpful for the teacher to indicate in advance that some portions of a report need to be written individually and some as a group. Individually written portions (with names attached) can ensure that each student has contributed more or less equally to the project. Those individually written portions can also help the student to find her/his own voice of expression. Some parts, however, can be written and edited as a group, so that students understand the importance of public rhetoric and become comfortable with sharing their writing and having it edited. When writing is only done for the eyes of the teacher, students miss out on the risks and benefits of shared writing.

Students also need experience in presenting their ideas orally to their own group and the rest of the class. This is not an activity that is a natural conclusion to all group activities, but students need to develop the art of presenting their ideas orally in an intelligent and interesting manner, and within a particular time frame. As with written responses, students should make clear to the teacher what responsibilities each member has had, individually and as a group. Initially, many students are afraid of giving an oral presentation — speaking in public is feared as much as visiting the dentist — and need the opportunity to overcome their hesitations and feel comfortable presenting their ideas. Teachers are sometimes surprised how much students do like to perform in front of the class, as long as they feel prepared. University lecturers and Fulbright Fellows in East Asia often complain that students do not readily enter into discussions; and yet these same students come alive and welcome the opportunity to make researched presentations in front of the class, even inventively (and with few inhibitions) turning that research into skits and short dramas. They are often less comfortable about role-playing for a class than in giving PowerPoint presentations, and teachers need to be sensitive to that distinction. In any case, the teacher needs to take the extra time to suggest how the structure of the presentation is similar to that of an essay, review how students can best engage the audience in spoken and body language, and indicate how visuals can be an especially effective part of the presentation.

As mentioned above, students show more creativity in writing essays and giving oral presentations when they are fully prepared and have had time to check the accuracy of their information. I cannot stress enough that accurate information and careful preparation are the keys to any presentation as they obviously make the audience pay close attention, and inaccuracy and carelessness quickly erode the audience's confidence and stand in the way of a successful presentation.

All students need this opportunity to present. The actual written amount or speaking time does not have to be identical, but should have some equivalency. It is all too common to let the "stars" — that is, those with the most confidence and ability in writing and speaking — do the final work, but this limits the possibility of everyone being heard and gaining the experience and confidence to undertake this task better the next time. Planning how to incorporate all the voices must become a key feature of each group's activity. There will certainly be some students with more flair for presenting, and they can be strategically placed, but all have the right to be heard.

In an oral presentation, most students will need an elaborate outline or a written script as a starting point, but these should not be the final step. Students need to be familiar enough with the research and to have worked on the presentation sufficiently so that they are not bound to a script (or by the outline of a PowerPoint presentation) or have their heads buried in print and facing the screen. A script read in its entirety without departure, embellishment, or extemporaneous examples does not work well. In certain humanities disciplines such as English and Cultural Studies, presenters usually read their papers, while, in medicine and social sciences, presentations are more conversational and delivered from notes. Even when a paper is read, however, the presentation usually fails if there are no ad hoc comments to invigorate the reading. Students need to understand that any kind of written or oral presentation needs careful structure and organization as well as other kinds of rhetorical assistance and audio-visual aids to make it interesting for the audience.

In writing up their material and/or in preparing for their oral presentation, students need to be reminded that they must:

- keep within the required length of the written or oral presentation;
- indicate what parts of the project have been completed by individual members and as a group;
- be prepared and ensure accuracy;
- give everyone an equal opportunity to speak;
- be familiar enough with the material to depart from a script;
- use appropriate structure, rhetoric, and audio-visual aids.

Evaluation and assessment

The final stage of any process and project in a student-centered classroom is evaluation and assessment. As will be discussed fully in Chapter 7, "Assignments and Assessments," students receiving marks for their work need to know the reasons for those marks, and, even in a pass-fail framework, require feedback on their participation and performance and opinions on how they can improve. More often than not, it is the teacher who assesses group work on the basis of the process and final presentations, and that mode of assessment is clearly essential.

While assessment is valuable and necessary at the end of a project, leaving it *only* until the end of the project limits its effectiveness. A better way to facilitate ongoing positive group dynamics is through the process of continuous self-assessment, and, if students are brought into that process, their evaluations can be immensely helpful in creating a sense of shared responsibility. Because, in working with one another, students are often aware of problems before the teacher is, they can help provide solutions if they are given a stake in the process. If, for instance, groups are assigned to work on projects over a month, team members might be asked to evaluate their own performance, as well as that of their fellow group members, on a regular, even weekly basis. If this process is formalized, so that students share their ideas first with each other and then with the teacher, the communication could make the process more open — but only if the assessment is carried on with good will and without antipathy for the rest of the group. One means of determining the effectiveness of the group is to develop categories for assessment, such as the following (again an adaptation of those by Arnold Bateman of the University of Nebraska 1990), and ask students to evaluate each category:

- Group goals
- Leadership
- Decision making
- Individual participation
- Group resources, talents, skills, knowledge, and experiences
- Problem solving
- Risk taking and creativity
- Group effectiveness
- Accord in working relationships
- Feedback

Yet another point can be made about the assessment procedures — students might well be asked to assess the value of the teacher as part of the final process. In that way, teachers will have feedback on their effectiveness in guiding group work. Indeed, having ways to evaluate effectiveness both of the group and teacher in working together is fundamental to any cross-cultural classroom experience.

Extending the Boundaries of the Student-Centered Classroom

Up to this point, I have focused on activities within a particular classroom, but the cross-cultural classroom can profitably extend the boundaries of learning outside conventional spaces. To enlarge international understanding, increase cross-cultural communications, and facilitate group work, the teacher can establish relationships with students and classes in other institutions, especially comparable cross-cultural classrooms in proximate locations and other countries. To accomplish this goal, schools, programs, and individual courses can engage in ongoing e-mail exchanges, videoconferencing networks, distance education programs, e-learning systems, field trips, and exchanges — whether in the summer, during the semester, or year-long.

E-mail exchanges

The simplest and easiest link among students is e-mail, and teachers can join them effectively through e-mail exchanges and electronic chat rooms.

Most students already communicate with friends through e-mail, but diversifying, structuring, and formalizing e-mail exchanges can enable students to meet other students and explore issues locally, nationally, and internationally. If these exchanges are between designated courses and programs at different universities, instructors at both institutions can work together to set up student partners, who can relate with one another socially and also work on mutual assignments.

There are many topics that can help students assess their world in diverse ways, whether on a social level (youth culture throughout the world), political level (attitudes to American interventionist policies), or corporate level (globalization and comparative business practices in the USA, Asia, and Europe). Students can be assigned readings in common, react to those individually, talk them out with their international partners, and draft essays together. On one occasion shortly after 9/11 and the beginning of the war in Iraq, classes at the University of Hong Kong and Yale University shared readings on the perception of the USA worldwide. American students at Yale were surprised and sometimes shocked to discover that the Hong Kong students held views so divergent from their own, and this led to profound discussions on national policies and identities. It is important that students from various cultures discover they have many similar views but equally important to recognize their differences that can be voiced and developed.

These discussions on e-mail lead to interesting essays about perceptions and opinions and, in many cases, to friendships lasting over several years. E-mail exchanges thus become a new instrument in helping students express their opinions in writing, first on a personal, informal, and almost confessional basis, then as a part of the process of researching and drafting an essay, and finally in producing a formal essay, either individually or jointly written and submitted. Having students keep copies of their e-mail exchanges and then explain how preliminary comments were written into formal presentations also help them understand and articulate the relationships of, and differences between, process and performance. These cognate assignments and inter-university relationships give students a sense of open discussion and shared community well beyond the classroom walls.

It is important to note that students do not always like being left completely on their own with e-mail exchanges and chat rooms any more than they like lectures posted on the course's webpage without being given in class. Students assume that the Internet should supplement basic classroom activity and not stand in lieu of it, and they sometimes see the virtual classroom as a lazy approach to education, even though every teacher knows it requires careful preparation. Teachers are sometimes shocked to discover that students do not necessarily share their appreciation of virtual materials, and this possibility reinforces a basic assumption about all classroom tools — it is necessary to position the teaching in a particular culture and be aware of relevant cultural sensitivities and student perceptions.

Videoconferencing

With the increasing sophistication of Internet telecommunications and videoconferencing technology, courses at one institution can be combined with those at another. In a recent experiment, a professor at the University of Hong Kong offered a History course on family behavior in Japanese culture and a professor at the College of William and Mary offered one in Anthropology on the process of socialization in rural Chinese culture entirely through teleconferencing, with both visual and audio links. To account for the time difference of 12 hours between east coast USA and China, students in Hong Kong met at 8 a.m. and those in Virginia at 8 p.m. Each location had an enrollment of about 10 students, and the professors and guests were able to give lectures and the students engage in discussion through audio and video teleconferencing at the same time a continent away. At the end of the course, students from Virginia came to Hong Kong for summary sessions and oral presentations, and, in the next iteration, students from Hong Kong followed the same procedure in going to the USA.

I myself have videoconferenced courses on (a) Asian American Culture and (b) Globalization and Americanization to students at the University of Hong Kong and the University of Southern Denmark-Kolding. I was able to lecture, sharing PowerPoint between the two institutions; I showed films and film clips to both classes simultaneously; and the two classes saw themselves and the other one at the same time. The use of cameras and portable microphones required a measure of extra formality in the classroom because everyone needed to sit still in the same location, but students quickly adapted to this challenge and engaged in fruitful discussions across continents.

Although advances in technology have made videoconferencing available at a low cost, there are occasional difficulties. For example, differences in equipment between the linked sites create functional disparities; that is, some equipment has better sound capabilities than others, and some allows for only a couple of microphones, so that having an easy discussion is difficult — someone has to run around with a microphone when another student wants to speak. Also, microphones pick up incidental conversation and movement in the classroom, causing background noise and sometimes embarrassment; and images may freeze for several seconds, so that the voice and the image are out of sync. More seriously, every now and again the videolink fails because of a power outage or system glitch and must be started again. In the big picture, however, these are small annoyances and do not detract significantly from the project.

These experiments in e-mail exchanges and videoconferenced courses can provide new educational opportunities and extend the frontiers of learning and the cross-cultural classroom indefinitely, giving students in various cultures an idea of how students elsewhere study and react to academic and social issues.

Distance education

E-mail exchanges and videoconferencing can also assist in distance education, so that students feel connected to other students and their instructors. More and more universities are developing distance courses, but students in these courses frequently feel disconnected from other students, their teachers, and their center of learning. With the opportunities provided by e-mail and tele- and videoconferencing, these students can connect with others, so that they gain a wider appreciation of the possibilities of their classes, course of study, and perceptions of classmates.

Although distance education is becoming more widely used all the time and many universities have extensive programs, it is unlikely that a new teacher abroad would be asked to participate in it at the outset. These are usually very site-specific programs and take a great deal of specific knowledge about facilities and programs.

E-learning systems

Part of the Internet technology that makes videoconferencing and distance education possible are e-learning systems such as Blackboard, a system that facilitates course delivery, including real-time chat groups, joint project development, electronic posting of course materials, and the marking and recording of course assessments. These systems provide excellent opportunities for local and transnational discussion groups and mutual projects and can further inter-institutional relationships through chat rooms, which can be monitored by instructors, allowing many new opportunities for interaction. Instructors can post their course outlines and readings on these sites, refer students to e-library links with access to full texts of articles, submit e-questionnaires to groups of students, send out questions and comments to the entire class, and assess and record the results. I have used Blackboard extensively over two years to put Hong Kong and Danish students together in the same virtual classroom and have found it an effective tool except on the occasion when the Blackboard system went down the weekend before the students were to give their joint oral presentations. Some faculty members and students, however, do have concerns about the surveillance permitted by these systems: teachers are able to tell who has been communicating on the system and read all of their comments, meaning that student comments are never private. This can be helpful insofar as the instructor can correct misinformed comments and make sure that professional standards are followed, but it can be regarded as an invasion of privacy and means that the teacher's monitoring can prevent honest communication among the students.

Field trips and exchanges

Cross-cultural understanding and respect is further deepened and expanded when students participate in short field trips or student exchanges lasting a term or a year. In a field trip, for example from China or Europe to the USA, students can get a good view of American culture by visiting a few cities throughout the country. These can include those on the Eastern seaboard (Williamsburg, Washington DC, New York City, Boston); the American heartland (Chicago, St. Louis, and Denver); the south (Charleston and New Orleans); and the West Coast (Los Angeles, San Francisco, and Seattle). The University of Copenhagen runs an annual trip to Washington and New York City for some 50 students, and several academic units (including American Studies, European Studies, and Geography) at the University of Hong Kong offer field trips to the countries represented in their programs. I have personally planned courses around field trips and escorted as many as 25 students at once from Hong Kong to the USA. In the most ambitious trip, we flew from Hong Kong to Toronto and rented a bus, first travelling east and south to Niagara Falls, Boston, New York City, Washington DC, Charleston, and Orlando. After Orlando, we drove across the south to New Orleans and up the Mississippi River to St. Louis and eventually Chicago. Less ambitious trips focused mainly on the important eastern cities of Boston, New York, and Washington DC, as well as a representative southern city, New Orleans.

These trips have many benefits in introducing students to American history, popular culture, and urban development. When students visit a country that provides a focus for their curriculum, especially when staying on university campuses, they can meet their e-mail partners and visit places they have read about or seen in the media, thereby vastly increasing their understanding of culture. Even students from the USA could profit by courses that take them to these American centers!

For students visiting a country other than their own, it is good to mix entertainment with historically and culturally focused materials. For example, students visiting Washington DC might stay at Georgetown University, saunter down the hill to Georgetown to eat and shop, and then hop on a subway to visit the many free cultural and political sites that Washington has to offer. The Capitol, the Mall, the Library of Congress, and the Smithsonian Museums (for example, in anthropology, aeronautical development, American and international art, and popular culture) provide an excellent overview of the USA at no cost because museums and galleries are free in the capital. Students can then visit the Kennedy Center for an evening of classical music.

A two-hour bus or train ride to Williamsburg, Virginia, allows students to visit a "living museum," in which employees of Colonial Williamsburg dress in the costume of eighteenth-century colonial Virginia in order to show visitors the innumerable historical properties there and indicate how life was lived during that period. This living museum brings students directly into contact with the issues of colonial Virginia in a way that books, documentaries, television, and the big screen cannot.

Although teachers may initially feel at a loss when organizing field trips and students may be daunted by the idea of going abroad, it is not such a difficult task with the information available on the Internet and a strong motivation to build bridges across cultures. In fact, organizing courses in the cross-cultural classroom with the intention of visiting cities that connect with them can be an excellent way of incorporating students into the actual planning of a trip. This can be one of the most enjoyable activities in a student-centered classroom and can provide a way for students to focus on their studies and to bond in special ways that will give classes and programs a unique spirit and identity.

Short field trips — such as day trips between Hong Kong and Macau or nearby spots on the Mainland — can usually be arranged without difficulty or great expense, but cost and accessibility are serious deterrents for large-scale field trips. In taking Hong Kong students to the USA, I was able to keep costs in a US$2,000–3,000 range that included airfare, accommodation at university residences, and site visits, but this figure was still out of range for many students. HKU did provide a subvention for students who held grants, but other students had to pay the entire amount out of their own pockets. This amount was reasonable for about half the students, but others who wanted to go were unable to afford it. Affordability is an even a greater problem for students in mainland China, where salaries and scholarships are much lower than in Hong Kong, Canada, or the USA. Without grants from foundations, most Chinese students cannot afford to go on such a trip to the USA, regardless of how inexpensive it might seem to Westerners. Affordability is also a concern for Danish students. Although university tuition fees are covered in Denmark and students get a substantial monthly government stipend, the high taxes (up to 60%) mean that students have little extra money to spend. In addition, because they are used to having educational expenses covered by the government, they are reluctant to pay for extra excursions.

Accessibility is also a significant deterrent, especially after 9/11. Governments in the West have become increasingly concerned about too-easy access for university students from other parts of the world. The USA has raised the bar on obtaining visitor and study visas: increased proof of academic programs and finances is required, and more time is taken to process applications. In effect, the US government admits a smaller percentage of students than a decade ago. Recently, however, it has relaxed the rules and speeded up the process, but students still find the procedure difficult.

In summary, extending the boundaries of the classroom through problem solving, group work, and presentations can make learning an ever more interesting process, but it is important to keep the students' opinions about these classroom activities uppermost in mind, while expanding their opportunities and capabilities. Sometimes a teaching model can run into steep opposition from students — for example, putting them into a large circle to facilitate discussion as discussed in Chapter 3 — or students themselves encounter conflicts in their class and subgroups. Certain students may complain of feeling under duress, daunted by professors sitting next to them, and exposed to the gaze and criticisms of other students. What is intended to ensure student involvement and student-centered learning can have unforeseen consequences, especially in the case of an international cross-cultural classroom. Not all pedagogical techniques can achieve the same unqualified positive results among all students in all locations and cultures. Cultural sensitivities must be taken into consideration in creating student-centered education within the cross-cultural classroom so that students and teachers alike save face and work together harmoniously.

One way to achieve an effective learning environment is to create group projects based on the principles of personal responsibility and problem solving. These principles are best employed when group work follows a sequence similar to that used for team-building, that is, group formation, self-definition, integration, performance, and evaluation. Each step of the process is valuable on its own, but the performance per se indicates to the entire class the value of the work itself. This performance can be a written report or essay and/or an oral presentation, as group projects, both written and oral presentations, help to build teamwork, literacy, and personal confidence. Other means of putting students together and giving them special opportunities for interaction and learning include e-mail exchanges, videoconferenced classes, distance education, e-learning systems, field trips, and student exchanges. Together, these can create an excellent student-centered learning environment.

6

Film in the Cross-Cultural Classroom

Student and teacher alike value an interesting and informative class, and courses need variety to maintain interest over the term or year. The time has passed when a textbook and a lecture would be adequate as the sole tools and methods of teaching in a classroom, although the kind and number of new tools and methods in the cross-cultural classroom depend upon the subject itself, adaptability of the teachers, and cultural expectations and possibilities.

Reading is a tried-and-true, absolutely necessary form of learning, but students whose first language is not English may have a much harder time with the vocabulary, concepts, images, and metaphors in a written text than those drawn from illustrations and pictures, documentaries, films, and music. In this sense, books are not universal and cannot be understood just by looking up vocabulary; it is fairly easy to get things wrong when readers only have a printed text and are not part of the culture that is under consideration. There are some famous instances of getting things wrong on the basis of print: for example, Chinese illustrations of the Brooklyn Bridge around 1890 showed massive pylons shaped like pagodas instead of the gothic arches to hold up the cables. Misperceiving another culture based upon assumptions about one's own culture is an issue that cross-cultural learning tries to address, and tools that can be used to prevent these misperceptions are welcome.

As mentioned in Chapter 5, e-mail exchanges, videoconferencing, distance education, e-learning systems, and field trips all provide excellent learning experiences, but films are also among the very best tools to mediate and integrate the humanities and social sciences. As David McFarland and Benjamin Taggie (1990, 232) note:

> Consider how empty is a history course on twentieth-century America that ignores the works of Arthur Miller, John Steinbeck, and Sinclair Lewis. It does not demand a great imagination to see how enriched students would be to see Willy Loman and Babbitt in an historical context, the products of the idiosyncratic features of American culture. Students could also examine the social values embedded in such literary works to better understand the history of the period. Steinbeck's *Grapes of Wrath* brings a realism to the horror and suffering spawned by the dust bowl that students do not experience from history books alone.

Although this comment is aimed at the incremental value of integrating printed fiction in history courses, it is easy to extrapolate that film, television, and other kinds of technology could enhance those examples just as well, and even more. As Mike Clarke remarks, the inclusion of cinema can discover "the production, circulation and consumption of *meanings* (i.e. the ideas and ideologies contained in films)" (1990, 70) useful for many disciplines.

Despite the validity of these assertions about the value of films as a teaching tool, many teachers have good grounds for objecting to their inclusion. Some argue that the use of films goes against basic educational values because they detract from students' ability to concentrate on reading, write with facility, and grasp abstract concepts. Others argue that, although films, television, and the Internet demonstrably situate various texts within specific cultural milieus, it is also necessary to critique them to facilitate a broader and deeper understanding, and too often that does not happen. For them, the issue is not an either/or impasse between reading and viewing or between fiction and the electronic media but the creative interplay of the two as well as cultural analysis and criticism.

The place of films within popular culture and the need for cultural critiques raise other objections. Some teachers and students view films as "easy learning" and "play" and think that only reading and analysis constitute "real" education. This is a common understanding in mainland China because films are not generally taught in universities and not commonly understood as anything other than a reflection of popular culture. These students do not have an understanding of film "grammar" — history, structure, and generic characteristics — and, consequently, are dependent on superficial readings.

Still others object that only trained specialists can teach films. In arguing that literature and film can complement history, however, McFarland and Taggie are not suggesting that historians need to teach these works as literary and film scholars would, but that their historical context and sociological descriptions fill in details missing from history texts. By arguing in this way, they presuppose that a history classroom does not have to employ a film specialist or embrace team teaching, and they assume that one can "view a topic (about which one has preconceived notions) through the perspective of another discipline (in which one may have no formal training). In doing so it forces a faculty member to take the same risks — the risks of finding those preconceived notions shallow in a public forum — that students are being asked to take. These risks are themselves intrinsic to interdisciplinary learning" (McFarland and Taggie 1990, 231).

This "call for open borders between disciplines" (Fuller 2003, 1) has "made the greatest inroads . . . at the elementary- and middle-school levels" (Grossman et al. 2000, 3) and may be unacceptable to adherents of strict disciplinary distinctions, but, at the university level, the concept of duty-free interdisciplinarity is, by and large, fallacious. In one sense, there is so much pressure towards disciplinarity that most faculty members do not undertake interdisciplinary collaboration easily. It is safe to stay within department or program walls for fear that colleagues and students will be too critical. In another sense, at the university level there is some form of disciplinary crossover almost everywhere: many humanities departments, for instance, share the same foundational research and teaching documents and similar methodologies. In English, Comparative Literature, Cultural Studies, and Film Departments, the current working methodologies come from linguistics (Ferdinand de Saussure); anthropology (Claude Levi-Strauss); psychology (Sigmund Freud and Jacques Lacan); Russian philosophy (Viktor Shklovsky, Mikhail Bakhtin); German philosophy (G. W. Hegel, Karl Marx, Martin Heidegger); French philosophy (Jacques Derrida, Paul de Man, Michel Foucualt); history (Stephen J. Greenblatt); feminism (Julia Kristeva, Hélène Cixous, Gayatri Chakravorty Spivak); and many others. In short, disciplinary walls are permeable — some postmodernists have attacked disciplines as being indefensible and oppressive communities of power without substance or merit (Grossman et al. 2000, 6) — and a knowledge of disciplines other than those in which faculty members have their degrees and teaching contracts can be acquired from a combination of background courses, personal research, and self-motivation, so crossing disciplinary boundaries is hardly a breach. It is quite possible for someone who has training in one area to research effectively in another, master the significant scholarship, become fluent in the ideas, and use different materials to enhance the classroom and integrate ideas. This is particularly true with the use of film. Almost everyone watches films and develops an understanding of how to read them sociologically, but it takes more research to discover particular ways they can be relevant interdisciplinarily.

Classroom time cannot be extended infinitely and hard choices have to be made about what kind of, and how many, materials to incorporate successfully. However, if a goal is to increase analytical skills across a broad range of cultural activities, cultivating those skills in current affairs, fiction, film, and music — in short, any part of culture — can accomplish that readily and make the students understand that these are not just academic but life skills. Identifying educational goals and skill sets that students need to cultivate is, thus, a primary requisite in deciding the total mixture of tools within the classroom.

Film and Cultural Contexts

In addition to the Internet and PowerPoint, the most productive technology for the classroom is the capability of showing films. Most students all over the world love films, although they may not have a chance to study them as part of university curricula. Because films are part of popular culture, students sometimes see them as having limited educational value or serious purpose; but, once they think of them as part of the larger cultural matrix, they discover films to be valuable additions in many different subjects, leading to creative interdisciplinary integration. Films can also be problematic, and I want to explore both the integrative possibilities and difficulties in this chapter. Insofar as I am especially interested in transnationalism and America in this book, I will focus on Hollywood films. My discussion here is of particular concern to studies in literature, film, and American studies, but the idea of comparing similar discourses has analogies in all areas.

As Mike Clarke notes in discussing media education, films are important as representation, form, and relationship of institutions and audience (1990, 74). In a cross-cultural classroom, representation (the relationship between the images, social groups, and ideas) is important to explore a variety of cultural considerations and is basic for interdisciplinary learning. The same is true of the relationship between institutions and audience, which establishes the "context of media production, circulation and consumption" (Clarke 1990, 75) in culture. However, form, "the various codes and conventions employed to create meanings in the different media, as well as the characteristics of particular genres" (Clarke 1990, 74), is more relevant to a specialized interdisciplinary analysis of film and literature.

Although teachers and students alike may think of films as easier to absorb than articles or books because they are visual and relatively short (usually up to two hours), their meaning may still be elusive. First, meaning can be hard to grasp when students do not understand the language, especially when the dialogue is in the viewer's second language rather than the first. The vocabulary may be relatively unfamiliar, the accents nonstandard, and the characters' voices difficult to understand. Then, too, the actors do not always speak so that the audience can see the front of their faces and thus do not have facial features or body language to help comprehension. Speakers of voice-overs cannot be seen at all, and this can be difficult for the audience. Second, they can be elusive if students are not able to position the content of the film or understand its genre. For instance, the iconographic *Easy Rider* with its characters hopped up on drugs may seem gratuitously violent to students abroad who cannot understand the dialogue, the American counter culture of the 1960s, or the genre of the road film. In short, while films may seem like the perfect medium to interest students and present accurate portrayals of people and times, students may have a surprisingly difficult time watching and understanding them.

In an international cross-cultural classroom, it is therefore helpful for films to be shown with subscripts in English (if the film is in English) or in the language of the majority of students in the class, so that they are able to hear and understand them. In the most popular Hollywood films, it is possible to buy DVDs and VCDs with subscripts in various languages. That is not true of older films on DVD, those out of circulation for a number of years, or the occasional VHS that can still be found in the video store or school and university library. Nor is it true of documentaries because these are produced on shoestring budgets, and distributors make few concessions to foreign viewers. For this reason alone, it is often problematic to include old films and documentaries in the international classroom because students may not be able to comprehend the language without the subscripts.

There is another important consideration in using films within classes — whether the object is to analyse the form and representation of the film as in an English or Cultural Studies class or its representation in support of some other subject. There are various kinds of sensitivities, cultural preferences, and social taboos that must be taken into consideration in the cross-cultural classroom. I discovered this issue quickly my first time in Hong Kong when I was assigned to talk about stories by Raymond Carver to first-year students. Teaching Carver within the university context normally does not present difficulties, but a problem did arise when I was asked to relate several of his stories to Robert Altman's film version, *Short Cuts*. The film is interesting and accessible and works well as a teaching aid in talking about Carver's disparate pieces of writing organized into one narrative, but the film is more edgy and cynical than the book and specifically has a scene with full-frontal female nudity. I knew that the edginess and cynicism could be nicely compared to the book, but I asked the department if the nudity would be a barrier to showing the film. The department debated the issue because students had not been exposed in the classroom to nudity in films. In the end, they did allow the screening of the film, but there are many other places in the world where it could not have been shown because of those nude scenes. In Hong Kong, this struggle was one of cultural sensitivity, but in mainland China Ang Lee's gay film *Brokeback Mountain* has been banned because the PRC government thinks it promotes an inappropriate lifestyle.

Sexuality is not the only culturally sensitive area to consider in thinking through cultural taboos. Excessive violence also ranks high. Although Martin Scorsese's *Gangs of New York* is an adaptation of Herbert Asbury's sensational written account, the highly orchestrated and choreographed violence gives the impression of being unnecessary and offensive, regardless of historical accuracy and aesthetic justification. Spike Lee's presentation of interracial conflict in *Do the Right Thing* is another case in point for, while it raises legitimate questions about race relations in New York City, the level of noise, aggressive behavior, and street violence goes counter to values of politeness in many international locations and leads to students' perceptions of New York City as a center of violence and African Americans the worst offenders in making life unsafe there. Certainly, in Scandinavia sexually explicit films would hardly raise an eyebrow, but unfettered violence would. Sweden bans films with too much violence, but almost none with sexually explicit scenes.

A teacher will therefore have to decide what is culturally sensitive in a given locale and whether it is important (or legal) to show a film that violates these sensitivities. Also, the instructor in a cross-cultural classroom will have to think seriously about what it means to engage or violate these sensitivities on a personal, cultural, or national level as American media come under international scrutiny and attack. As Nathan Gardels and Mike Medavoy argue in "Hollywood in the World " (2006), "we are witnessing a mounting resistance, particularly from Asia and the Muslim world, to the American media's libertarian and secular messages." This resistance is particularly against "the blockbuster formula of action, violence, sex and special effects" as examples of "moral decay, promiscuity and pornography" and a "Ramboesque parochial populism that displays naïveté, ignorance and arrogance in its portrayal of the rest of the world." These charges against the American media are currently played out in local presses and in the streets, but they could just as easily be played out in the classroom.

Open sexuality and excessive violence are two reasons that films are problematic or that students reject them, and another in Hong Kong concerns social realism and rural life. For that reason, John Steinbeck's films find little support among students, even though applicable to central interdisciplinary issues. Although *Of Mice and Men* effectively portrays unemployment problems and inadequate care of the emotionally ill, and although *Grapes of Wrath* shows the underlying situation of the Dust Bowl during the Great Depression and the consequent great migration of mid-westerners to the southwest, concentrating on the lives of the unemployed and homeless goes against cultural expectations and aspirations of the upwardly mobile Hong Kong students. Many of these students are the first from their families to attend universities and have few means, so they find limited value in studying the homeless or socially deviant because they think university study should be uplifting and train their minds in the excellences of knowledge and possibilities for social development, not in the worst features of human behavior and social instability. Thoroughly urbanized Hong Kong and mainland Chinese students also sometimes have difficulty identifying with rural life, which is outside the range of their experience and beyond their interest. Those from non-urban areas may value that rural life and identify with its problems and beauty, but those from cities of 10 million people often find it irrelevant and quaint. Such preferences should not disqualify films for inclusion in class, and it is the teacher's job to extend the students' range of normative sympathies and cultural understanding, but teachers need to know why films taught successfully in some places may generate lukewarm interest in the cross-cultural classroom and be prepared to deal with that issue in appropriate ways.

Many students, perhaps especially those in developing countries, also are not interested in things old and tawdry; they want sophistication and modernity in all its guises, and that usually does not include black and white technology or genres that focus on the problems of urban or rural life, so something like Howard Hawks' version of Raymond Chandler's *The Big Sleep* bemuses them. Their unfamiliarity with hard-boiled detective fiction and inability to grasp Chandler's playfulness in handling the slang and argot of non-standard English makes them feel that they are reading inferior literature and studying the lives of immoral and disreputable people in a corrupt society. Moreover, when they watch Hawks' noir film, they often cannot understand what the fuss is all about. It is, after all, in black and white, and even though they can grasp the relationship between noir techniques and the narrative itself, that explanation does not always sustain their interest. So, despite an awareness of the basic social issues, technological developments, and aesthetic reasons, students may still dislike black and white films that seem archaic and old-fashioned. Teachers may have good reasons to teach social realism and unfashionable forms, but they should be aware that students may not share their academic preferences and cultural assumptions.

Film Adaptation as a Cross-Cultural Tool

The use of film in the classroom is now quite common, and I strongly believe in the special value of film adaptation to help students develop and hone reading, viewing, analytical skills, and language acquisition in ways that history, film, or fiction/drama by themselves do not. Very simply, in film adaptation, the director takes a short story, novel, or drama — or sometimes a combination of them — and adapts it to film. Sometimes this is a loose adaptation in which the director takes great liberties with the foundational text, and sometimes it is a faithful adaptation, utilizing the most important features and many of the details in the original story. The study of film adaptation is particularly valuable for students in the cross-cultural classroom — for example, the study of American texts outside the USA by ESL students — but I also think that the resources for these courses must be chosen carefully with the local culture in mind because these environments generate particular preferences and dislikes and because history, film, fiction, and pedagogy are not value free or ideologically neutral.

It was in Hong Kong, Denmark, and mainland China that I fully realized the value and difficulties of film adaptation for the cross-cultural classroom. In my first term of teaching at the University of Hong Kong in 1995, I taught a course on contemporary American fiction and assigned a new novel every two weeks, a reasonable, if slightly aggressive schedule in view of the students' native Cantonese linguistic and cultural background. I discovered, however, that the amount of reading was beyond most of the students' abilities.[5] An additional problem was the complexities of

---

5 It is important to note that students generally take six courses a term and that these courses meet for lectures two hours a week in addition to small group tutorials at regular intervals.

postmodern fiction, which can be taxing for any reader, but especially for those trained, as these students were, more or less exclusively in traditional modes of writing. The biggest problem by far was the students' inadequate knowledge of American language and culture — that is, vocabulary and diction were not only unfamiliar to them, but cultural referents were beyond the register of their experience. In asking questions, I quickly discovered that, because students were not able to attach particular images to descriptions, they were misconstruing imaginative details of the book and unable to use images to help construct an adequate understanding of the plot and larger networks of relations. Moreover, distorted visual associations and lack of comprehension of vocabulary constrained their abilities to understand the culture. Because everything about a text and classroom is contextually embedded, students had difficulty in grasping the cultural complexity unless they had the tools to do so, and those tools went beyond the simple reading of the text. In other words, because novels and other kinds of creative writing are not predictably, if ever, transparent, timeless, and universal, a film version of the written text can facilitate the students' ability to read fiction and to understand it and the culture. I found that by using both the film and the story it was based upon, students could grasp the images, increase their understanding of the language, develop a better understanding of the printed text and film, and become critical of the process and value of adaptation.

In the international cross-cultural classroom, studies of adaptation can be more helpful than studies of film as such, for many non-native English speakers cannot understand conversations in films and, if they exist, have to depend upon inadequate, and sometimes misleading, subscripts for meaning. As noted before, many students in China who are fluent in English have a difficult time understanding speakers in films unless there are subtitles, but those subtitles are sometimes inaccurate and elliptical.

Depending on how it is set up, film adaptation can deal with three important issues:

- Establishing and illustrating the development and range of culture in history
- Exploring the changes and variety in novels, short fiction, and film
- Teaching students filmic conventions or "grammar" and, hence, how to read, analyze, and respect fiction and films, how to write and talk about them, and how to respond to various kinds and degrees of adaptation.

Since not all students in cross-cultural institutions are likely to have studied the same culture, history, literature, or film, in detail, this kind of study must teach these in an integrated and systematic way.

What are the issues to consider and conclusions to draw about film adaptation in the cross-cultural classroom? Among the principle issues are:

- reading and analytical skills;
- choices of fiction and film;
- kinds of film adaptation;
- cultural preferences and restrictions; and
- educational goals.

Among the first and most important features of film-adaptation in the cross-cultural classroom are concerns about the amounts and kinds of reading. Because non-native-English speakers have varying degrees of facility with the language, the instructor needs to choose texts that can develop the students' reading skills, neither underwhelming nor overwhelming them with the kind and amount of reading. Shorter novels and stories ensure adequate variety, but only if reading lists are given well in advance could novels like *Moby Dick* and *Grapes of Wrath* be incorporated, and, even then, students would probably need a great deal of time to discuss them. While a novel such as *The Age of Innocence* is on the long side, its conventional plotting and standard English make it relatively easy to read and understand. However, even this decision should not be taken lightly as Chinese students, for instance, are taught from an early age to read small amounts of writing very carefully and, with dictionary in hand, to translate and annotate words they do not know. As students are often discouraged from reading quickly or trying to skim fiction or essays, assigning a long text may stretch their abilities and work against cultural norms. In the Chinese classroom, the emphasis on reading and mastering of short texts as opposed to longer narratives is not merely based on personal preferences or reading abilities but comes from years of training and deeply held ideological values about carefulness and precision and about how and what to read.

In the cross-cultural classroom, fiction also needs to be chosen with an eye to vocabulary, diction, and style, and the instructor needs to think out course goals in this regard. Does he/she want one particular style, for example with the goal of improving students' abilities to read, understand, and speak normative English, or might the goal be to show diversity in the vernacular use of English so that students understand that "normative" may be a false ideal in itself? The instructor also has to think about the actual level of difficulty students have with vocabulary, diction, and style, especially in unconventional narratives. The turgid style of William Faulkner's *The Reviers*, the pronounced Southern black dialect and illiteracy of the main character in Alice Walker's *The Color Purple,* or the crazy, drug- and alcohol-induced style of Hunter S. Thompson's *Fear and Loathing in Las Vegas* might not be the best examples for readers struggling with the intricacies of the English language. Even the hard-boiled detective style of Raymond Chandler might raise questions in *The Big Sleep,* unless the instructor is willing to spend time deciphering slang, playful metaphors, and situational humor. However, novels by Jane Austen, Charles Dickens, Edith Wharton, and John Steinbeck might be perfectly appropriate in giving students a complex and full understanding of standard English and comprehensible narratives.

The reputation of the fiction and film themselves is another consideration. If students are persuaded that these are representative literary works and important film pieces, they can understand the need to prepare them for class. If the study focuses only on good fiction or good film and ignores the other half, students will be less committed to the project and get less out of the comparison. But therein lies the trick — to find excellent fiction matched by excellent film because poor fiction sometimes makes good film, and good fiction sometimes makes poor film.

Sometimes, too, many important kinds and styles of writing are excluded from the film industry. Although scriptwriters frequently turn to novels and stories for creative sources, postmodern fiction, according to Brian McFarlane, is highly resistant to being turned into film (1996, 6). Wayne Wang's treatment of Paul Auster's short story — "Auggie Wren's Christmas Story" (1995) — in *Smoke,* however, gives the lie to the assumption that films cannot be produced from postmodern fiction, as does Stephen Daldry's transformation of Michael Cunningham's *The Hours.* Nevertheless, it does seem odd that many of the best postmodern films such as *American Beauty, Magnolia, In the Bedroom,* and *Far from Heaven* have no prototype in fiction. Although certain fictional or film strategies can be taught when there is an imbalance in quality between fiction and film, it may defeat some of the purposes of the classroom and diminish students' enthusiasm when one form is clearly better than the other.

To argue in another way, insofar as the cross-cultural classroom can teach analytical skills for both fiction and film, poor examples may serve a useful purpose in teaching students how to critique and write about film apart from literature. Students generally take written fiction quite seriously, and English, Comparative Literature, Cultural studies, Media studies, and American studies spend considerable time developing students' abilities to read and analyze fiction. A range of issues — such as the differences between story, plot, and theme, different kinds of plot and characterization, the use of narrators, supporting symbol patterns, and other such matters — are normally valued in classes in almost every country. Analysis of film, however, is not so common, particularly in countries outside North America, and students may need an introduction to the basic grammar of film, including *auteur, montage, mise-en-scène*, establishing shot, and so forth. In addition, they need to learn the importance of studying film. Because film has become such a popular form of entertainment, students often think that it does not need to be, or even deserve to be, studied and critiqued; although film's place in popular culture renders it accessible to everyone, it also mitigates against being taken seriously as an art form or perhaps even as a legitimate way to talk about culture. I have been told repeatedly by colleagues that students automatically assume that films, especially American ones, are completely transparent and do not require explanation or evaluation. This cultural assumption means that studies in film adaptation need to teach the tools of analysis, so that students are able to understand films as art, cultural products, and critiques of both art and culture. In the case of films adapted from fiction, it is very important to explore the cultural milieu that produces a text, the milieu that is being described, and why the fiction and film were especially appropriate at the time of their publication or release. In short, issues of artistic and cultural production and consumption are equally important for both fiction and film, and the students in the cross-cultural classroom need to develop the tools of analysis to study both.

Another important aspect for students to learn is the kind of adaptation and its particular characteristics, integrity, and value. Students can explore the positive and negative effects of greater and lesser fidelity to the fiction. Jack Clayton's *The Great Gatsby,* for example, provides a superb example of the strengths and limitations of faithful adaptation of a novel. Based upon Francis Ford Coppola's script, this film carefully and lovingly explores many of the smallest details of the novel, although even here many things are altered. For example, the decision to use Robert Redford and make Gatsby's character blonde and blue-eyed, the change of style and color of the mansions, the external and internal whiteness of Daisy and Tom's house, and the alteration of the order of events should all be considered in a generally faithful adaptation. At the opposite end of the spectrum is Wayne Wang's *Smoke,* an adaptation of Paul Auster's charming Christmas story that was short enough to have been published in the *New York Times.* As there simply was not enough substance in the original story to create a feature length film, Paul Auster, at Wayne Wang's suggestion, embedded the original story in a new narrative that shows the realistic fabric of Brooklyn and its inhabitants. This adaptation shows the creativity of both scriptwriter and director in shaping a story in such a different way, but is also of special interest because, from it, Wayne Wang generated another quixotic film, *Blue in the Face*, a free-flowing postmodern take-off on *Smoke*. From both of these films, students could see the progress of a short story embedded within one film, which in turn is embedded in another film, and discover compelling reasons for certain kinds of adaptation as well and inter- and intra-textuality. In brief, students can look seriously — and sometimes humorously — at decisions directors take in adapting fiction to film.

Finally, it can be important in a cross-cultural classroom to consider choosing films that can represent the ethnicity of the students themselves and raise important questions about identity in general. For instance, in a Hong Kong classroom, choosing films in order to talk about the representation of Chinese in American society helps students to recognize early forms of prejudice against Chinese and basic stereotypes of Asians. Chandler's and Hawks' versions of *The Big Sleep* work extremely well in raising questions about how Chinese were conventionally represented in literature and film at the middle half of the twentieth century and also how *The Big Sleep* manages a new perspective by focussing on the corruption of the whites in Los Angeles and not of the Chinese (Slethaug 2000). Amy Tan's novel and Wayne Wang's film of *The Joy Luck Club* update those images in showing the model-minority status of Chinese in American culture, although many Chinese feel that both the novel and the film provide a simplistic and even faulty portrayal of both traditional Chinese culture and the model minority. Part of the criticism by those in Hong Kong and mainland China, however, may be based on an assumption that any representation of the Chinese by a Westerner — especially one of mixed heritage like Amy Tan — is likely to be faulty. A discussion of this kind of assumption can present an opportunity to talk about the Chinese view of Americans or others of their own race who migrate to the USA. A most important opportunity for the cross-cultural classroom is for students to critique their own cultural perceptions, beliefs, and practices, while assessing those of other countries.

Comparing two kinds of ethnicities and identities is often a way of moving to a consideration of ethnicity and identity in general. One group of people may feel discriminated against but may not always sense ways in which their society discriminates against anyone whose color is darker than theirs or whose society is not technically or socially advanced. Northern

Europeans may consider themselves open and accepting societies until challenged by racial and ethnic issues and discrimination in their own cultures. Harper Lee's classic novel and Robert Mulligan's adaptation of *To Kill a Mockingbird* provides an excellent way to view racial discrimination in the USA, its effects, and its cultural heroes, but as much to the point is the need to show the lives of ethnic groups in today's society, not 50 or more years removed. Consequently, while Frederick Douglass's depiction of slavery provides a good starting point for issues of integration and assimilation, a consideration of *Malcolm X* would bring that into the conflicts of the Civil Rights movement in the 1960s, while Spike Lee's *Do the Right Thing* takes it into the 1980s. Branching out to look at the ethnicity of today's Japanese Americans, African Americans, and Native Americans can begin to break down social stereotypes and cultural misperceptions. David Guterson's *Snow Falling on Cedars* (and Scott Hick's adaptation), Alice Walker's *The Color Purple* (and Steven Spielberg's adaptation), and Sherman Alexi's *The Lone Ranger and Tonto in Heaven* (and Chris Eyre's adaptation called *Smoke Signals*) can explore the various historical perspectives on racial disharmony in the USA and ways of re-viewing that in terms of the advances and perceptions of the current generation.

To conclude, using different kinds of media can help make the classroom an interesting and vibrant place, and film adaptation in the cross-cultural classroom can give students an opportunity to study some of the best examples of fiction and film, see how fiction leads to film, and consider the sort of choices that contribute to excellence. Students also have a chance to explore the grammars of fiction and film and to learn about terms and techniques required to become sensitive readers and interpreters of culture. The instructor has an array of choices and can organize the materials to explore the development of history, culture, fiction and film as well as considerations of gender, ethnicity, urban life and other relevant themes.

I would stress, however, the need to develop reading skills and cultural awareness in the cross-cultural classroom through a careful choice of relevant materials. I would also emphasize the value of taking into consideration perceptions and personal preferences and dislikes as well as cultural values and prohibitions, opening students' eyes to important and subtle differences in cultures. Film adaptation in the cross-cultural classroom can do just that in an effective and interesting way, and the following is a list of film adaptations (listed roughly according to the chronology of the historical period they describe) that might serve the complex purposes of many cross-cultural classrooms as they engage American culture and American films:

Early American

- *The Crucible* (play, Arthur Miller, 1953; film, Nicholas Hytner, 1996)

  Based on a play about the Salem witch trials in the Puritan America of the 1630s, this film explores bigotry and intolerance with implications not only for early America but for the McCarthy period in the 1950s as well.

- *The Last of the Mohicans* (novel, James Fennimore Cooper, 1826; film, Michael Mann, 1992)

  This film explores the relationship of Indians and whites during the British and French Wars some 20 years before the American Revolution. It is primarily a love story but also shows the Indian's difficulty in negotiating and surviving this conflict between European powers.

Civil War

- *Red Badge of Courage* (novel, Stephen Crane, 1895; film, John Huston, 1951)

  Long considered the first great American narrative about the actual chaos and carnage of war, this film depicting the Civil War of 1861–65 finds battle filled with brutality rather than nobility and heroism mainly a fraud.

- *Gone with the Wind* (novel, Margaret Mitchell, 1936; film, Victor Fleming, 1939)

  A favorite of students everywhere, this romance of a selfish, wilful woman and a wayward man is a story of survival dealing with the historical sweep of the South from the ante-bellum period, through the Civil War, and into Reconstruction.

- *Cold Mountain* (novel, Charles Frazier, 1998; film, Anthony Minghella, 2003)

  This tragic story opens before the Civil War but mainly concerns the separate but intertwined destinies of a couple in love — the hardship of the wounded Confederate soldier, Inman, as he deserts the war and makes his treacherous way home to Cold Mountain and the difficulties of his fiancée as she forms an alliance with another woman and survives the war by learning how to farm her dead father's land.

- *Gangs of New York* (historical account, Herbert Asbury, 1928; film, Martin Scorsese, 2002)

  Only partly based on Asbury's account, this film is not so much concerned with the Civil War per se as with destructive conflicts created by hundreds of thousands of penniless and starving Irish immigrants landing on American soil from the 1840s onward and fighting among themselves and American racists during this traumatic period of American history. It also indicates New York's ambiguous position during the Civil War.

The Gilded Age (post-Civil War to 1900)

- *Daisy Miller* (novel, Henry James, 1878; film, Peter Bogdanovich, 1974)

  This film about the 1870s explores the unmannered, spoiled, newly rich Americans flaunting their wealth abroad after the Civil War, but it also gives a sympathetic portrayal of the young teenaged Daisy who does not deserve the scorn and hostility she receives from the bigoted Europeans in her travels there.

- *Washington Square* (novel, Henry James, 1880; film, Agnieszka Holland, 1997)

  Set in the fashionable Washington Square area of 1870s New York City, this story explores the love of the naïve and wealthy Catherine Sloper for the sophisticated but insolvent Morris Townsend, a match bitterly opposed and thwarted by her father. The film faithfully depicts the New York of this period.

- *Age of Innocence* (novel, Edith Wharton, 1920; film, Martin Scorsese, 1993)

  Set in the New York City of the 1870s and '80s, this film highlights the conflict of conventional values and unconventional love affairs of the very richest New Yorkers at a time that the USA was coming of age as an international power.

- *The Wizard of Oz* (novel, L. Frank Baum, 1900; film, Victor Fleming, 1939)

  Set in Kansas during the 1890s, the first part of this film contrasts the suspicious-looking Depression-era farm with the fantastic and colorful world of "over the rainbow" Oz. The story of Dorothy Gale who wants nothing more than to get home after a tornado picks her and her dog up from Kansas and deposits them in Oz, the story simultaneously appeals to everyone's wish to escape and the need to cope with difficulties that appear around every corner of the Yellow Brick Road.

Early twentieth century, including the iconic Great Depression

- *The Great Gatsby* (novel, F. Scott Fitzgerald, 1925; film, Jack Clayton 1974)

  Another New York story, this film explores the longings of Jay Gatsby who sets out to accumulate a fortune and live in a fabulous mansion to attract Daisy, his former lover who left him for a much richer man. This film is about the swinging '20s, urban gangsters, and the American Dream at the same time that it is about a passionate love affair.

- *Of Mice and Men* (novel, John Steinbeck, 1937; film, Gary Sinise, 1992)

  A sad story of two drifters who try to get along by traveling to various farms during the Depression to find work, the film shows the lives of the dispossessed agricultural underclass whose difficulties are compounded by one of them being mentally retarded and inadvertently killing the farmer's wife.

- *Grapes of Wrath* (novel, John Steinbeck, 1939: film, John Ford, 1940)

  Steinbeck's epic account of farm families fleeing Oklahoma and other drought-ridden states during the Great Depression, the film shows the Joad family's difficult migration to California by jalopy on Route 66, their hope for the family's future, and their commitment to the social and economic welfare of other migrants.

- *To Kill a Mockingbird* (novel, Harper Lee, 1960; film, Robert Mulligan, 1962)

  Set in the Great Depression, this film is unusual in addressing racial rather than the economic and class issues of the period. The story of an idealistic lawyer Atticus Finch who defends a black man unjustly accused of raping a white woman, this is a gentle and sensitive account narrated through the eyes of Finch's six-year-old daughter.

• *The Big Sleep* (novel, Raymond Chandler, 1939; film, Howard Hawks 1946)

In this depiction of Los Angeles in the Great Depression, the private detective Philip Marlowe agrees to work for the wealthy General Sternwood and solve crimes, which turn out to involve his youngest daughter. In exploring the lives of the corrupt rich, this film establishes some of the basic conventions of film noir.

• *Death of a Salesman* (play, Arthur Miller, 1949; film, László Benedek, 1951)

Generally considered Arthur Miller's best work, this play has resulted in the 1951 film as well as three television productions in English (1966, 1985, 2000). Also set in the iconic Great Depression and 1940s, this tragedy of the salesman Willy Loman critiques American business people who abandon their values in pursuit of money and end up destroying themselves and their families in the process.

Mid-century USA, including World War II

• *Streetcar Named Desire* (play, Tennessee Williams, 1946; film, Elia Kazan, 1951)

Following the play meticulously, including Williams' script and with most of the actors from the Broadway production, this film focuses on the escalating tragedy of Blanche DuBois, who sometime in the 1930s and '40s seduces the young men and boys of her hometown, loses the Louisiana family plantation, and ends up reliant on her sister Stella and brutal brother-in-law Stanley, but who is also sensitive, poetic, and pathetic in her psychological entrapment and descent into madness.

• *The Color Purple* (novel, Alice Walker, 1982; film, Steven Spielberg, 1985)

This film documents the life of Celie, a young black girl raped by her father and pregnant at 14, who manages to pull herself out of Depression poverty and illiteracy into a stable middle-class existence with her female partner. Rather than a tragic film about racism, this is tale of systemic family abuse and redemption resulting from self-discovery and sexual and financial independence.

- *Snow Falling on Cedars* (novel, David Gutterson, 1995; film, Scott Hicks, 1999)

  A story that explores anti-Japanese sentiments in the northwest, which exploded into politically sanctioned racism after the raid on Pearl Harbor in 1941, this film about the trial of Kabuo, a returning war hero suspected of killing a fellow fisherman, covers the period leading up to the American involvement in World War II, the internment of the Japanese in camps, and their resettlement after the end of the war in 1945.

- *Old Man and the Sea* (novel, Ernest Hemingway, 1952; film, John Sturges, 1958)

  A timeless story — though probably set in the 1940s — that explores three days in the life of an aging, lonely fisherman who catches a huge marlin off the coast of Cuba, only to have it eaten by a shark, this film shows the difficulty and loneliness of Santiago's seemingly pointless adventure, even while it points up his endurance, strength of character, and existential heroism.

- *A Raisin in the Sun* (play, Lorraine Hansberry, 1961; film, Daniel Petrie, 1961)

  An account that explores a black family's anxious decisions about raising themselves through higher education and a move from the inner-city to the suburbs in the pre-civil-rights Chicago of the 1950s, this film is not only about the personal heroism of African American family members but also the need for the legislation of the civil rights period that banned legally enforced racism.

- *Malcolm X* (autobiography, Malcolm X, 1972; film, Spike Lee, 1992)

  Based on the *Autobiography*, various speeches of Malcolm X, and his subsequent assassination, this film examines the life of one of the most powerful and controversial of the black nationalist leaders of the 1950s and '60s, who advocated violence and the bullet over accommodation and the ballot in race relations.

Late twentieth century

- *Short Cuts* (various stories, Raymond Carver, 1960–1983; film, Robert Altman, 1993)

  Based on short stories that detail the lives of people in California and Washington state during the 1960s and '70s, this loose adaptation locates the action entirely in late twentieth-century Los Angeles, putting over 20 characters from a dozen stories together, creating a sense of alienation and interdependency, and giving characters the kind of film noir edginess tainted with dishonesty, infidelity, and death that characterizes this sun-drenched and violent city but that also carries some redemption.

- *The Joy Luck Club* (novel, Amy Tan, 1989; film, Wayne Wang, 1993)

  A sentimental story of four immigrant women from China and their American daughters, this film covers their tough lives in China during the Chinese Revolution of the 1930s and '40s, migration to California and adaptation to the USA following the war, and the difficult relationship with their Chinese American daughters (during the '90s) whose lives and values have become so different from their own.

- *Fear and Loathing in Las Vegas* (novel, Hunter S. Thompson, 1971; film, Terry Gilliam, 1998)

  Based on Hunter S. Thompson's own wacky, drunken, psychedelic road trip from Los Angeles to Las Vegas, the film is a period piece from the drug culture of the 1960s and '70s focusing on the search for the American Dream and discovery, instead of fear and loathing. This is a film that plays with the road conventions established by the earlier *Easy Rider* and its abortive search for the American Dream throughout the south and southwest.

- *Glengarry Glen Ross* (play, David Mamet, 1984; film, James Foley, 1992)

  Set in Chicago in the 1980s, this film follows the play meticulously in focusing on four realtors and exploring the pressures, inhumanity, and duplicity of American business, in this case, real estate sales. It seems that these salesmen, like the earlier Willy Loman, will do anything to make a sale and the furthest thing form their minds is the well-being of the unsuspecting buyer.

- "Auggie Wren's Christmas Story," *Smoke* (short story, Paul Auster, 1990; film, Wayne Wang, 1995), and *Blue in the Face* (film based on *Smoke*, Wayne Wang, 1995)

  A liberal adaptation of a six-page short story, *Smoke* and its sequel *Blue in the Face* put a humane and compassionate face on a relatively gritty part of Brooklyn in the 1990s. In some sense also a response to *Do the Right Thing*, these films show that different races and classes can get along in a small space and that racism, bigotry, and crime are insignificant parts of the big picture.

- *Smoke Signals* (from short stories in *The Lone Ranger and Tonto Fistfight in Heaven*, Sherman Alexi, 1993; film, Chris Eyre, 1999)

  The first film written, directed, and acted by Native Americans, *Smoke Signals* weaves several stories by Sherman Alexi into a narrative about two Indian youths who have to come to terms with each other, their parents, and heritage (forefathers). Taking place in the 1980s and '90s, the film corrects many of the stereotypes so common about Native Americans in literature and film.

Early twenty-first century

- *The Hours* (novel, Michael Cunningham, 1998; film, Stephen Daldry, 2002)

  A successful film about the beauty and tragedy of gay relationships, the story takes the viewer back to Virginia Woolf's 1920's *Mrs Dalloway* as a connecting point for the lives of three characters (a 1950's housewife, a 1990's lesbian editor, and a 1990's young man dying of AIDS) who are having difficulty working out their sexual and emotional relationships.

- *Brokeback Mountain* (short story, Annie Proulx, 2000; film, Ang Lee, 2005)

  Based on a single short story, this film portrays the love of two young men herding sheep in Wyoming. The beauty, ruggedness, and treachery of the landscape complements their intense and ultimately tragic relationship.

- *Blade Runner* (novel, *Do Androids Dream of Electric Sheep*, Philip K. Dick, 1968; film, Ridley Scott 1982)

  Set in a dystopian Los Angeles of the future, this deeply unsettling neo-noir film explores the relationship between androids or "replicants" and their masters, asking basic questions about industrialization, automation, cybernetics, and the ethics of human control.

7

Assignments and Assessments

Everyday assignments and reading loads, end-of-term projects, examinations, and assessments or evaluations are of critical importance in every classroom, but these take on an added dimension in the cross-cultural classroom because teachers may have one kind of expectation drawn from their own culture and students may have different expectations from their own cultures. Such requirements need to be thoroughly considered and interrogated individually by the classroom teacher, but also be balanced by the recommendations of other teachers.

In certain East Asian cultures, daily and weekly assignments are expected, but as they carry less weight — in terms of marks and regard — than the examination at the end of the term, students do whatever they can to get good marks on the exam. As a result, foreign lecturers at Asian universities often complain that students will read the material only after the teacher has talked about it so that they can get an authoritative opinion before reading it themselves. This response might be based upon customary study habits or perceived views of efficiency, but it results in the teachers' giving lectures rather than attempting to have informed class discussions, or valuing work at the end of the term at the expense of ongoing projects. By contrast, in a classroom with a Western, and specifically North American character, the emphasis is usually upon a combination of participation, projects, oral and written presentations, and examinations. It is uncommon for American classrooms to have a final exam for the entire course, but in Asian classrooms (and, it should be noted, in the traditional British empire classroom of only a few decades ago or even now) there is often a final examination worth most of the marks. Each way — everyday readings and continuous assessment or final written examination and end-of-term evaluation — has its strengths and limitations, but teachers have strong feelings about this issue, and faculties and universities often take a united stand on it, so it is best to think carefully about the issue when choosing institutions to teach in and constructing requirements.

Appropriate Kinds and Levels of Assignments

The final examination

Because students in a cross-cultural classroom are likely to have differing levels of familiarity with the language of instruction and differing understandings of the value of assignments, the kind of assignments and amount of reading required on a daily basis can be crucial for a student's development, as can a final examination. This weighting of final examinations determines the balance of everything else that goes on during the term (Morris 1991, 40), and "the assessment tail wags the educational dog the world over" (Tang and Biggs 1996, 159).

The pervasive use of year-end finals frequently relates to the use of public examinations that serve as gateways both to educational and employment opportunities, and students may have "as many as eight sets of competitive examinations in their school years" (Salili 1996, 90). In speaking of this phenomenon in China in 1991, Morris and Marsh note, "in a country where only 1 per cent of the working population obtain university degrees, it is little wonder that university entrance examinations are seen as a very important springboard. It is also important to note that the reputation and material rewards for schools in the PRC is based upon the performance of their students in the public examinations" (1991, 260). Even though a much higher percentage of students are now educated in Chinese universities than in 1991, the emphasis on finals and public examinations has changed little over the years: examinations were the "means by which even the poorest could gain entry into the powerful mandarin class" of many centuries, and they are highly regarded today (Tang and Biggs 1996, 159). With such a strong emphasis upon public examinations, schools are expected to train students in the culture of examinations, meaning that teachers and students think of themselves as bound to this pattern.

If the final examination counts heavily (75% in Hong Kong in the not-too-distant past for all universities and between 50% and 100% in mainland China), then students know that nothing else carries much value. In practice, too, an emphasis on the final examination may mean that students put off comprehensive reading until the end of the term, so that information will be fresh in their minds at the time of the examination. It also means that they may not wish to read material until they have the instructor's views on it — this may be considered strategic in saving time, or it may mean that students believe they are going to get the "right" interpretation of the material before they read it. Where a single course runs for an academic year — formerly the standard for the Commonwealth countries — students study much less during the first half of the year than the second, and, as a result, instructors may come to expect less of them in the classroom during the final period as well. In a semester arrangement, the same pattern may hold, but the time is shorter, and students may discover after only a few weeks that they have to put in effort on a regular basis or fall irretrievably behind. Short terms may lead to short and fragmented assignments, but they also push students along in their work.

The notion of the examination thus governs the entire arrangement of the course. When an examination is heavily weighted, term papers and other projects are relatively devalued by comparison, meaning that instructors characteristically assign few and short essays, and students do not put much time into their preparation. It can also mean that students do not place much value on discussion or oral presentations in the classroom because they do not translate directly into answers for the examination.

Teachers who want to develop a variety of skills in their students therefore need to think seriously about examinations in relation to other assignments. The educational system may well dictate what can be done — Denmark's *studieordning* (or study regulations) lays out examination requirements very precisely well in advance, but if instructors do have a choice in the matter, they must think carefully and creatively about the balance they wish to achieve.

Equal emphasis on in-term assignments and end-of-term examinations

Options other than a heavily weighted exam include equalizing the value of all essays and projects, examinations, oral presentations, and discussions, or rewarding progress by staggering their value. A technique that can work well is to require short essays of a page or two at the beginning of the term leading to a long essay at the end, a process that gives students an opportunity to gauge the instructor's expectations about content and style of written work. Class discussions and oral presentations perhaps need less deliberate strategies, but, nevertheless, students need explicit instructions, especially from teachers who have recently come abroad to teach. Some students, for example, are hesitant about taking classes from visiting Fulbright professors teaching for a term or a single year at a guest university because the professors do not know the students or the culture and often set requirements that fall outside of students' knowledge or expectations and do not give the kind of instructions that is necessary for full understanding. This is not a matter of students being lazy, unwilling, or unable to do the work, but of not understanding how to do something they have never done before. As a result, they may not trust the instructor's abilities to assess their inexperience in relation to past expectations and/ or need more than one semester to get skills up to speed. In general, students worry whether visiting teachers mark too severely, are difficult to understand, and are aware of cultural differences.

As discussed in Chapter 5, class discussion can also be incorporated within the classroom, but must be carefully monitored and fairly assessed. When essays, discussion, and examinations are valued equally or relatively highly, then students work hard to meet those expectations. Effective class discussion depends upon students' preparedness from topics given in advance and course readings for the period. Giving the topic in advance does have advantages insofar as the student can think about it carefully beforehand, but announcing the topic in class can also be useful in teaching students to respond spontaneously.

Reading assignments

It is important to note that students in different cultures have different attitudes to reading on a daily basis and different levels of ability. For instance, although English is one of the two official languages in Hong Kong, students are used to communicating regularly in Cantonese and hardly speak English outside of class. This means that verbal and written fluency differs greatly from person to person, and even very bright students in prestigious programs and universities may not be able to read and absorb more than 30 pages of reading a week. Even that amount may be far too much for most ESL students. Diane Schmitt thinks that reading assignments beyond 1,000 words in English may be difficult for such international students (2005, 64). By contrast, in settings abroad such as Singapore where English is one of the key languages, students can handle more, and more complex, reading on an everyday basis.

Many students in East Asia are taught in their primary and secondary schools to sit with a dictionary in hand and read small amounts of material. Every word they do not know is annotated. They place value on reading slowly and carefully, translating exactly, memorizing vocabulary, and mastering a small amount of material perfectly. Because of this practice, most students have not been taught to read vast amounts quickly. Consequently, instructors need to teach them how to skim — to make their way quickly through a text by reading the first and last sentences of paragraphs and not stopping to look up every word, but letting previous knowledge and the context determine their understanding. By learning that technique, students can discover the main arguments of the text and then go back to pick up the details in a second reading, if they wish. The ability to read large amounts of materials is both a value and a skill. Teachers in particular cultures may choose not to teach it as a skill because they do not consider it of value, believing that it leads to glib and unfounded generalizations. By contrast, other cultures may not value the limitations imposed by systematic close reading because that process limits students' ability to explore facts and ideas comprehensively.

What a student can read will depend upon how theoretical it is, how many other courses he/she is taking at the same time, and the overall workload. This question of theory-based readings is important. Some cultures are practice-oriented and do not engage with theory in the same way as North Americans do, so readings based on theory might be extremely difficult and all but incomprehensible. In any case, the instructor must be careful not to use the classroom "at home" as a measure of what students have to do abroad and must try to assign enough to challenge, but not overwhelm, them.

Costs and availability of materials

The issue of reading also raises the question of texts that an instructor chooses. If a teacher requires more texts than a student can read, then the student pays a financial penalty. Even well-to-do students may not be able to afford texts easily, and requiring them to buy more than they can read may jeopardize the entire teaching and learning experience. Before ordering texts, teachers should find out what is available, what the cost will be, and what students can realistically afford. If texts cost too much, then the instructor should seek out alternatives, for example by photocopying relevant handouts, articles, and chapters of books (without violating international copyright regulations), having students access materials online, or sharing books with the students. It is often frustrating for teachers to go abroad and discover that their favorite teaching materials are not available or will take months to order. Any instructional materials that the teacher believes to be critical should be carried abroad on the plane to ensure that the teaching goes well and that students have what the teacher thinks is necessary to read, view, and learn. It can take months for boxes to arrive by mail, and some go missing; to repeat, anything essential must be hand-carried.

Teachers who go abroad should also not count on materials being available in school, university, or city libraries. Some countries censor politically or culturally sensitive materials; most libraries have small budgets; and some may not allow materials to be checked out. Also, as some have very strict policies about how much and what kind of materials can be photocopied, planning on resources being easily accessible can be a big mistake. Also, students themselves might not have easy access to research materials, even through interlibrary loan, so projects that require particular kinds of research materials may not be possible.

Written assignments

Every teacher probably believes that he/she knows exactly what goes into an essay — a central topic, a main argument, evidence to support the argument, an account of available research in the area, an appropriate structure, and good use of language. Within the English language tradition, this is presented in a linear style and logically deductive form — at least in arts subjects — but, as Kaplan observes (as cited in McLean and Ransom 2005, 57), there are at least four other alternative styles: circular (Chinese), digressive (Romance languages), parallel (Middle Eastern languages), and a variable of parallel (Russian and German). These various styles are all ways of arguing a point, but the focus and organization will differ radically from case to case, meaning that teachers from abroad may well misunderstand the local values of expression and ways of writing and how to present meaningful alternatives. It is also the case that because of language difficulty, apart from culturally different ways of writing, second-language students will require more time to organize material, will write more slowly, and, in most instances, will write shorter papers. Since writing is rarely taught in university outside English courses — and then only as a secondary consideration in most places — students may not understand what it takes to write an essay in a mode required by the teacher. The teacher needs to be quite explicit about what the writing assignment entails as this cannot be taken for granted.

Related to expectations about the quality of essays is the function and phrasing of the questions themselves that are put to the students. The questions should "set clear expectations and give detailed instructions" (McLean and Ransom 2005, 59), but the presentation and understanding of that clarity varies from place to place. In Hong Kong, questions are often of a general nature, and students are expected to define their topics and establish the direction on their own. In mainland China, the students expect the questions themselves to give direction and to be very explicit in setting out goals and steps to meet them. In both places, students are often overwhelmed when too many choices of question are given, for each one requires some mental planning; and, in the case of an essay examination, it takes time for students to eliminate questions and focus on the one to discuss. Teachers going abroad may also assume that their way of phrasing question is transparent and that the students will automatically understand what they mean. As Mary Scott has noted, however, "terms such as 'analyse', 'argue', 'discuss' and 'evaluate' . . . serve to encode particular modes of enquiry within particular fields" (2004, 57) and presume strategies of critical thinking that are not universally acknowledged or comprehended.

Because of cultural differences in the directions and the essay writing itself, teachers should be prepared to spend more time on writing instructions themselves, giving explicit directions in advance about the terms, goals of the essay, terminology, the amount of research required, and the parts of the essay itself. Such terms as "argument," "argumentative essay," and "discuss" may have to be defined and elaborated upon, if the students are to understand precisely what is required. "Reflective writing" might be used instead of "argumentative essay" or "discussion" to convey a better sense of what is needed. Sample essays should be given in advance to illustrate both excellent and poor quality. It is also a good idea to increase the required length and value of the essays throughout the term, as the student gains skills and confidence.

Cultural Considerations in Student Assessments and Marks

As students' attitudes toward heavily weighted final examinations suggest, grades and marks loom large in every system. For some teachers, giving anything other than "Pass" or "Fail" seems arbitrary — and perhaps even a pass-fail system is arbitrary — but for others nothing but fine distinctions and precise calculations will do. Most students want to know how well they have done, want to improve, and look for care in the examination process and awarding of marks. Some students are private about their results and never share them with friends, but others like to compare results and ascertain that the whole process has been even-handed.

My own preference for the cross-cultural classroom is for marks based on a combination of class participation, essays, projects, oral presentations, and examinations. I have experimented with many different forms and combinations, ranging from term assessments only (projects, essays, and presentations) to mainly final examinations. All have advantages and disadvantages. Final examinations or mid-term and end-of-term examinations together assist students in thinking in macro or global ways about courses, tying material together into coherent segments or a whole. Although this assessment pattern does help students comprehend larger patterns and issues, it can also work against those who cannot respond well to the pressure of an examination situation, or are ill at the time of the examination. It may also disadvantage those less adept in the language medium of the class. The aspect of language can be a concern for the cross-cultural classroom if students are coming to grips with an unfamiliar language while also trying to understand and communicate particular forms of subject matter. For instance, if a student's native language is Polish but he/she is in the preliminary stages of studying in an English-speaking classroom, that student may not be very successful under the pressure of a time-restricted examination. As McLean and Ransom note, students struggling with the language may require more time simply to make out the question itself (2005, 58) for expression is never as transparent as the instructor thinks and is open to misinterpretation. Basing assessment mainly upon examinations can thus present significant handicaps for some bright and competent students.

Ongoing or continuous assessment of essays, projects, and presentations during the term offers additional advantages and disadvantages. One advantage is that they can give individuals and groups an opportunity to work on writing and presentation skills without the pressure of examinations. Some students love to study a particular topic and work without significant pressure on a nicely focused and expressed essay or oral presentation. This form of assessment may not have the advantage of comprehensiveness, however, and students may come away from courses feeling that they have enjoyed the individual bits but do not grasp the unifying purposes and ideas, or that they are not being well prepared for other kinds of examination situations. As a result, it is not uncommon for parents to pull students out of schools because they are not "learning enough," meaning that their knowledge is segmented rather than unified, that memorization is not required routinely, and that they do not have enough experience of the pressures of rigidly structured examinations to compete for entrance into universities or within particular university structures. All in all, in the cross-cultural classroom, a combination of forms serves students well so that they have a variety of results, a sense of the big and small pictures of the material at hand, and the ability to compete successfully in any assessment situation. The cross-cultural classroom may be unique in this respect because of the need to address the expectations of diverse cultures at the same time.

In all of these instances, there are several related issues that need to be considered. As Jude Carroll (2005a, 32) observes, "students being assessed usually welcome explicit instructions on:

- the length of submissions (and the fact that longer is not better);
- the format (with explanations of what a report, poster, essay or précis might be and possibly a chance to try out new formats such as oral presentations and viva voces);
- what the assessment criteria mean and how they are applied;
- what is being assessed (especially the percentage of the mark allocated to English language proficiency; and
- which aspects of the assessment brief are compulsory and which are guidance or suggestions.

Depending on the student and the context, each of these is more or less important, but all of them affect the way a student prepares an assignment and the way a teacher assesses it.

Marks

An important aspect of the assessment process is, of course, the kind of marks or grades that are awarded to students. There are significant differences in marking systems from country to country. For example, note this comparison:

USA	Canada	Hong Kong	Denmark
A = 90–100	A = 80–100	A = 70–100	A = 10–13
B = 80–90	B = 70–80	B = 60–70	B = 7–9
C = 70–80	C = 60–70	C = 50–60	C = 6
D = 60–70	D = 50–60	D = 40–50	D/F = 5
F = 0–60	F = 0–50	F = 0–40	F = 0–3

A large discrepancy exists in these ranges, and, on the face of it, an A would be the most difficult for students to achieve in the USA and the easiest to achieve in Hong Kong or Denmark. (Incidentally, Denmark is in the process of changing its marking system to accord with other EU countries.) In practice, this is not the case because marks in the USA are, on the whole, higher than in Canada, Hong Kong, and Denmark, with the majority of students receiving As and Bs. In Commonwealth and former Commonwealth societies, including Australia and Hong Kong, faculties or colleges within universities often set percentile quotas of the number of students who can get As, Bs, Cs, Ds, or Fs. Most are supposed to get Cs (50–60) (McLean and Ransom 2005, 58), with the rest allocated as As (10%), Bs (20%), and Ds and Fs (20%).

Each system, however, has ways of evaluating assessments, that is, setting limits and interpreting and explaining differences in distinctions. In the USA, educators look carefully at the range of marks within a given category. That is, a 92 (or A-) is regarded differently than a 95 (an A), and a student with a string of As might not be accepted to a prestigious program or school, whereas a student with all 95s probably would. Similarly, a 90 might be regarded as a gift to a student who was on the border between a B+ and an A- and, as a result, in the viewer's perception, might carry significantly less weight than a 91.

In most places in the USA, marks are assigned individually by the teacher, and one teacher might give high marks and another low marks, with the understanding that the law of averages will even things out. In Commonwealth countries, by contrast, universities and/or departments often have a very formal evaluation process involving first and second readers as well as external assessors on final examinations. Furthermore, they often have rigid grids for marks, as mentioned above. This spread of marks may vary from college to college or faculty to faculty, however. The same is somewhat typical of Denmark, where, although a 13 is possible, a 10 or 11 tends to be the highest mark given to only a few students, 8s and 9s to the rest of the best, and 6s and 7s to those in the average or high average range. A 5 is a very bad mark, but few students get a 5 or anything below it because the system is still somewhat elitist as regards admission. In Denmark and Hong Kong, a C or equivalent is still a respectable mark, but students in Canada and the USA complain bitterly if they are awarded a mark of C — tantamount to getting an F in other cultures (McLean and Ransom 2005, 58).

Letters of recommendation

Many cultures depend on letters of recommendation to explain the system and clarify the marks. This is particularly true in the USA, where letters of support are increasingly required for applications and academic promotions, but there are also particular cultural features to these letters of recommendation. Americans typically give enthusiastic letters of recommendation, and those skilled in reading them look for cautionary phrases among the positive comments. Canadian and Hong Kong letters are often reserved and diffident, and the readers of these letters must be careful not to disadvantage students who come from those cultural dispositions and propensities when putting them side by side with American versions. Denmark rarely uses letters of recommendation, and students applying for jobs or further education must depend on the recipients of the applications having a general knowledge of the system and perhaps even specific knowledge of the school or university and personal experiences of the candidate when making decisions. This may be easier to do in places like Hong Kong and Denmark with small and relatively homogeneous populations and normative educational systems than it is in a multi-cultural, multi-system place like the USA.

In short, awarding and interpreting marks is located within a culture in particular ways. Teachers in the cross-cultural classroom will need to spend considerable time understanding the particular cultural context of the school or university and making sure that students and parents do as well. It is not easy for teachers to change systems in this respect for not only are the valuations of the marks different, but the percentage of those receiving them will differ from country to country. Assigning marks, then, is a big issue for the cross-cultural classroom.

Cultural Considerations and Plagiarism

Teachers base marks on honest effort and earned achievement, so students' cheating on examinations and passing others' work off as their own creates a deep sense of personal injustice and violation of professional standards. There is grave concern that cheating and plagiarism are mounting problems in high schools and universities at home and abroad. In a 2005 report on academic cheating and plagiarism from the Center for Academic Integrity, the American researcher Don McCabe (2005) notes that "studies of 18,000 students at 61 schools," conducted from 2001 to 2005,"suggest cheating is . . . a significant problem in high school — over 70% of respondents at public and parochial schools admitted to one or more instances of serious test cheating and over 60% admitted to some form of plagiarism." University campuses share that trend: "70% of students admit to some cheating," and 77% state that "cheating is not a very serious issue" (ibid.). The percentiles of student cheating released by the Center for Academic Integrity differ little from John Walker's 1998 survey of 200 American business students in which 80% confessed to cheating, but, while only 19% confessed to plagiarizing at that time, the figure is now 60%. This upward drift suggests that plagiarism has become more serious, and instances of "unpermitted collaboration at nine medium to large state universities [have] increased from 11% in a 1963 survey to 49% in 1993" (McCabe 2005).

Although Jude Carroll from the United Kingdom believes that "most cases of plagiarism arise from misuse of print-based resources" (2002, 14), McCabe (2005) finds that Internet plagiarism has been accelerating: "most students have concluded that 'cut and paste' plagiarism — using a sentence or two (or more) from different sources on the Internet and weaving this information together into a paper without appropriate citation — is not a serious issue. While 10% of students admitted to engaging in such behavior in 1999, almost 40% admit to doing so in the Assessment Project surveys." The accessibility of research material on the Internet, the ease of interweaving sources electronically, and the purchasing of research essays online have made the improper use of the Internet a significant part of plagiarism.

This is a strong indictment of students' lack of ethics, but not all faculty members have reacted strongly to the issue or even responded at all. McCabe comments that many faculty members have not given "clear direction" to students and "are reluctant to take action against suspected cheaters. In Assessment Project surveys involving almost 10,000 faculty in the last three years, 44% of those who were aware of student cheating in their course in the last three years, have never reported a student for cheating to the appropriate campus authority" (2005). Some faculty members do not want to acknowledge that the problem exists; others do not want the amount of work required to move forward on plagiarism prevention or charges; others want the authority to handle all forms of cheating on their own and do not want the issue to go beyond their classroom; and still others are afraid of litigation arising from charges against a student (McCabe et al. 2006, 20, 24). This is the case for American- and Canadian-based teachers, but it probably applies elsewhere as well.

For many teachers internationally, the issue of plagiarism is new and uncertain. For some, it is a relatively new phenomenon; for others, universities are only just beginning to recognize the scale of the existing problem and to implement policies; and for still others, the problem is well recognized, and universities have policies in place. As an example of the relatively new phenomenon, it was only in the latter half of the twentieth century that universities in Great Britain and the Commonwealth began to base some course marks on essays and class presentations and, consequently, open the doors to plagiarism. Traditionally, students took their examinations at the end of the degree program and were awarded an academic standing on the basis of those written examinations. Questions were handled confidentially through a central body, and the answers were written in essay form and often read by multiple readers. The structure of the examining process kept cheating to a minimum and hardly allowed for plagiarism, so the trust inherent in the relationship of teachers and students was kept intact.

Statistics on plagiarism suggest that teachers at home and abroad have been the unwitting victims of student cheating, but this can go both ways, and there have been several stories of late about dishonest faculty members who plagiarized the work of other educators and students and falsified their own research. It has happened in some of the most respected universities across the planet. In 2002 the Vice Chancellor of Monash University was accused of plagiarism and subsequently stepped down, and in 2004 the Harvard Law School had three separate instances of professors who were accused of copying passages from other works. By far the most notorious recent case has been South Korean embryonic stem cell scientist who invented or altered research data so that he could gain recognition and millions of dollars in research grants. Ranking highly, but not quite so sensationally, are several cases concerning Chinese professors: one from Jiao Tong University, who stole chip designs from Motorola, passing them off as his own research and invention (Barboza 2006); another from Wuhan University, who plagiarized the work of his students; a third from Shantou University, who plagiarized the work of a PhD student at another university; a fourth from Sichuan University, who published fraudulent biomedical research in an issue of *Nature Biotechnology*; and, finally, one from Tianjin Foreign Studies University, who plagiarized 10 articles for his book (Johnson 2006). These latter are all instances of educators and scientists whose research was so fraudulent that the universities had little choice but to take action, and all but one professor lost his job.

The effect of such revelations has been to create a deep concern about the ethics of students, professors, and the academic systems that support them. According to Reed Hundt, formerly chairman of the Federal Communications Commission in the USA, "the underlying problem" in China "is that the Chinese government has not established a rule of law for research and development" (Barboza 2006), but that cannot be said of the West. Another underlying problem is that, obsessed with rankings, universities and academics worldwide are under increasing pressure to publish research papers because the academic systems reward "scholars for prolific results in publishing and [pay] little regard to quality" (Johnson 2006). Where there are no guidelines from the government, where there is undue pressure to publish, where universities are inconsistent on cheating regulations and legal infrastructure, and where there is no established tradition of authorship and publication, then no single standard is considered sacred, consistency is compromised, and faculty and students alike suffer from ambiguity. At the heart of the matter is a feeling that for too many, it does not really matter. According to Choi Kai Yan, a young assistant professor at Shantou University, "in China there is a kind of climate of temptation to use other people's work and put your name on it" because "no one takes plagiarism very seriously"; and, according to the government news agency Xinhua, as many as 60% copy others' work (Johnson 2006). If no one wants to take plagiarism very seriously and if so many faculty members plagiarize, it may be because there is too much tolerance in general of academic cheating and intellectual property theft, as has been the case in China in the recent past. This can be upsetting for academics when they unexpectedly encounter these problems at home and abroad.

As a result of such revelations, universities globally are implementing firm guidelines and penalties on academic cheating at student and faculty levels, though policies tend to be targeted mainly at students. Universities want to head off problems with plagiarism at the outset and create a mechanism for fair and enforceable legal action on campus. In most Western countries, committees of students and teachers have worked together in drawing up exacting regulations about plagiarism, and boards with student and faculty representatives commonly enforce them. This practice is democratic, shows that all parties are equally concerned about policies and violations, and invests everyone as stakeholders in the process. Nonetheless, because this is "a culturally determined concept" (McLean and Ransom 2005, 59), how plagiarism is defined and the actual penalties do differ from place to place in the world, and that inconsistency can be confusing for the teacher abroad.

According to McCabe et al., one of the strongest single deterrents to cheating and plagiarism is the teacher's statements about academic integrity at the beginning of the term. These include "lectures during orientation sessions, website pages and chapters in student handbooks devoted to ethical standards, and admonishments in course syllabi" — all of them "effective in undergraduate schools" (2006, 3). For the individual teacher abroad, then, the very first step is to find out the institutional definition of plagiarism and to take that up with the students at the beginning of class and include an admonishment against plagiarism in the course outline or syllabus. McCabe himself indicates that "cheating is higher in courses where it is well known that faculty members are likely to ignore cheating" (2005). Confronting the issue in the classroom at the beginning of term, indicating that there is a strict policy in force, and stressing the importance of personal responsibility in engaging in scholarship does therefore discourage cheating and plagiarism. This introductory session should go still further, however, by going over particular examples so that students can see how to recognize plagiarism and discussing citation rules so that they know what has to be done.

Most agree that "plagiarism is passing off someone else's work, whether intentionally or unintentionally, as your own for your own benefit" (Carroll 2002, 9), but that needs further elaboration. Institutions assume that "someone else's work" refers to work in general, not specifically to language theft, and includes "constructions, images, organisational structures, compositions, and ideas," whether literary and artistic, critical, scientific, etc. that can be used to get a higher "mark or grade but it might include a promotion, stronger bid for funds, or enhanced professional reputation" (ibid., 10). In short, there is cheating at all levels, whether student plagiarism, cheating in examinations, or faculty abuse of other people's "ideas, structures, and work" (ibid., 11), and students need to know that the university will not tolerate cheating and plagiarism from its faculty members any more than from students.

Students also need to know the penalties for cheating and plagiarism. Because there are no national standards on cheating, teachers need to go over institutional policies very carefully and counsel students that they will hold them to a strict standard. At the least, a plagiarized paper usually carries a penalty of a 0 for the assignment, or, as a middle ground, a 0 for the course, and, at the most, expulsion from the program of study and/or the university. The latter is seen as an extreme measure, but colleges and universities do expel students, and in North America they even have "the legal authority to revoke or rescind an academic degree" in cases of plagiarism (Standler 2000, section 7). According to Standler, no faculty member or student judged guilty of plagiarism in the USA ever won a court appeal against such a university decision, but that may not be true abroad.

Although many universities are strong in condemning plagiarism, they may be elusive about specific penalties for students who cheat and plagiarize — importantly because many institutions have none — so teachers need to indicate what their expectations are and make certain that they conform to any governing institutional requirements. Sometimes, university regulations are relatively open-ended and need clarification. As a case in point, the "Regulations Governing Conduct at Examinations" of *The University of Hong Kong Calendar 2005–2006*, state that a student "shall not engage in plagiarism nor employ nor seek to employ any other unfair means at an examination or in any other form of work submitted for assessment as part of a University examination" (2005, 132), but the regulation does not give precise limits to plagiarism or stipulate penalties. The *Calendar*, however, contextualizes that comment by stating:

> In conducting research, a candidate shall not engage in any misconduct which shall include, but not [be] limited to, fabrication; falsification; plagiarism; infringement of another person's intellectual property rights; misleading ascription of authorship including the listing of authors without their permission, attributing work to others who have not in fact contributed to the research, or the lack of appropriate acknowledgement of work primarily produced by another person; and other practices which seriously deviate from those commonly accepted within the academic community for proposing, conducting or reporting research.

In addition to this *Calendar* statement in Hong Kong, each college or faculty sends memos to students about the meaning of plagiarism and possible penalties. The Dean of Arts' letter, for example, indicates that the penalties "can be severe, up to and including the withholding of a degree and not in any case less than failure in the paper where plagiarism has occurred." Another University document called "What Is Plagiarism?" warns that serious cases of plagiarism will be referred to the University Disciplinary Committee, consisting of three faculty members and two students, and could result in expulsion. Although it is rare that cases are sent beyond the faculty level to the University Disciplinary Committee, it does happen, and students have been expelled.

Some universities are more prescriptive about the nature of plagiarism and penalties than is an institution like the University of Hong Kong, but the net effect could be more confusing. In the instance of Shantou University in China, the regulations, while overly lenient, are spelled out for students in some detail: "Undergraduates who plagiarize under four sets of conditions will be expelled. Specifically, they involve: an essay in which 50% of the content [is] copied; the undergraduate thesis has at least 30% or more of the content plagiarized; to express other people's viewpoints as the total, core or major viewpoints of one's own work; and letting others write one's thesis or writing someone else's thesis" (Cheng 2006). Nothing in Shantou's regulations includes faculty members, but, in any case, allowing 50% of an essay to be plagiarized before serious action seems too permissive, while expulsion may seem too severe. This standard may seem fair in mainland China, however, where there may be no history of policies against plagiarism, an issue that in itself raises ethical questions for teachers abroad. When, after a professor's resignation for plagiarism, Shantou students were asked to review their own regulations and consider Harvard's more stringent code on plagiarism, they were shocked, thinking Harvard's very severe (Cheng 2006).

Because the cross-cultural classroom includes a variety of international students from different backgrounds, teachers need to be especially careful about communicating policies on cheating and plagiarism. Carroll finds that "research does not generally support the view that cultural differences make plagiarism more likely in international student groups" (2002, 20), but the differences in background mean that communication about regulations and expectations is absolutely necessary. Although many universities share comparable attitudes, policies, and strategies (for example, those in the Center for Academic Integrity — Great Britain, Europe, Australia, and New Zealand, Canada, and the USA), experiences with and perceptions about cheating may differ considerably. In some societies, students might never think of cheating in an examination or plagiarizing a paper, and plagiarism is not seen as a significant problem; this is my experience in Denmark where students take honesty for granted as the basis of a relationship of trust, and most would not jeopardize this. However, as students in other societies might have a different attitude, it is necessary to be up front at once about the issue.

In considering whether international students pose particular problems for plagiarism or require special kinds of help, many academics raise questions about students who come from cultures that value the progress of the group rather than the individual and think it necessary for students to help one another in all kinds of circumstances. In the Middle East and China, for example, students commonly support the group over the individual, frequently study together to promote "deeper learning" and "social relationships" (Robinson and Kuin 1999, 194), and may not think it an offence to share information at any point in the process (Storti 1994, 26). At the same time, these students are highly competitive and are usually aware of rules against plagiarism in their home universities but are "unsure *how to act on this requirement* when writing coursework" (Carroll 2002, 21). The teacher abroad needs to take on board these deeply held cultural views, figure out ways that they can be helpful in the classroom, and yet articulate and instil values of academic integrity and the need for independent work and responsibility so that they are not compromised either.

Teachers' concerns for academic integrity, breeches in assessment regulations, and fair penalties mean that circumstances in student behavior need to be well thought out to ensure natural justice. It is important to be consistent in approaches to academic integrity and penalties, but it is not possible to have "predetermined penalties for plagiarism" (Carroll 2002, 74) because individual cases and circumstances always differ, and there are special factors that can be taken into consideration. According to David Gardner of the English Centre, the University of Hong Kong (2005), many students in Hong Kong commit "plagiarism accidentally. They were getting confused about how to make use of the information in the books they were reading (the sources) and they were getting frustrated because they knew they were doing a bad job of their academic writing." Most institutions indicate that intention cannot be considered in judging plagiarism, but student confusion over the use of information could be a mitigating circumstance arising from lack of information or previous research practices. More than one Hong Kong student has said that in high school they were taught to sit down with four or five texts, extract relevant materials, and weave those together. The putting together of those materials into a coherent form was sufficient proof of their individual research and writing skills, and they were not expected to put it in their own language or to comment on it. This confusion about the use of information suggests little intention to deceive and, therefore, reason to be cautious in determining penalties. If this is a likely scenario, it also suggests that the teacher needs to address the issue early on.

According to David Watkins, another reason for carefulness in considering penalties for plagiarism may be the Chinese view that the pupil should seek the most authoritative sources and replicate those (1996, 116). This explanation may account for some plagiarism in writing, but it probably pertains more to practices in calligraphy and art. Still, that frequently repeated comment might say something about different attitudes toward originality. Within the traditional pedagogy of the East, personal originality often did not have the same currency as in the modern West. Children were taught that their family unit was foremost, and that they must learn to conform to the opinions of the family and peers. Standing out with a personal voice — especially if they had no real knowledge of the subject — was consequently not of high value.

Another reason to exercise care in penalizing students is that, according to Jude Carroll, students plagiarize mainly because they cannot manage their time well (*Handbook* 2002, 19) and do not cheat on a regular basis. This reason, too, does not suggest deliberate deceit so much as the need to get an assignment completed on schedule, and a lack of previous offences should provide grounds for leniency.

There is at least one other and especially important reason to think carefully about the issue of plagiarism within the cross-cultural classroom — that is, students whose specialty does not lie in the area may assume they have inadequate knowledge and need to copy others who do. Although students who have adequate information and understanding also resort to plagiarism, it is much more likely to occur among those whose background and academic experience lie outside the immediate assignment. In one humanities course at the University of Hong Kong taught to students whose majors were in other areas — social science, business, medicine, dentistry, and engineering rather than arts — a high percentage of the students downloaded material from the Web without adjustments or attribution. In one case, a visiting professor claimed that up to 50% of his students had downloaded substantial amounts of material directly into essays without any kind of attribution. This extreme case eventually revealed an even greater problem — these students had come through specialized science or business programs in high school and had never written a humanities or social sciences paper and, in many cases, had never had to write an essay of any kind in high school. All their assessments had been based on final examinations or certain kinds of lab experiments and problem solving. In short, having to write an essay for the university classroom, they had no "scaffold" of ideas or rhetorical understanding (Schmitt 2005, 70) upon which to construct an argument, and they panicked or did the best that they could, which for many was to plagiarize.

There are various other reasons for plagiarism, including disinterest in the subject matter and course (or belief that the tutor and instructor show disinterest in the course) and fear of expressing ideas in anything but perfect English. And there are the very bad cases in which students are simply lazy or corrupt and do not want to spend the time or effort to get their own personal response together. Unfortunately, it is sometimes hard to know if these form the majority or minority of the plagiarizers. They are the ones, though, for whom teachers have little or no sympathy.

Every teacher wants to know the best way to counteract plagiarism and cheating in examinations. There are no foolproof methods, but studies indicate that there are a few particularly effective ones, some located at the policy level and some in practice. Aside from the teacher establishing the basis for academic integrity at the beginning of the term, as discussed above, an especially effective deterrent is the use of honor codes and student involvement. As McCabe indicates, "serious test cheating on campuses with honor codes is typically 1/3 to 1/2 lower than the level on campuses that do not have honor codes. The level of serious cheating on written assignments is 1/4 to 1/3 lower" (2005). These are impressive statistics, but obviously even student involvement in prevention does not entirely eliminate the problem.

The use of an honor code also suggests that students respond to internalization of values. That can be a problem if acceptance of plagiarism accelerates the tendency, but it can be a solution if the students put pressure on each other to prevent plagiarism. "When peers are seen cheating, cheating may come to be viewed as an acceptable way of behaving and of getting ahead," but when students agree together through honor codes and other signs of personal integrity that they will not cheat, then that reduces the likelihood of cheating (McCabe et al. 2006, 8).

Another deterrent is "plagiarism-resistant assessments" (Carroll 2002, 6). First of all, the onus is on instructors to think carefully about what is readily available in the library and on the Internet and how best to use them in course requirements. Instead of restricting research to older, well-researched topics, instructors can choose up-to-the-minute topics with limited available resource materials, ask students to relate that to their own experience, or request evaluation and analysis to show their own understanding. In being aware of "plagiarism opportunities" and "collusion opportunities" on essays (ibid., 24–25), teachers can go beyond those perils by asking for outlines in advance and multiple drafts and requesting student interviews at the time of final submission. Teachers also need to go beyond conventional topics in examinations, so that answers are unlikely to conform to one another, either accidentally or intentionally. If many students study and memorize material together for a conventional examination dependent on memory skills alone, it can be difficult to determine what is copied from another student's paper in an examination or what simply reflects classmates studying together, so thinking up unique questions is necessary. I had such an experience in mainland China when I gave a question that depended too much upon memorized results from the lectures and readings, and I found a dozen almost identical answers, though many of the students were not even sitting together. To circumvent that kind of response subsequently, I gave problem-based questions in which students were asked to apply course readings to unique contemporary situations or to their own experiences, and that prevented students from copying each other.

Yet another deterrent is the use of electronic detection. This deterrent normally has to be implemented by the department or university as a whole because the cost of the service is too much to bear on an individual basis. The University of Hong Kong subscribes to Turnitin.com, and students in some departments submit all their essays on line to this site; this instrument compares each essay to all public online materials in addition to the essays of other students who have previously submitted electronically. By explaining the site and its capabilities in advance and going through the procedure, instructors have found that the rate of plagiarism goes down at once to almost nothing. This deterrent, then, is the most straightforward and successful when teacher and student are both aware of the procedure and its implications. It is not a complete solution, however, because there are limitations to the system.

Plagiarism, then, is of critical concern for the cross-cultural classroom, and teachers will need to make certain that there is a school or university policy, know what it contains, and make sure students have copies and understand its importance. Taking time to go over this policy at the beginning of class will send a strong signal for academic integrity and save embarrassment later on. Teachers will also need to make sure that they spend the required amount of time going over examples of plagiarism so that students have no remaining doubts about the varieties or about the teacher's attitude toward them. Having students agree to codes of personal integrity also assists in preventing cheating and plagiarism. Finally, if it is, indeed, a class of students (or even some of a class) who have never previously had to undertake a particular kind of assignment, then the teacher must spend the required amount of time talking about how to write such a paper and integrate material so that students understand what to do. Talking about researching and writing of such an assignment can take a great deal of time, and it may mean that every teacher ultimately has to talk more about the writing than the content, but, if ignorance of writing skills for this particular discipline really is the issue, that must be addressed in the fullest possible fashion in advance of the problem. It is not good enough to blame the students when they have no knowledge or understanding of the task.

Classroom Assessment

In addition to student marks and plagiarism, the issue of assessment needs to include the entire classroom and the students it produces. An assessment of the classroom should look at the experiences, learning, and attitudes of the staff and students, but, in a related sense, some thought must also be given to graduates of these programs and the difficulties they might have in their society as a result of these experiences.

Assessing the classroom is not the same as assessing the students in it. While it is a teacher's duty to make judgments on the merits of the students and indicate whether they have passed or failed, the classroom itself needs to be assessed, and, in this process, everyone needs to participate. The need for everyone to be involved is particularly true in the cross-cultural classroom when students and teachers from different nations and cultures are put together. In a single culture with a homogeneous population, many things are taken for granted and implicitly understood. However, in a cross-cultural classroom, assessing the classroom at least at the end of the year is essential as it is too easy for things to be misunderstood and not successfully communicated.

Every classroom and institution will have to come up with a process of evaluation that it considers fair. The teacher needs a primary say in the process and perhaps should write a simple statement about the goals of the class and how well they have been achieved. Students, too, should be asked what they assume the goals to be and whether they have been fulfilled. A form with questions that can be scored easily is ideal as part of the response, but in a secondary school or university, students should be asked to express their opinions, both as to what has happened during the year and what their recommendations are for the next offering of the class or course. All teachers recognize the inherent limitations of such questionnaires, but they do provide at least one glimpse into the classroom activities by everyone who has been involved.

Taken together, assignments and assessments are concrete representations of the values of the cross-cultural classroom. The first embodies the expectations that teachers have for their students, and the second the judgment that they and the students put upon the realization of those expectations. Schools and universities need to challenge the students, neither "dumbing down" the requirements nor expecting too much, and everyone must share in evaluating the results of those expectations. It is an age-old view that teachers should evaluate students, but it is an important modern addition that students should have a fair say in evaluating the education process as well — the courses, the teacher, and the classroom as a whole. In that way everyone becomes a stakeholder in the process of education.

8

Conclusion:
Descent, Consent, and
Cross-Cultural Affiliations

Globalization, internationalization, and transnationalism have accelerated in the last two decades, and, as noted throughout this study, the cross-cultural classroom has shared strongly in this phenomenon, enhancing simple enjoyment, facilitating teaching and learning, and aiding in the construction of identity. Opportunities for cross-cultural teaching exist in every country but are particularly well illustrated in China's rapidly changing educational culture. Chinese education has a long and venerable history, but as existing programs have been transformed and new ones opened, curriculum requirements of faculties and colleges have changed, and universities have taken on a new character. Change at the structural level has driven the effort to re-examine and refresh the quality of teaching and learning as well.

Given this emphasis on pedagogy and learning in the international classroom, teachers need to be aware how culture is configured locally and internationally. Without understanding the priorities and values of the differing cultures present in the modern cross-cultural classroom, teachers and students alike can make unwise decisions. As previously discussed, one primary consideration in strengthening the cross-cultural classroom is attentiveness to the relationship of the individual to the group. This is a complicated matter and bears strongly upon aspirations and restrictions, hierarchical arrangements, politeness, and styles and degrees of participation in the classroom. Whether the teachers and students come from communitarian or individualist societies, and whether they are able to understand differing perspectives on the group versus individual dynamics impacts strongly upon the classroom atmosphere and, ultimately, everyone's identity. Adjusting to the demands of teaching abroad, learning how to respect the students, and receiving respect from them in turn, however, goes beyond the relationship of the individual to the group and beyond multiculturalism: it is dependent upon what Werner Sollers in *Beyond Ethnicity* defines as descent and consent in culture — that is, cultural codes, beliefs, rites and rituals that are inherited through blood or ideology (descent) in interaction with those that are chosen, contracted, or self-realized (consent). As Sollers (1986, 39) remarks in defining his terms against conventional assessments of ethnicity and multiculturalism:

> I propose that for the purposes of investigating group formation, inversion, boundary construction and social distancing, myths of origins and fusions, cultural markers and empty symbols, we may be better served, in the long run, by the vocabulary of kinship and cultural codes than by the cultural baggage that the word "ethnicity" contains. My concern has therefore shifted from ethnicity to the cultural construction of the codes of consent and descent . . .

Although Sollers makes his observations about American culture within the context of ethnicity theory, his view that the relationship between inherited and chosen traditions creates personal and social identities is decidedly relevant for the international cross-cultural classroom as well.

Within the rhetoric of nation-building from the settlement of America, Sollers points out that consent and adjustment to local values are valued over descent and adherence to old-world cultures and mores; however, in assessing the contemporary scene, David Hollinger in *Postethnic America* does not value the new world over the old but argues that his "postethnic perspective favors voluntary over involuntary affiliations, balances an appreciation for communities of descent with a determination to make room for new communities, and promotes solidarities of wide scope that incorporate people with different ethnic and racial backgrounds. A postethnic perspective resists the grounding of knowledge and moral values in blood and history, but works within the last generation's recognition that many of the ideas and values once taken to be universal are specific to certain cultures" (1995, 3). He further argues that postethnic affiliation is valuable in debating "issues in education and politics" (ibid.). He favors voluntary *cosmopolitan* postethnic affiliation (as opposed to a *pluralist* one based on ethnocentrism and fixed ethno-racial groupings) that "promotes multiple identities, emphasizes the dynamic and changing character of many groups, and is responsive to the potential for creating new cultural combinations" (ibid., 3–4). By "affiliation," Hollinger refers to acts of individual will and volition in forging identities, and by "cosmopolitan" he means "recognition, acceptance, and eager exploration of diversity" (1995, 84) as an important part of that volition. I do not think that the term "identity" is as bound to stasis as Hollinger claims, but I also take his point that a term is needed to reflect the desired diversity, multiplicity, and dynamic process of change in identity formation. I will, then, link affiliation to identity and refer to "affiliated identities" to represent these evolving identities.

Cross-Cultural Affiliated Identities

More than a century ago, W. E. B. DuBois (1897, 195–96) saw that living as a black person in the USA required a "double-consciousness":

> [T]he Negro is a sort of seventh son, born with a veil, and gifted with second-sight in this American world — a world which yields him no self-consciousness, but only lets him see himself through the revelation of the other world. It is a peculiar sensation, this double-consciousness, this sense of always looking at one's self through the eyes of others of measuring one's soul by the tape of a world that looks on in amused contempt and pity. One ever feels his two-ness, an American, a Negro; two souls, two thoughts, two unreconciled strivings; two warring ideals in one dark body, whose dogged strength alone keeps it from being torn asunder.

For DuBois, a black or Negro consciousness was expressed through family and the immediate racial community, but another — an American consciousness — was required for interactions in the larger economic, social, and political sphere. Later, Malcolm X and others in the black community objected to this idea of a double-consciousness, arguing that blacks were racially different from the whites and had to be singular in their commitment and allegiance to their own race and community. In Malcolm X's mind, an identity or consciousness could not be bifurcated between private and public or black and white spheres.

While Malcolm X's position appeals to those like Richard Rodriquez who believe in the importance of a single undifferentiated identity — either the complete rejection of, or, alternatively, complete assimilation into, the mainstream culture — DuBois' pluralism continues to resonate with many "hyphenated" Americans (e.g. Asian-Americans) who find that rejection of their racial and ethnic descent would be destructive of their family identity and social heritage. For them, complete consent and "achieved identity" as opposed to "ascribed identity" (Sollers 1986, 37) is neither desirable nor possible. Instead, many who value cultural pluralism argue that it is necessary to conjoin descent and consent in what the Hawaiians call a Hapa mentality, the marriage of opposites. These double identities may be used for different purposes, giving rise to what Amy Iwasaki Mass refers to as "situational identity," in which, as Paul R. Spickard reflects, the Asian identity is a private, subdominant identity, and the American identity the public and dominant one (2000, 257–60). These are uneasy alliances. There are those like Joy Nakamura who, rather than juggling oppositions or pairing dominant and subdominant identities, opt for a third that "mixes the languages, values, and symbol systems of their two parental cultures" (Spickard 2000, 262). Each of these positions confirms ethnic harmony, and each is also situational, cultural, and experiential, but only the latter comes close to affirming Hollinger's identities based on choice.

Many now accept the view that culture and identity differ, and that neither is fixed. As Jan English-Lueck notes, "culture and identity are different concepts, but they overlap, making it difficult to carefully define the distinctions between them. Identity is one piece of culture. Identity refers less to what we do — our behavior — than to who we believe ourselves to be. Identity is reflexive, reflecting several dimensions; it is how we categorize ourselves to ourselves. Identity is theatre; it is how we present ourselves to others. Finally, one aspect of identity is passive; it is how others classify us" (2002, 117). Hollinger's idea of conjoining descent and consent confirms English-Lueck's observation that identities are neither essentialist nor stable, but, rather, diverse, malleable, and dependent on cultural context. Hollinger, however, separates identity from affiliation on the basis that "*identity* implies fixity and givenness" (1995, 7), while *affiliation* performs personal choice and participates in the social dynamics of that action. By this definition, affiliation can be subdivided into the personal (personal views, personality, individual reactions and responses); the familial (ways of relating to parents, siblings, and partners and preferences for domestic arrangements); the community or communal (where to live and what feels comfortable in public); and the national (not only things that make Americans, Canadians, or Chinese but attitudes towards those that affect social relationships).

Affiliation is created through the fusion of home and society or descent and consent, and schools and universities are the crucible in which the private, the public, and the national are mixed strategically. This blending is useful in thinking out teaching in a foreign classroom because the classroom reflects the way the culture positions identity and learning.

Learning consists of many things, but, in the cross-cultural classroom, it is referenced by politics of descent and consent in an unstable relationship between teacher and students. At certain moments the teacher might well be avowing descent and the students consent, whereas in other ones this might be reversed.

Intelligence, learning, and the educational context of the cross-cultural classroom are thus intricately intertwined in the construction of cross-cultural affiliated identities. Robert Sternberg (1985) maintains that intelligence consists of three elements — the componential, the contextual, and the experiential. Componential intelligence, he argues, concerns the process of thinking, planning, and realizing thoughts and executing plans. Contextual intelligence concerns the ability to apprehend and adapt to the basic needs and requirements of the context. Finally, experiential intelligence allows the individual to make use of experiences, build upon them in creative ways, and incorporate them into actions. These are all practical forms of intelligence as opposed to theoretical constructs, and relate directly to the *development* and *performance* of affiliation in the classroom as opposed to the *understanding* of it.

Because the classroom shapes identity, it is important to build a strong foundation. The classroom is critical as the site where many first become aware of who they are, how their affiliations are constituted, and how these affiliations are performed, but the cross-cultural classroom is even more central because it requires a bifurcated vision, an awareness of and adaptation to the new "layered" environment and "flexible, evolving and differentiated" multiple identities (Kim, 2001, 38, 66). Students who learn in this layered cross-cultural classroom need to feel socially, culturally, and linguistically connected, part of local kinship networks, and able to maintain their "own culture, traditions and values, starting from family values" and extending to national characteristics (Deshpande 2004), but they also should be able to embrace others coming from outside and generate interest and enhance their knowledge base and skills set. In other words, the cross-cultural classroom performs ethnicity, as Sollers might say, as the teacher and students bring their inherited ideas and attitudes into the social realm and yet adapt to different kinds of people, situations, and contexts. Teachers must feel connected to the classroom, even if their students vary considerably in cultural background and understanding from their own. They need to feel that their personal and public affinities are maintained even as they change, adapt, and accommodate to new forms. This ability to change and adapt should serve students and teachers well in future situations.

That situational identity is marked nationally as American, Canadian, Chinese or something else. Even though the nation state is a contested notion, it is fair to say that culture, educational training, and identity assume a national character, if not always a national curriculum, and pedagogy, too, tends to be marked nationally, although usually with a range of choices. Students who are part of these systems thus find that their individual and social affiliated identities are defined at least in part by these preferences. That means that students in China will see and value their educational experiences differently than do students in the USA. This is not a matter of being better or worse, superior or inferior, but rather of being appropriate to the culture. Students who have been exposed to other educational systems and pedagogical alternatives may, then, feel that their identity in the cross-cultural classroom is affected and altered by this new classroom situation.

Students and teachers alike may find this change exhilarating as they affirm a multiple national affiliation, but they may also find it problematic because they are simultaneously insiders and outsiders, of their own country and another, of a foundational ideology and an adopted one, of one governing pedagogy and another, creating a new kind of learning opportunity and shifting identity. This might seem obvious for teachers and students who mix the cultures of East and West and their differing social patterns and pedagogies, but it is an important characteristic and applies to any transnational situation and sometimes to a thoroughly domestic one. Each person is first located in a particular culture, probably a middle-class American culture for any teacher who has gone abroad from the USA and the local or host culture for students who enroll in the course/school/university, but must change as a result of these new encounters. Stable identities will be transformed to new and flexible affiliated identities by an encounter with, and regard for, new practices and beliefs.

Taken together, descent and consent create the ingredients for a new cultural awareness, and, given the right attention and nurturing, new organizational dynamics and personal affiliated identities. Both teacher and students must partly suspend belief in (or deconstruct) their own culture and traditional training in order to embrace this new classroom dynamic. Although the experience of adaptation will have difficult moments, the nurturing of a cross-cultural affiliation should succeed relatively well when, as Ruben and Kealey (1979) observe, individual competence is perceived as productive and affirming.

As mentioned in previous chapters, in helping to shape this dynamic cross-cultural classroom, create the best opportunity for an interaction of stability and change, and mould flexible affiliations, teachers and students have to be willing to learn, experiment, share, and show respect for the opinions of others. The academic, cultural, and social dimensions to education need to be recognized and modified in each case. In Geert Hofstede's language, students and teachers alike must be willing to have their mental software modified to cope with this new environment. They both need intellectual space to develop a classroom dynamic appropriate to this particular group in this particular place. All must be willing to share in what they know intuitively from their own culture and what they learn from others in the cross-cultural classroom.

Students and teachers in this new cross-cultural classroom who learn to manage stability and change readily develop the characteristics of leadership. As Debashis Chatterjee notices, "leaders shape reality. They do so by combining change and stability. This involves the synthesis of two innate human competencies: creation and construction. Whereas creation is a living and changing process, construction is a structure of stability that controls this process. Creation is multidimensional and dynamic; construction is sequential, progressing step by step" (2002, 222). In the cross-cultural classroom, these leaders will be both teachers and students. Certainly, one of the values attributed to the classroom is the cultivation of leadership, and involvement in the cross-cultural classroom on its own creates strategies for incorporating stability and change, creativity and construction.

Affiliated Identity and Cultural Markers in the Classroom

There are many factors that serve as ingredients for successful affiliated identities and cross-cultural classrooms, but the most important is the respect between teacher and student and between students themselves. Unless the teacher adapts to the culture in important ways and also respects the basic identity of the students, including their collective rights and individual opinions, and unless the students respect the teacher's knowledge, attitude, and identity, basic learning is jeopardized and educational opportunities sacrificed.

Although this may seem superficial, the image of the teacher and of her/ his professional identity in a given cultural context is fundamentally important. This is as basic as our clothing. Americans students have fairly casual relationships with their instructors, and teachers in American classrooms often dress in a correspondingly relaxed way. While a generation ago, the teacher-student relationship was more formal and a dress or suit required of teachers, now jeans and other kinds of casual apparel are common for women and men. Casual relationships and dress are also common in many countries in Europe, especially in Great Britain and Scandinavia, where societies as a whole value that.

Other countries may expect something different. Lecturers typically dress up in China, where they are given high regard and expected to dress correspondingly. Men and women alike wear high-quality casual clothing, and women often wear dresses, but, in many places, anything that fits too tightly is inappropriate, and, in parts of India, the Middle East, and Northern Africa, Western-style dresses — even with skirts well below the knees — are often considered inappropriate, and the women will be stared at by everyone and refused entry to some public places.

Not only apparel but also voice and actions must be approached with caution in working in another part of the world. The loudness of Americans in conversation, their tendency to sit on the desk when lecturing or put their feet on furniture, their playful jostling in public places — these are cultural traits and personal characteristics that can strain cross-cultural relationships where soft-spoken speech and personal restraint are valued. The image of the teacher, as well as those in other occupations, is context- sensitive, and Westerners need to be cautious about professional dress and personal conduct for, as outsiders, they are under scrutiny outside and inside. One of my colleagues said that most local Hong Kong people thought expatriates were crazy anyway, so being careful of dress and conduct was not essential, but this easy attitude might get people into trouble in many cities where a host population might not so easily discount or forgive actions not in keeping with their cultures.

In the cross-cultural matters of dress, custom, religion, and politics, it is always best for foreign professionals to be careful, if not reserved, in and out of the classroom in order to be accepted. It is always important to recognize that teachers, as foreigners, are guests in the country, and regardless of private opinions, are not in the position to change a country's culture. Americans who dislike smoking and complain openly about public smoking in France will not keep any of the French from smoking but will convey a sense of intolerance. Or, within the classroom, if there is a pervasive pattern of students coming late, the instructor's shouting at the students to be on time will not change the culture but can alienate students. Of course, instructors should talk with their classes about matters of tardiness, but if they are working against deeply engrained cultural habits, it is unlikely to have much effect. Teachers are in the position to modify the subject matter and pedagogy, but not deeply held practices or views of behavior. Continuing to fight unwinnable battles will leave everyone angry and frustrated.

An important battle that teachers in Asia often face is with the students talking in class. This phenomenon can also be observed at movie theatres, conferences, and other public events. In many cases, students do talk because it has become a pattern in class, whether or not they are vitally interested in the lecture. Having sat in these audiences, I have, however, observed that students in the cross-cultural classroom often have difficulty in understanding all the terms or concepts and try to ask their friends for clarification before the lecturer moves too far along. This can create a noisy buzz in the classroom that is very unnerving for presenters and can seem rude. For the most part, students do not see it as rude, and it continues whether the speaker is high profile and interesting or not. Having enough handouts with the keywords should eliminate some of the need for buzz, but the teacher will have to develop his/her own technique to keep the students quiet.

Key to keeping students interested is having an interesting style, but, even more importantly, keeping abreast of new developments in the field and so having something to say. That requirement is equally important for basic knowledge and classroom pedagogy. Only with the required knowledge can teachers be sufficiently confident of their material to cultivate appropriate means of presentation. Although it is not my purpose to dwell on basic knowledge and academic credentials here, a "wing and a prayer" style is clearly bad pedagogy and inadequate preparation for the classroom. Because internationalized parents and students often value excellent education highly and because international teachers and students are exposed in a kind of fish-bowl, cross-cultural teachers need to be even better prepared than when in their own country and very careful in thinking through potential difficulties in understanding the material.

When going abroad, it is crucial for teachers to study the culture carefully in order to find their right place within it. When teachers and students go abroad, there will be a period of adjustment to the new social conditions outside the classroom as well as the expectations of the classroom. Various people, particularly those in intercultural communications and intercultural psychology, have talked about the culture shock that teachers and students can expect (Gabrenya 1998, 57), and some people approach new cultures neutrally, but others have strong and immediate reactions — either loving or hating them. Even those who immediately love the culture will usually experience some disillusionment after about six weeks and then gradually move to an acceptance of the positive aspects and difficulties.

This process of adaptation also applies to the classroom itself. Gao and Gudykunst find that the main difficulties in foreign students' adaptation center on the degree of cultural distance from their home cultures, insufficient knowledge of the new culture, and a poor social network. These characteristics are not limited to students, but other key factors for teachers include personal and professional expectations, age, status and change of status, previous cross-cultural experience, personality traits, social skills, living arrangements, and knowledge of the job itself.

One of the most important goals in the classroom is the understanding, accepting, and enhancing of the identity of the students and the culture in which the school or university is located — whether personal, regional, national, or ethnic. John Stephens asserts that an important value of American studies programs in the USA is "to gain self-knowledge, to understand ourselves" (1996, 6), and I would add that one reason to teach and study in the cross-cultural classroom is to accept our own identities and those of others. This is a fundamental starting point and goal for education. In major American centers of immigration like New York City or Los Angeles, it is not unusual to have a dozen different nationalities in the same classroom, so individual and collective affiliated identities can be a complicated matter, and this can be doubly so in the foreign cross-cultural classroom. A consideration of student affiliated identity begins with the students' and/or teacher's national and ethnic background and the degree to which they are deculturated from their mother culture, and enculturated or absorbed into the host or receptor culture (Kim 2001, 53). An unresolved national debate continues in the USA about whether it is best for immigrants to *assimilate* into the "melting pot," surrendering their native identity and blending into the American social landscape, or whether it is best for them to *acculturate* and embrace the "salad bowl" or "quilt" ideal, retaining important features of their national and cultural background and becoming only as "American" as they wish (Hollinger 1995, 65; Sollers, 1986, 66–101). But the USA is by no means the only country where this is an issue.

It is always helpful for instructors who are teaching abroad to bear in mind the national and ethnic backgrounds of their students and routinely ask them to reflect on their own national background. This has the advantage of alerting the teacher to differences in attitudes and making issues more relevant and interesting for the students. Without including the local context in their teaching, teachers sometimes make false assumptions about what class material the students are absorbing because they lack the ability to see international connections. Pamela George notes that many Fulbright professors going abroad find that only by comparing their course materials about the USA to local conditions can students understand it (1995, 75–77). International law, for instance, may only be comprehensible within the context of the students' understanding of their own national laws. International positions on the environment make better sense when compared to local views. International youth culture makes sense only when students reflect on the youth culture of their local environment. By reflecting on the global in relation to the local, students perceive cross-cultural values with regard to their own particular cultural practices and through that process become aware of their own values. This process should make both teachers and students alike more understanding and accepting of each other's positions, and it should also give them pride in their "home" culture.

In an international cross-cultural context, some of the students might not have a strong sense of their home culture but rather see themselves as "third culture kids" (Pollock and Van Reken 2001) or nationals of one country transplanted to another and, therefore, not completely of one culture or another, but sharing elements of both. Those who live outside what Julie Kidd and Linda Lankenau call their own "passport culture" inevitably discover that they cannot be wholly comfortable in either their adopted or home cultures (no date). Discovering that they are third-culture people complicates their lives but also liberates them to feel that they have a unique identity not completely congruent with any given culture. Third-culture students can be among the most enjoyable to teach because they can readily identify with various cultural contexts and positions and are quite adaptable.

This is abundantly clear in Hong Kong, which has seen a change in sovereignty in the last 10 years. In Hong Kong, citizens at large have often experienced a conflict about the primacy of the once-dominant British culture and the newly emerging dependency on the culture, politics, and economics of mainland China. There, students "see themselves as 'in between' in tangible ways," (Ford and Slethaug 1999, 152), reinforcing Ackbar Abbas's cautions that, in Hong Kong, national and personal identities "are not stable, they migrate, metastasize" (1997, 2). While being "in between" in immediately-post-handover 1997 Hong Kong bore the complications of the British, Chinese, and Hong Kong identity, a decade later Hong Kong people are no less conflicted, although mainly about Hong Kong and Chinese identities. As C. K. Lau of the *South China Morning Post* reported in 2005, "54.8 percent felt more Hongkongese than Chinese, while

31.9 percent more Chinese than Hongkongese. Another 11.2 percent said they regarded themselves as both Hongkongese and Chinese . . ." These figures all suggest multiple affiliated identities.

Blending Creative Opposites: The Best of All Possible Worlds?

This sense of multiple-consciousness, respect for diverse cultures and nations, and blend of creative opposites carried to leadership levels is reminiscent of what Larry Wang describes of Westerners who come to Hong Kong and China for work:

> It's no secret that Greater China is flourishing. Its surging economy is creating tremendous, long-awaited chances for multinationals bold and smart enough to meet the demands of rapidly developing markets. . . . To grow and succeed, these multinationals are in dire need of qualified staff. They're hungry for professionals with a foot in both the East and the West. They want people who possess the best of both worlds in terms of culture, language, education, and professional training, and who can effectively implement western corporate business strategies within local markets. (1998, ix)

Wang's admiration for an innovative East and West mixture of "culture, language, education, and professional training" gets precisely at the cross-cultural classroom that sets out to marry the differing institutional, pedagogical, personal, and national identities. It is, of course, fitting that he sees this as the best strategy for multinational companies that are increasingly global and visible.

Many see an opportunity for Chinese Americans who come to China with the skills of the new world combined with their partial Chinese identity. As Jun Wang writes, returning Chinese "are discovering better career opportunities at home. 'They are promoted much faster back in China,' says Steve Orlins, chairman of the private, non-profit making National Committee on United States-China Relations" (2005). They are not imperilled by a glass ceiling. As Larry Wang (1998, 8) also notes:

> In many ways, Greater China is evolving into a mix of the best of two worlds, the East and the West, which reflects the exact make up and abilities that many Chinese Americans possess. Increasingly, business in the region encompasses a broad spectrum of scenarios, from the entirely Asian to the entirely western and everything in between. Chinese

Americans are finding themselves among those capable of adapting to the range of situations that are encountered.

The implication is clear. Bilingual and bicultural Chinese Americans are finding themselves with a distinct competitive advantage. It's not about having either Asian abilities or western professional training alone, but the combination of both that's at a premium.

The mixture of affiliated identities can work to the advantage of those who have been raised with multi-ethnic, multi-cultural, and cross-cultural perspectives and can easily be seen as a metaphor for the generative constructing and blending of different affiliated identities in the cross-cultural classroom. Embracing the formation of affiliated identities in the classroom can have long-term beneficial effects for companies requiring creative, resourceful and independent thinkers willing to solve problems, communicate well, and cooperate with others.

Teaching and learning in the cross-cultural classroom thus involve a process of "selves-discovery," for ideally they present everyone with multiple possibilities, and each can adapt differently. As Salman Rushdie remarked about his own adaptation to new cultures and nations and the literature that grew out of such border-crossings: "Our identity is at once plural and partial. Sometimes we fall between two stools. But however ambiguous and shifting this ground may be, it is not an infertile territory for a writer to occupy. If literature is in part the business of finding new angles at which to enter reality, then once again our distance, our long geographical perspective, may provide us with such angles" (1992, 15). These angles of vision are the result of the processes of learning discussed in this book.

In concluding, it is important to note that, as with so many things, there can be problems. As Young Yun Kim comments, "all individual experiences of cross-cultural adaptation, long-term or short-term, are both problematic and growth producing . . . Cross-cultural adaptation is thus a double-edged process, one that is simultaneously enriching and troublesome. Despite, or rather because of, the difficulties crossing cultures entails, people do and must change some of their old ways so as to carry out their daily activities and achieve improved quality of life in the new environment" (2001, 21). This must also be the case with the identity of the cross-cultural classroom and those who inhabit it — there will be stresses and gains as well as losses, and it is the teacher's role to be perceptive enough to be aware of these disturbances and negotiate them.

One of my former students from Hong Kong recently reminded me of the gains of the cross-cultural classroom. She remarked that other classes had not required students to "voice out" on a regular basis, whereas that was part of the American studies classroom. Finding her voice and being able to speak her mind was thus a profound discovery made possible by the cross-cultural classroom. Indeed, the verb "voice out" describes this particular phenomenon well for it clearly differs from just learning to speak up or speak out: voice out incorporates a notion of the affiliated identity discovered in this classroom. This experience resonates with others in Southeast Asia, as noted by a Thai mother who sent her children to an international school, "'we didn't learn how to express our ideas,' she recalled of her days in Thailand's national school system. 'We learned from our teachers that we're not supposed to stand in front of the public and say anything'" (Gatsiounis 2006, 10). She wanted her children to be given the opportunity to voice out in an international school.

There can be real advantages to this environment, but it is important not to disregard the stresses and losses. The stresses and losses experienced in institutional and personal identities are often related to the process of acculturation and becoming comfortable with a new environment and habit of being, and also to deculturation as well. Transforming oneself psychologically and socially and acquiring new affiliated identities requires giving up or unlearning something that previously had value. This can be difficult. A few decades ago, for example, the American government did not allow Americans moving to Canada to take out Canadian citizenship unless they gave up their US citizenship, whereas the British could hold dual nationalities in Canada. The British usually felt little loss in taking out that new Canadian passport and identity, but as Americans sometimes did, the rate of taking out Canadian citizenship was much lower for Americans. Fear of deculturation and cultural loss thus can be daunting. By contrast, highly qualified Asian Indians have come to the USA in ever-increasing numbers since the Indian and US governments have allowed them to hold dual citizenship.

Even when deculturation is successful in the short term, it may still be disconcerting over the long run. Communications experts often talk about stress that can accompany deculturation and transformation to identity. In that vein of thought, some of the short-term advantages of the cross-cultural classroom might be disadvantageous in the long-term. One of the students exposed to American-style teaching in Hong Kong may serve as an example here. "Shari" was taught in the Chinese way in her public school education and was not encouraged to speak in the classroom unless specifically asked. After taking courses with American instructors who favored class reports, discussions, and on-going assessment, she overcame her reticence and became comfortable speaking to her fellow students and teachers in the classroom. After graduation, she worried about this new identity because she found that her habits had been so modified that she did not exactly fit into the Asian patriarchal family and workplace. The hierarchical workplace required certain forms of submission to authority, and what initially had been liberating began to seem a liability because she could not be entirely happy in that particular constrained environment. On the whole, she still thought of her new-found abilities as positive, but there is a lesson here: education moulds and shapes, but, if values in the classroom differ substantially from those in society at large, students and their parents may come to believe that they have not been well served. In one such case, a Thai mother was happy that her son learned to think for himself in an international school, but less pleased that "he doesn't listen to us as much as he should" and that he is less "humble" than he should be (Gatsiounis 2006, 11). Teachers need to be aware of what they want to accomplish, what they have accomplished, and the cultural ambiguity they have created for all of this impacts on the students' sense of their cultural identity.

In conclusion, then, the cross-cultural classroom concerns the things that make teachers and students human and humane and that mark personal, social, and national affiliated identities in particular ways, whether in the cultures of East or West. These include: the creation of a classroom that can develop a lifelong interest in learning and important skill sets; the ability to construct dreams and try to achieve them; the desirability of transcending the restrictions of a single culture and mode of education; the ability to relate and work with others, regardless of ideology, race, ethnicity, class, family, gender, religion, and age; and the power to change, assess, adapt, and create.

Works Cited

Abbas, Ackbar. 1997. *Hong Kong: Culture and the Politics of Disappearance.* Hong Kong and Minneapolis: University of Hong Kong and University of Minnesota.

Ady, Jeffrey C. 1998. "Negotiating Across Cultural Boundaries: Implications of Individualism-Collectivism and Cases for Application." In *Teaching about Culture, Ethnicity, and Diversity: Exercises and Planned Activities.* Ed. Theodore M. Singelis. Thousand Oaks, London, and New Delhi: Sage Publications. 111–20.

Alexander, Miles. 2004. "Beyond 9–11: Realities and Wishful Thinking." Pre-publication of the English Department of Odense University, the University of Southern Denmark. 131 (April).

Amey, Marilyn J. and Dennis F. Brown. 2004. *Breaking Out of the Box: Interdisciplinary Collaboration and Faculty Work.* Greenwich, CT: Information Age Publishing.

Auster, Paul. 1995. "Auggie Wren's Christmas Story." In *Smoke and Blue in the Face.* New York: Hyperion. 151–56.

Barboza, David. 2006. "In a Scientist's Fall, China Feels Robbed of Glory." *The New York Times.* May 15. http://www.nytimes.com/2006/05/15/technology/15fraud.html?ex=1305345600&en=33a5549ea70aebdd&ei=5088&partner=rssnyt&emc=rss

Bateman, Arnold. 1990. "Team Building: Developing a Productive Team." Nebraska Cooperative Extension CC352, University of Nebraska, Lincoln. http://ianrpubs.unl.edu/misc/cc352.htm#eytd

Becker, Bert. 2002. "The 'German Factor' in the Founding of the University of Hong Kong." In *An Impossible Dream: Hong Kong University from Foundation to Re-establishment, 1910–1950.* Eds. Chan Lau Kit-Ching and Peter Cunich. Oxford and New York: Oxford University Press. 23–37.

Bhikkhu, Mettanando. 2005. "Anna and the Retarded Education." *Bangkok Post.* Friday, May 6. Section 1: 10.

Biggs, John. 1995. "Learning In and Out of School." In *Classroom Learning: Educational Psychology for the Asian Teacher.* Eds. John Biggs and David Watkins. Singapore: Prentice Hall, 1995. 3–17.

Biggs, John. 1996. "Western Misperceptions of the Confucian-Heritage Learning Culture." In *The Chinese Learner: Cultural, Psychological, and Contextual Influences.* Eds. David A. Watkins and John B. Biggs, Hong Kong: Comparative Education Research Centre, the University of Hong Kong, 1996 (rpt. 2005). 45–67.

Biggs, John and David Watkins. Eds. 1995. *Classroom Learning: Educational Psychology for the Asian Teacher.* Singapore: Prentice Hall.

Bosworth, Kris. 1994. "Developing Collaborative Skills in College Students." In *Collaborative Learning: Underlying Processes and Effective Techniques.* Eds. Kris Bosworth and Sharon J. Hamilton. San Francisco: Jossey-Bass Publishers. 25–31.

Bosworth, Kris and Sharon J. Hamilton. Eds. 1994. *Collaborative Learning: Underlying Processes and Effective Techniques.* San Francisco: Jossey-Bass Publishers.

Boyer, Ernest L. 1990. "Making the Connections: The Search for Our Common Humanity." In *Rethinking the Curriculum: Toward an Integrated, Interdisciplinary College Education.* Eds. Mary E. Clark and Sandra A. Wawrytko. New York: Greenwood Press, 1990. 13–21.

Bryson, Bill. 1998. *Made in America.* Reading, Berkshire: Black Swan (imprint of 1994 edition).

Carroll, Jude. 2002. *A Handbook for Deterring Plagiarism in Higher Education.* Oxford: Oxford Centre for Staff and Learning Development.

Carroll, Jude. 2005a. "Strategies for Becoming More Explicit." In *Teaching International Students: Improving Learning for All.* Eds. Jude Carroll and Janette Ryan. London and New York: Routledge. 26–34.

Carroll, Jude. 2005b. "Multicultural Groups for Discipline-Specific Tasks: Can a New Approach Be More Effective?" In *Teaching International Students: Improving Learning for All.* Eds. Jude Carroll and Janette Ryan. London and New York: Routledge. 84–91.

Carroll, Jude and Janette Ryan. Eds. 2005. *Teaching International Students: Improving Learning for All.* London and New York: Routledge.

Casmir, Fred L. 1998. "The Transferability of Knowledge." In *Teaching about Culture, Ethnicity, and Diversity: Exercises and Planned Activities.* Ed. Theodore M. Singelis. Thousand Oaks, London, and New Delhi: Sage Publications. 9–13.

Chan Lau Kit-Ching and Peter Cunich. Eds. 2002. *An Impossible Dream: Hong Kong University from Foundation to Re-establishment, 1910–1950.* Oxford and New York: Oxford University Press.

Chapman, David W. and Ann E. Austin. Eds. 2002. *Higher Education in the Developing World: Changing Contexts and Institutional Responses.* Westport, CT, and London: Greenwood Press.

Chatterjee, Debashis. 2002. "Really Leading: Leadership That Is Authentic, Conscious, and Effective." In *Business: The Ultimate Resource*. Ed. Daniel P. Goleman. Cambridge, MA: Perseus Publishing. 222–23.

Cheng, Qijin. 2006. "The Lesson from the Hu Xingrong Plagiarism Affair at Shantou University." Translated from *Southern Weekend*. *EastSouthWestNorth*. January 5. http://www.zonaeuropa.com/20060109_1.htm

Chidester, David. 2005. *Authentic Fakes: Religion and American Popular Culture*. Berkeley: University of California Press.

Chinese Service Center for Scholarly Exchange. 2001. "General Situation of International Students Education." Downloaded 1.10.2004. http://www.cscse.edu.cn/laihua/

Clark, Mary E. and Sandra A. Wawrytko. Eds. 1990. *Rethinking the Curriculum: Toward an Integrated, Interdisciplinary College Education*. New York: Greenwood Press.

Clarke, Mike. 1990. "Media Education: Critical Times?" In *The New Social Curriculum: A Guide to Cross-Curricular Issues*. Ed. Barry Dufour. Cambridge: Cambridge University Press. 69–83.

Costanza, Robert. 1990. "Escaping the Overspecialization Trap: Creating Incentives for a Transdisciplinary Synthesis." In *Rethinking the Curriculum: Toward an Integrated, Interdisciplinary College Education*. Eds. Mary E. Clark and Sandra A. Wawrytko. New York: Greenwood Press. 95–106.

Deeney, John J. 1996. "Summary Report on the Visits of the HK Delegation to PRC American Studies Centers during the Summer of 1996." Hong Kong: Hong Kong-America Center.

Deshpande, Shekhar. 2004. "Whose Identity Is It Anyway?" From *The Diaspora: A Symposium on Indian-Americans and the Motherland*. Seminar, 1–13 June. Downloaded 31.10.2006. http://www.india-seminar.com/semsearch.htm

De Vita, Glauco. 2005. "Fostering Intercultural Learning through Multicultural Group Work." In *Teaching International Students: Improving Learning for All*. Eds. Jude Carroll and Janette Ryan. London and New York: Routledge. 75–83.

Disch, Estelle.1998 "Multicultural Literacy Assignment." In *Teaching about Culture, Ethnicity, and Diversity: Exercises and Planned Activities*. Ed. Theodore M. Singelis. Thousand Oaks, London, and New Delhi: Sage Publications. 47–55.

Du Bois, W. E. Burghardt. 1897. "Strivings of the Negro People." *Atlantic Monthly*. 80. August: 194–98.

Duch, Barbara. 2006. University of Delaware Problem-Based Learning website. Downloaded 2.11.2006. http://www.udel.edu/pbl/

Dufour, Barry. Ed. 1990. *The New Social Curriculum: A Guide to Cross-Curricular Issues*. Cambridge: Cambridge University Press.

Dyrbye, Helen, Steven Harris, and Thomas Golzen. 1997. *The Xenophobe's Guide to the Danes*. Horsham, West Sussex: Ravette Publishing Limited.

Eisner, Elliot W. 1994. *The Educational Imagination: On the Design and*

Evaluation of School Programs. New York: Macmillan College Publishing Company.

English-Lueck, Jan A. 2002. *Cultures@Silicon Valley.* Stanford CA: Stanford University Press.

Finder, Alan. 2005. "Foreign Student Enrollment Drops." *New York Times.* November 14, nytimes.com

Ford, Stacilee and Clyde Haulman. 1996. "'To Touch the Trends': Internationalizing American Studies: Perspectives from Hong Kong and Asia." *American Studies International.* 34.2 (October): 42–58.

Ford, Stacilee and Gordon Slethaug. 1999. "Hong Kong Students Look at the U.S.A.: American Studies in Hong Kong." *American Studies.* 40.2 (Summer): 151–81.

French, Howard, W. 2005. "China Luring Scholars to Make Universities Great." *The New York Times.* October 28. Downloaded 28.10.2006. http://www.nytimes.com/2005/10/28/international/asia/28universities.html

French, Howard W. 2006. "As Chinese Students Go Online, Little Sister Is Watching." *The New York Times.* May 9. Downloaded 9.05.2006. http://news.com.com/As+Chinese+students+go+online,+Little+Sister +is+watching/2100-1028_3-6070073.html

Friedman, Thomas L. 2004. "China's Challenge." *International Herald Tribune.* Friday, June 25: 7.

Fu, Charles Wei-hsun. 1990. "Toward a Creative East-West Dialogue in Moral Education and Value Orientation." In *Rethinking the Curriculum: Toward an Integrated, Interdisciplinary College Education.* Eds. Mary E. Clark and Sandra A. Wawrytko. New York: Greenwood Press. 135–49.

Fuller, Steve. 2003. "Interdisciplinarity. The Loss of the Heroic Vision in the Marketplace of Ideas." In *Rethinking Interdisciplinarity.* 1–5. Downloaded 15.6.2006. http://www.interdisciplines.org/interdisciplinarity/papers/3

Gabrenya, William K., Jr. 1998. "The Intercultural Interview." In *Teaching about Culture, Ethnicity, & Diversity: Exercises and Planned Activities.* Ed. Theodore M. Singelis. Thousand Oaks, London, and New Delhi: Sage Publications. 57–63.

Gage, Nathaniel L. Ed. 1976. *The Psychology of Teaching Methods.* Chicago: National Society for the Study of Education (distributed by the University of Chicago Press).

Gao, Ge and William B. Gudykunst. 1990. "Uncertainty, Anxiety, and Adaptation." *International Journal of Intercultural Relations,* 14.3 (1990): 301–17.

Gardels, Nathan and Mike Medavoy. 2006. "Hollywood in the World: The Fast-Fading Luster of the American Story." *International Herald Tribune.* Thursday, June 15: 6.

Gardiner, Lion F. 1999. "The Lecture Method — How Effective?" July 9. Downloaded 30.10.2006. http://www.hi.is/~joner/eaps/wh_lecte.htm

Gardner, David. 2005. *Plagiarism and How to Avoid It.* Hong Kong: English Centre, the University of Hong Kong. Downloaded 30.10.2006. http://ec.hku.hk/plagiarism/author.htm

Gatsiounis, Ioannis. 2006. "Broader Education Gains Appeal in Asia." *International Herald Tribune*. Tuesday, October 17: 10–11.

Gelfand, Michele J. and Karen M. Holcombe. 1998. "Behavioral Patterns of Horizontal and Vertical Individualism and Collectivism." In *Teaching about Culture, Ethnicity, and Diversity: Exercises and Planned Activities*. Ed. Theodore M. Singelis. Thousand Oaks, London, and New Delhi: Sage Publications. 121–31.

George, Pamela Gale. 1995. *College Teaching Abroad: A Handbook of Strategies for Successful Cross-Cultural Exchanges*. Boston: Allyn and Bacon.

Goleman, Daniel P. Ed. 2002. *Business: The Ultimate Resource*. Cambridge, MA: Bloomsbury Publishing.

Graff, Gerald. 1992. *Beyond the Culture Wars: How Teaching the Conflicts Can Revitalize American Education*. New York: W. W. Norton.

Greenlees, Donald. 2006. "International Schools Grapple with 'Staggering' Demand." *International Herald Tribune*. September 30–October 1: 18.

Grossman, Pam, Sam Wineburg, and Scott Beers. 2000. "Introduction: When Theory Meets Practice in the World of School." In *Interdisciplinary Curriculum: Challenges to Implementation*. Eds. Sam Wineburg and Pam Grossman. New York and London: Teachers College Press, Columbia University. 1–16.

Hafner, Katie. 2004. "In Class, the Answer Is Just a Click Away: Clickers Spur Classroom Participation." *International Herald Tribune*. Friday, April 30–Sunday, May 2: 15.

Hayden, Mary and Jeff Thompson. 1995. "International Schools and International Education: A Relationship Reviewed." *Oxford Review of Education*, 21.3. September: 327–45.

Hayhoe, Ruth. 1999. *China's Universities 1895–1995: A Century of Cultural Conflict*. Hong Kong: Comparative Education Research Centre, the University of Hong Kong.

Heath, Shirley Brice. 1982. "Questioning at Home and at School: A Comparative Study." In *Doing the Ethnography of Schooling: Educational Anthropology in Action*. Ed. George Spindler. New York: Holt, Rinehart and Winston. 102–31.

Ho, David Yau-Fai. 1976. "On the Concept of Face." *American Journal of Sociology*. 81: 867–84.

Hofstede, Geert. 1980. *Culture's Consequences*. Beverly Hills, CA: Sage.

Hofstede, Geert. 1997. *Cultures and Organizations: Software of the Mind — Intercultural Cooperation and Its Importance for Survival*. New York: McGraw-Hill.

Hollinger, David A. 1995. *Postethnic America: Beyond Multiculturalism*. New York: BasicBooks (HarperCollins Publishers, Inc.).

Ickstadt, Heinz. 1996. "Teaching American Studies Abroad: The European Experience." *U. S. Society and Values*. 1.15, October: 11–15.

Jackson, Philip. 1990. *Life in Classrooms*. New York and London: Teachers College Press, Columbia University.

Johnson, Tim. 2006. "In China, Faculty Plagiarism a 'National Scandal.'" Knight Ridder/Tribune Information Services: March 22.

Kember, David. 2004. "Misconceptions about the Learning Approaches, Motivation, and Study Practices of Asian Students." In *The RoutledgeFalmer Reader in Higher Education*. Ed. Malcolm Tight. London and New York: RoutledgeFalmer. 39–55.

Kidd, Julie K. and Linda L. Lankenau. "Third Culture Kids: Returning to Their Passport Country." No date. Downloaded 2.11.2006. http://www.state.gov/m/dghr/flo/rsrcs/pubs/4597.htm. This article originally appeared in *Syllabus*, a publication of Phi Delta Kappa, Chapter 1144.

Kim, Min-Sun. 1998. "Conversational Constraints as a Tool for Understanding Communication Styles." In *Teaching about Culture, Ethnicity, and Diversity: Exercises and Planned Activities*. Ed. Theodore M. Singelis. Thousand Oaks, London, and New Delhi: Sage Publications. 101–9.

Kim, Young Yun. 2001. *Becoming Intercultural: An Integrative Theory of Communication and Cross-Cultural Adaptation*. Thousand Oaks, London, and New Delhi: Sage Publications, Inc.

Klein, Julie Thompson. 1990. *Interdisciplinarity: History, Theory, and Practice*. Detroit, MI: Wayne State University Press.

Klein, Julie Thompson. 2005. *Humanities, Culture, and Interdisciplinarity: The Changing American Academy*. Albany: State University of New York Press.

Klein, Julie Thompson and William G. Doty. Eds. 1994. *Interdisciplinary Studies Today*. San Francisco: Jossey-Bass Publishers.

Koh, Tommy. 1999. "Asian vs European Values." Second Informal Asia-Europe Meeting on Human Rights. Beijing. June 27–29. Downloaded 29.10.2006. http://apollo4.bournemouth.ac.uk/si/tjolley/teaching_materials/ethics/asian_values.htm

Krupat, Arnold. 1983. "The Indian Autobiography: Origins, Type, and Function." In *Smoothing the Ground — Essays on Native American Oral Literature*. Ed. Brian Swann. Berkeley and Los Angeles: University of California Press. 261–82.

Kuhn, Thomas S. 1996. *The Structure of Scientific Revolutions*. Chicago: University of Chicago Press.

Lang, Gretchen. 2004. "Cross-Cultural Training: How Much Difference Does It Really Make?" *International Herald Tribune*. January 24–25: 13.

Lau, C. K. 2004. "Identify Yourself." *South China Morning Post*. October 1: A14.

Lee, Wing On. 1996. "The Cultural Context for Chinese Learners: Conceptions of Learning in the Confucian Tradition." In *The Chinese Learner: Cultural, Psychological, and Contextual Influences*. Eds. David A. Watkins and John B. Biggs. Hong Kong: Comparative Education Research Centre, the University of Hong Kong (rpt. 2005). 25–41.

Levin, Richard C. 2003. "Let the Chinese Students Come." *International Herald Tribune.* December 11: 8.

Lin, Alfred H. Y. 2002. "The Founding of the University of Hong Kong: British Imperial Ideals and Chinese Practical Common Sense." In *An Impossible Dream: Hong Kong University from Foundation to Re-establishment, 1910–1950.* Eds. Chan Lau Kit-Ching and Peter Cunich. Oxford and New York: Oxford University Press. 1–22.

Lincoln, Kenneth. 1983. "Native American Literatures." In *Smoothing the Ground — Essays on Native American Oral Literature.* Ed. Brian Swann. Berkeley and Los Angeles: University of California Press. 3–38.

Lingenfelter, Judith and Sherwood G. Lingenfelter. 2003. *Teaching Cross-Culturally: An Incarnational Model for Learning and Teaching.* Grand Rapids, MI: Baker Academic.

Lionnet, Francoise. 1989. *Autobiographical Voices: Race, Gender, Self-Portraiture.* Ithaca and London: Cornell University Press.

Louie, Kam. 2005. "Gathering Cultural Knowledge: Useful or Use with Care." In *Teaching International Students: Improving Learning for All.* Eds. Jude Carroll and Janette Ryan. London and New York: Routledge. 17–25.

Luk, Thomas Y.T. and James P. Rice. Eds. 2000. *Before and After Suzie: Hong Kong in Western Film and Literature.* Hong Kong: Chinese University Press.

Lynch, David J. 2003. "More of China's Best, Brightest Return Home." *USA Today.* March 7: 6–7A.

Ma, M. Elaine. 2000. *Paper Daughter: A Memoir.* New York: Perennial.

McCabe, Don. 2005. "Center for Academic Integrity Assessment Project." June. http://www.academicintegrity.org/cai_research.asp

McCabe, Donald L., Kenneth D. Butterfield, and Linda Klebe Treviño. 2006. "Academic Dishonesty in Graduate Business Programs: Prevalence, Causes, and Proposed Action." Unpublished.

McFarland, David and Benjamin F. Taggie. 1990. "Cutting the Gordian Knot: Secrets of Successful Curricular Integration." In *Rethinking the Curriculum: Toward an Integrated, Interdisciplinary College Education.* Eds. Mary E. Clark and Sandra A. Wawrytko. New York: Greenwood Press. 229–41.

McFarlane, Brian. 1996. *Novel to Film: An Introduction to the Theory of Adaptation.* Oxford: Clarendon Press.

McLean, Patricia and Laurie Ransom. 2005. "Building Intercultural Competencies: Implications for Academic Skills Development." In *Teaching International Students: Improving Learning for All.* Eds. Jude Carroll and Janette Ryan. London and New York: Routledge. 45–62.

McLeish, John. 1976. "The Lecture Method." In *The Psychology of Teaching Methods.* (Yearbook of the National Society for the Study of Education). Ed. Nathaniel Lees Gage. Chicago: University of Chicago Press. 252–301.

Malone, Robert W. 1990. "The Need for Global Education." In *Rethinking the Curriculum: Toward an Integrated, Interdisciplinary College Education.* Eds. Mary

E. Clark and Sandra A. Wawrytko. New York: Greenwood Press. 167–79.

Marsh, Colin and Paul Morris. 1991. *Curriculum Development in East Asia*. London, New York, and Philadelphia: The Falmer Press.

Marton, Ference, Gloria Dall'Alba, and Tse Lai Kun. 1996. "Memorizing and Understanding: the Keys to the Paradox?" In *The Chinese Learner: Cultural, Psychological and Contextual Influences*. Eds. David A. Watkins and John B. Biggs. Hong Kong: Comparative Education Research Centre, the University of Hong Kong (rpt. 2005). 69–83.

Matthews, Robert. 2006. "Where East Can Never Meet West." *Financial Times*, Friday, October 21: 8-Business Life section.

Min, Weifang. 1997 "Chinese Higher Education Reconsidered from the U.S. Experience." *International Higher Education*. March. Downloaded 2.11.2006. http://www.bc.edu/bc_org/avp/soe/cihe/newsletter/News07/text3e.html

Min, Weifang. 2001. "Current Trends in Higher Education Development in China." *International Higher Education*. Winter. Downloaded 28.10.2006. http://www.bc.edu/bc_org/avp/soe/cihe/newsletter/News22/text014.htm

Ministry of Education Statistics (Xinhua). 2005. *South China Morning Post*. Education Section. May 28: E3.

Montessori website. "Home" section. Downloaded 30.10.2006. http://www.montessori.com/index_home.html

Mooney, Paul. 2006. "The Long Road Ahead for China's Universities." *The Chronicle of Higher Education*. 52.37. May 19: A42.

Morris, Paul. 1991. "Assessment." In *Curriculum Development in East Asia*. Eds. Colin Marsh and Paul Morris. London, New York, and Philadelphia: The Falmer Press. 37–57.

Morris, Paul and Colin Marsh. 1991. "Patterns and Dilemmas." *Curriculum Development in East Asia*. Eds. Colin Marsh and Paul Morris. London, New York, and Philadelphia: The Falmer Press. 255–71.

Newell, William H.1994. "Designing Interdisciplinary Courses." In *Interdisciplinary Studies Today*. Eds. Julie Thompson Klein and William G. Doty. San Francisco: Jossey-Bass Publishers. 35–51.

Nisbett, Richard E. 2003. *The Geography of Thought: How Asians and Westerners Think Differently — and Why*. New York: Free Press.

Nowotny, Helga. 2003. "The Potential of Transdisciplinarity." In *Rethinking Interdisciplinarity*. Downloaded 16.06.06. http://www.interdisciplines.org/interdisciplinarity/papers/5.

Nye, Joseph S. 2004. *Soft Power: The Means to Success in World Politics*. New York: Public Affairs — Perseus Books Group.

O'Meara, Patrick, Howard D. Mehlinger, and Roxana Ma Newman. Eds. 2001. *Changing Perspectives on International Education*. Bloomington and Indianapolis: Indiana University Press.

Pike, Graham. 1990. "Global Education: Learning in a World of Change." In *The*

New Social Curriculum: A Guide to Cross-Curricular Issues. Ed. Barry Dufour. Cambridge: Cambridge University Press. 133–49.

Pollock, David C. and Ruth E. Van Reken. 1999 and 2001. *Third Culture Kids: The Experience of Growing Up Among Worlds.* Yarmouth, ME: Intercultural Press.

Postiglione, Gerard A. 2001. "Globalization and Professional Autonomy: The Academy in Hong Kong, Shanghai and Beijing." *Education and Society.* 19.1: 23–43.

Postiglione, Gerard A. 2002. "Chinese Higher Education for the Twenty-First Century: Expansion, Consolidation, and Globalization." In *Higher Education in the Developing World: Changing Contexts and Institutional Responses.* Ed. David Chapman and Anne E. Austin. Westport, CT, and London: Greenwood Press. 149–66.

Qian, Ning. 2002. *Chinese Students Encounter America.* Trans. T. K. Chu. Hong Kong: Hong Kong University Press.

Reckmeyer, William J. 1990. "Paradigms and Progress: Integrating Knowledge and Education for the Twenty-First Century." In *Rethinking the Curriculum: Toward an Integrated, Interdisciplinary College Education.* Eds. Mary E. Clark and Sandra A. Wawrytko. New York: Greenwood Press. 53–64.

"Record Number of Foreign Students." 2006. *South China Morning Post.* Tuesday, June 6: A7 National Section.

Reid, T. R. 1999. *Confucius Lives Next Door: What Living in the East Teaches Us about Living in the West.* New York: Vintage Books (Random House, Inc.).

Roberts, Priscilla. 2004. "The Love-Hate Relationship: China and the United States Since 1970 and the Impact upon American Studies in China." In *Re-reading America: Changes and Challenges.* Eds. Zhong Weihe and Han Rui. Cheltenham, England: Reardon Publishing. 423–31.

Robinson, Viviane. M. J and Lai Mei Kuin. 1999. "The Explanation of Practice: Why Chinese Students Copy Assignments." *International Journal of Qualitative Studies in Education.* 12.2: 193–210.

Ruben, B. D. and D. Kealey. 1979. "Behavioral Assessment of Communication Competency and the Prediction of Cross-Cultural Adaptation." *International Journal of Intercultural Relations.* 3.1: 15–47.

Rushdie, Salman. 1992. *Imaginary Homelands: Essays and Criticism 1981–1991.* New York: Penguin.

Ruzaite, Jurate. 2004. "Cross-Cultural Differences in Professional Settings: Vagueness in British and American Academic Discourse." Paper delivered at Ninth Nordic Conference for English Studies. Aarhus, Denmark. May 27–29. 23 pages. Downloaded 19.10.2006. http://www.hum.au.dk/engelsk/naes2004/show_abstract.html?ID=51

Ryan, Janette. 2005. "Improving Teaching and Learning Practices for International Students: Implications for Curriculum, Pedagogy and Assessment." In *Teaching International Students: Improving Learning for All.* Eds. Jude Carroll and Janette Ryan. London and New York: Routledge. 92–100.

Ryan, Janette and Jude Carroll. 2005. "'Canaries in the Coalmine': International Students in Western Universities." In *Teaching International Students: Improving Learning for All*. Eds. Jude Carroll and Janette Ryan. London and New York: Routledge. 3–10.

Salili, Farideh. 1996. "Accepting Personal Responsibility for Learning." In *The Chinese Learner: Cultural, Psychological and Contextual Influences*. Eds. David A. Watkins and John B. Biggs. Hong Kong: Comparative Education Research Centre, University of Hong Kong (rpt. 2005). 85–105.

Satloff, Robert. 2003. "American Schools Abroad Have a Big Part to Play." *International Herald Tribune*. December 23: 9.

Schmitt, Diane. 2005. "Writing in the International Classroom." In *Teaching International Students: Improving Learning for All*. Eds. Jude Carroll and Janette Ryan. London and New York: Routledge. 63–74.

Sciolino, Elaine. 2003. "School Scarf Ban Backed in France." *International Herald Tribune*. December 12: 1, 6.

Scollon, Ron and Suzanne Wong Scollon. 2001. *Intercultural Communication: A Discourse Approach*. Malden, MA: Blackwell Publishing, second edition.

Scott, Mary. 2004. "Student, Critic and Literary Text: A Discussion of 'Critical Thinking' in a Student Essay." In *The RoutledgeFalmer Reader in Higher Education*. Ed. Malcolm Tight. London and New York: RoutledgeFalmer. 56–67.

Singelis, Theodore M. Ed. 1998. *Teaching about Culture, Ethnicity, and Diversity: Exercises and Planned Activities*. Thousand Oaks, London, and New Delhi: Sage Publications.

Singelis, Theodore M. and Richard W. Brislin. 1998. "The Distribution of Rewards." In *Teaching about Culture, Ethnicity, and Diversity: Exercises and Planned Activities*. Ed. Theodore M. Singelis. Thousand Oaks, London, and New Delhi: Sage Publications. 67–72.

Siskin, Leslie Santee. 2000. "Restructuring Knowledge: Mapping (Inter)Disciplinary Change." In *Interdisciplinary Curriculum: Challenges to Implementation*. Eds. Sam Wineburg and Pam Grossman. New York and London: Teachers College Press, Columbia University. 171–90.

Slethaug, Gordon E. 1996. "Report on HKAC American Studies First Trip to China: April 3–10, 1996 [and] May 5–7, 1996." Hong Kong-America Center.

Slethaug, Gordon E. 2000. "The Exotic and Oriental as Decoy: Raymond Chandler's *The Big Sleep*." In *Before and After Suzie: Hong Kong in Western Film and Literature*. Eds. Thomas Y. T. Luk and James P. Rice. Hong Kong: Chinese University Press. 161–84.

Slethaug, Gordon E. 2001. "American Studies and the Pedagogy of East and West." *Journal of American Studies*. 33.2. Winter: 149–64.

Sollers, Werner. 1986. *Beyond Ethnicity: Consent and Descent in American Culture*. New York and Oxford: Oxford University Press.

Spaulding, Seth, James Mauch, and Lin Lin. 2001. "The Internationalization of

Higher Education." In *Changing Perspectives on International Education*. Eds. Patrick O'Meara, Howard D. Mehlinger, and Roxana Ma Newman. Bloomington and Indianapolis: Indiana University Press.190–212.

Spickard, Paul R. 2000. "What Must I Be? Asian Americans and the Question of Multiethnic Identity." *Asian American Studies: A Reader*. Eds. Jean Yu-wen Shen Wu and Min Song. New Brunswick, NJ: Rutgers University Press. 255–69.

Spindler, George. Ed. 1982. *Doing the Ethnography of Schooling: Educational Anthropology in Action*. New York: Holt, Rinehart and Winston.

Staff Reporter. 2003. "Arts Losing the Fight for Funding to Sciences." *South China Morning Post*. March 15:A5.

Standler, Ronald B. 2000. *Plagiarism in Colleges in USA*. Downloaded 30.10.2006. http://www.rbs2.com/plag.htm

Stephens, John F. 1996. "American Studies in the United States." *U.S. Society & Values*. 1.15. October: 5–10.

Sternberg, Robert J. 1985. *Beyond IQ: A Triarchic Theory of Human Intelligence*. New York: Cambridge University Press.

Storti, Craig. 1994. *Cross-Cultural Dialogues: 74 Brief Encounters with Cultural Difference*. Yarmouth, ME: Intercultural Press, Inc.

Swann, Brian. Ed. 1983. *Smoothing the Ground — Essays on Native American Oral Literature*. Berkeley and Los Angeles: University of California Press.

Tang, Catherine. 1996. "Collaborative Learning: The Latent Dimension in Chinese Students' Learning." In *The Chinese Learner: Cultural, Psychological and Contextual Influences*. Eds. David A. Watkins and John B. Biggs. Hong Kong: Comparative Education Research Centre, the University of Hong Kong (rpt. 2005). 183–204.

Tang, Catherine and John Biggs. 1996. "How Hong Kong Students Cope with Assessment." In *The Chinese Learner: Cultural, Psychological and Contextual Influences*. Eds. David A. Watkins and John B. Biggs. Hong Kong: Comparative Education Research Centre, the University of Hong Kong (rpt.2005). 159–82.

Tibbitts, Felisa. 2006. "Tips for Leading Discussions." Human Rights Education Association. Downloaded 29.10.2006. http://www.hrea.org/pubs/tips-discussion.html

Tight, Malcolm. Ed. 2004. *The RoutledgeFalmer Reader in Higher Education*. London and New York: RoutledgeFalmer.

Ting-Toomey, Stella. 1999. *Communicating Across Cultures*. New York and London: The Guilford Press.

Toohey, Susan. 1999. *Designing Courses for Higher Education*. Buckingham, England: The Society for Research into Higher Education and Open University Press.

Tyler, Ralph W. 1949. *Basic Principles of Curriculum and Instruction*. Chicago and London: University of Chicago Press.

The University of Hong Kong Calendar 2005–2006. 2005. Hong Kong: The University of Hong Kong.

Volet, Simone and Peter Renshaw. 1996. "Chinese Students at an Australian University: Adaptability and Continuity." In *The Chinese Learner: Cultural, Psychological and Contextual Influences*. Eds. David A. Watkins and John B. Biggs. Hong Kong: Comparative Education Research Centre, the University of Hong Kong (rpt. 2005). 205–20.

Walker, John. 1998. "Student Plagiarism in Universities: What Are We Doing about It?" *Higher Education Research and Development*. 17.1: 89–106.

Wang, Jun. 2005. "Return of the 'Sea Turtles.'" *South China Morning Post*. September 30: A17.

Wang, Larry. 1998. *The New Gold Mountain: the Success of Chinese Americans in Greater China . . . and What You Need To Know To Get There*. Hong Kong: Andiremar Publications.

Watkins, David. 1995. "Student Self-Esteem." In *Classroom Learning: Educational Psychology for the Asian Teacher*. Eds. John Biggs and David Watkins. Singapore: Prentice Hall. 69–81.

Watkins, David. 1996. "Hong Kong Secondary School Learners: A Developmental Perspective." In *The Chinese Learner: Cultural, Psychological and Contextual Influences*. Eds. David A. Watkins and John B. Biggs. Hong Kong: Comparative Education Research Centre, the University of Hong Kong (rpt. 2005). 107–17.

Watkins, David and John B. Biggs. Eds. *The Chinese Learner: Cultural, Psychological and Contextual Influences*. Hong Kong: Comparative Education Research Centre, the University of Hong Kong (rpt. 2005).

Webb, Graham. 2005. "Internationalisation of Curriculum: An Institutional Approach." In *Teaching International Students: Improving Learning for All*. Eds. Jude Carroll and Janette Ryan. London and New York: Routledge. 109–18.

Welch, Anthony R. 2002. Preface. *Third Delight: The Internationalization of Higher Education in China*. By Rui Yang. New York and London: Routledge. xi–xiii.

Wilcox, Kathleen. 1982. "Differential Socialization in the Classroom: Implications for Equal Opportunity." In *Doing the Ethnography of Schooling: Educational Anthropology in Action*. Ed. George Spindler. New York: Holt, Rinehart and Winston. 268–309.

Wineburg, Sam and Pam Grossman. Eds. 2000. *Interdisciplinary Curriculum: Challenges to Implementation*. New York and London: Teachers College Press, Columbia University.

Winter, Sam. 1995. "Student Interaction and Relationships." In *Classroom Learning: Educational Psychology for the Asian Teacher*. Eds. John Biggs and David Watkins. Singapore: Prentice Hall. 34–50.

Wong, Sandra Leslie. 2001. *Managing Diversity: Institutions and the Politics of Educational Change*. Lanham, MD: Rowman and Littlefield Publishers, Inc.

Wu, Frank. H. 2002. *Yellow: Race in America Beyond Black and White*. New York: Basic Books.

Wu, Jean Yu-wen Shen and Min Song. Eds. 2000. *Asian American Studies: A Reader*. New Brunswick, New Jersey: Rutgers University Press.

Yang, Rui. 2002. *Third Delight: the Internationalization of Higher Education in China*. New York and London: Routledge.

Yang, Rui. and King Hau Au Yeung. 2002. "China's Plan to Promote Research in the Humanities and Social Sciences." *International Higher Education*. Spring. Downloaded 10.28.2006. http://www.bc.edu/bc_org/avp/soe/cihe/newsletter/News27/text012.htm

Zhong, Weihe and Han Rui. Eds. 2004. *Re-reading America: Changes and Challenges*. Cheltenham, England: Reardon Publishing.

Zia, Helen. 2000. *Asian American Dreams: The Emergence of an American People*. New York: Farrar, Straus and Giroux.

Index